T0335671

The 2-tuple Linguistic Model

Luis Martínez • Rosa M. Rodriguez
Francisco Herrera

The 2-tuple Linguistic Model

Computing with Words in Decision Making

 Springer

Luis Martínez
Department of Computer Science
University of Jaén
Jaén, Spain

Rosa M. Rodriguez
Department of Computer Science and AI
University of Granada
Granada, Spain

Francisco Herrera
Department of Computer Science and AI
University of Granada
Granada, Spain

ISBN 978-3-319-24712-0   ISBN 978-3-319-24714-4   (eBook)
DOI 10.1007/978-3-319-24714-4

Library of Congress Control Number: 2015957246

Springer Cham Heidelberg New York Dordrecht London

Printed on acid-free paper

Springer International Publishing AG Switzerland is part of Springer Science+Business Media (www.springer.com)

This book is dedicated to all people who have enjoyed studying and researching the 2-tuple linguistic model and approaches based on it; they have encouraged us to reach this point. Thanks to all researchers who have contributed to developing and applying the model.

To our families.

Preface

This book presents a comprehensive view of the 2-tuple linguistic model, its extensions, and their application to different types of real-world linguistic decision-making problems. Linguistic decision making makes use of linguistic information to model and manage the uncertainty related to the vagueness of meanings that usually arises when linguistic preferences/opinions are elicited in *ill-defined* decision situations. The focus of this book is on providing a clear timeline and explanation of the necessity, concepts, models, methodologies, and tools based on the 2-tuple linguistic model that have been introduced over the last 15 years.

We remark, despite the existence of other linguistic models and their corresponding computational processes, that the 2-tuple linguistic model and its related models and tools present a series of advantages which have made this model probably the most widely used within the linguistic decision-making area. The most important advantages presented by the 2-tuple linguistic model are highlighted below:

- It follows the fuzzy linguistic approach by keeping the fuzzy representation of the semantics and providing a syntax for each 2-tuple linguistic value. But additionally, it provides extra information by a numerical parameter which converts the linguistic representation into a continuous one that facilitates obtaining more accurate linguistic results.
- The 2-tuple linguistic model fulfils all the requirements of the *Computing with Words* methodology, providing easily understood linguistic outputs from linguistic inputs.
- All 2-tuple linguistic based approaches also provide accurate linguistic results that are easy to understand, despite the complexity of the decision definition framework (decision situations).
- The development of an associated software suite (Flintstones), presented in this book, that facilitates the automation and implementation of 2-tuple linguistic decision-support tools and also the comparison among different decision approaches makes the 2-tuple linguistic model a powerful proposal not only because of its complete and well-founded theoretical machinery, but also because of its associated software.

This book is structured in eight chapters. Chapter 1 explains the necessity and importance of linguistic information in decision making and how the fuzzy linguistic approach is able to model the linguistic information by means of linguistic variables. It reviews a methodology to carry out the Computing with Words processes in linguistic decision making and briefly introduces classical linguistic computational models. Afterwards, a comparative analysis among such models is carried out.

Chapter 2 introduces a new fuzzy linguistic representation model based on symbolic translation and its computational model to accomplish the Computing with Words processes in linguistic decision making. It solves a linguistic decision-making problem by using the 2-tuple linguistic model and compares the results obtained with classical linguistic computational models to show its adequacy to deal with linguistic information in decision making. Different aggregation operators for the 2-tuple linguistic model which have been classified by operators' families are reviewed.

Chapter 3 presents a review of some symbolic approaches based on the 2-tuple linguistic model and its concepts that aim at overcoming some specific limitations of the 2-tuple linguistic model.

Chapter 4 explains the need for dealing with complex decision contexts in which the linguistic information provided by experts can be modeled using multiple linguistic scales or different types of information. This chapter reviews several 2-tuple linguistic based approaches to deal with heterogeneous contexts in decision-making problems, such as multigranular linguistic information and nonhomogeneous information. Different examples are introduced to understand such approaches easily.

Chapter 5 shows the necessity of managing not uniform or symmetrically distributed terms in a linguistic scale and presents a representation model for unbalanced linguistic information along with its computational model which guarantees accurate and linguistic results using the 2-tuple linguistic model.

Chapter 6 goes a step further for dealing with linguistic information and reviews the concept of hesitant fuzzy linguistic term sets that allows modelling the experts' hesitation and facilitates the generation of more flexible and richer linguistic expressions than single linguistic terms. A multicriteria decision-making model that deals with comparative linguistic expressions and carries out the computing processes by using the 2-tuple linguistic model is described.

Chapter 7 makes a comprehensive review of different decision applications and related areas in which the 2-tuple linguistic model or any of the 2-tuple linguistic based approaches have been used to solve real-world problems.

Finally, Chapter 8 shows a fuzzy linguistic decision tool enhancement suite, called Flintstones, which solves linguistic decision-making problems based on the 2-tuple linguistic model following the Computing with Words paradigm. Furthermore, this chapter also presents the *Flintstones* website in which the current release can be downloaded along with a repository of datasets for linguistic decision-making problems.

Due to the broad coverage of the material proposed in this book and its importance in multiple areas of application (see Chapter 7), this book can be very useful for master's degree students or senior undergraduate students in management information systems, computer based systems, courses, and so forth. Of course the book can be also very interesting for researchers in the areas of decision making, fuzzy systems, decision-support systems, and the like, and eventually for managers who can apply the methods and software introduced to solve their own decision-making problems.

We would like to acknowledge the support from the Spanish Ministry of Economy and Finance Postdoctoral Training (FPDI-2013-18193).

We wish to thank our colleagues M. Espinilla, F.J. Estrella, E. Herrera-Viedma, and D. Ruan (in memory) for their support over the last 15 years in the development and application of the 2-tuple linguistic model.

Jaén, Spain   Luis Martínez
Granada, Spain   Rosa M. Rodriguez
Granada, Spain   Francisco Herrera
July 2015

Contents

Chapter 1
Linguistic Decision Making and Computing with Words

1.1 Introduction

Human activities are very broad and diverse, but in their daily lives people commonly face tasks and activities in which it is necessary to use decision-making processes. Decision making (DM) is a key activity proper to human beings and a complex process, because it may involve different and specific difficulties that can come from various sources [16], such as the inherent complexity and uncertainty of the decision situation or the existence of multiple and conflicting objectives in the decision problem; additionally DM becomes more complicated because nowadays the need for quick decisions dealing with huge amounts of information and alternatives is continuously growing. Some authors claim that DM in complex situations is a clear distinction between human beings and animals [8].

Generally, DM is a cognitive process based on different mental and reasoning processes that lead to the choice of a *suitable* alternative from a set of possible alternatives in a decision situation [24]. Despite the existence of different DM processes in the literature composed of different phases [16, 37], this book considers a DM process composed of at least five phases (see Figure 1.1). All models presented in this book follow this DM process, although the *intelligence* phase is implicitly assumed.

- *Intelligence*: It observes reality to identify the problem, alternatives, and objectives to be achieved by its solving process.
- *Modelling*: It builds a model that defines a *framework* establishing the problem structure, preferences, uncertainty, and so on.
- *Information gathering*: It obtains the information, knowledge, and preferences provided by decision makers according to the model previously defined.
- *Analysis*: It analyses and *aggregates* the information gathered according to the objectives and constraints, and reports results to be considered in the selection phase.

© Springer International Publishing Switzerland 2015
L. Martínez et al., *The 2-tuple Linguistic Model*, DOI 10.1007/978-3-319-24714-4_1

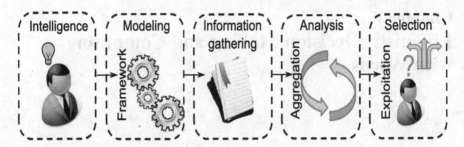

Fig. 1.1 A decision-making process

- *Selection*: According to the results obtained in the analysis step, an *exploitation* process in which decision makers can choose the solution alternatives for the decision problem is carried out.

It should be stressed that DM is a core area in a wide range of fields and disciplines such as *engineering* [13, 15, 40], *psychology* [23, 25], *operations research* [6, 11], *artificial intelligence* [14, 31, 58], and so on, hence DM has been the subject of study from different points of view and can be understood in different ways depending on the situation and area of application. Therefore, in decision theory, different classifications of decision problems attending to different aspects have been developed [22], such as number of decision makers, criteria, and so forth. But paying attention to the decision definition framework in the *modelling* phase, it is common to distinguish between:

1. Well-structured decision problems defined under certainty in which all states of nature related to the decision problem are perfectly known and the decision-solving process is straightforward using an algorithmic approach that obtains the optimum solution. These situations are called *well-structured problems*.
2. Decision problems, called *ill-structured problems* [80], that cannot be solved so straightforwardly, because the decision framework might be either defined in changing environments or related to the existence of vagueness, uncertainty, and so on.

The latter case is fairly common in real-world complex decision-making problems of any of the previous scientific disciplines. Therefore, for solving ill-structured decision-making problems dealing with vague and imprecise information, that is, decision making under uncertainty, classical decision theory provides probabilistic models to manage uncertainty in such problems. In many of them, however, it is easy to observe that many aspects of these uncertainties have a nonprobabilistic character, because they are related to imprecision and vagueness of meanings provided either by experts or by decision makers when they elicit their knowledge about the decision-making problem [41]. In such situations the use of linguistic descriptors, to elicit knowledge and preferences about the alternatives or criteria, is often utilised by experts and decision makers involved in the decision-making problem, raising the concept of *linguistic decision making* (LDM) to indicate that the decision-making problem deals with linguistic information. The elicited linguistic descriptors are fuzzy judgments rather than probabilistic values, hence for modelling and managing their inherent uncertainties and vagueness there exist different methodologies and approaches [36, 46, 56, 69]. However, this book is mainly focused on the use of fuzzy logic, fuzzy set theory [32], and fuzzy linguistic approaches [74] to facilitate the modelling and managing of uncertainty in LDM [12, 37] and provide a direct way to represent the linguistic information by means of linguistic variables.

The use of linguistic information in DM implies operating with such types of information. Hence, different computational models and methodologies have been presented in the literature to operate with linguistic information in DM. Within fuzzy theory the "Computing with Words" (CW) methodology stands out; its roots are based on the fuzzy logic and fuzzy linguistic approach, and it provides a direct way to accomplish linguistic computational processes. CW aims at dealing with words or sentences defined in a natural or artificial language instead of numbers to emulate human cognitive processes in order to improve solving processes coping with uncertainty. Consequently, CW has been applied as a computational basis to decision-making problems with linguistic information [39, 42] because it provides tools close to human reasoning processes related to decision making, enhances the reliability and flexibility of classical decision models, and improves the resolution of decision making under uncertainty with linguistic information [43].

Among the different models and methodologies for dealing with LDM, this book is devoted to the *2-tuple linguistic model* introduced by Herrera and Martínez [29] which is one of the more widely used methods for working with linguistic information in LDM and that fulfils the requirements of CW methodology [46]. Therefore, to facilitate comprehension of the core of this book, this chapter introduces some basic and necessary concepts about LDM. The fuzzy linguistic approach is then reviewed, because it is the conceptual basis of the 2-tuple linguistic model for representing linguistic information and carrying out CW processes. Eventually, different linguistic computational models to carry out CW processes within DM are analysed and compared to justify the importance of the 2-tuple linguistic model from the CW perspective in DM.

1.2 Linguistic Decision Making

Complex real-world decision-making problems are often *ill-structured* problems whose definition framework involves uncertainty, vagueness, and incomplete information that many times cannot be well modelled by probabilistic models. There are different possibilities that can be used to model and manage such types of uncertain information such as interval values [51, 53, 59], belief degrees [30, 70], and so on. Notwithstanding that previous choices deal with decision-making problems under nonprobabilistic uncertainty, the use of linguistic information is rather common in decision-making problems originating another concept in decision theory namely, *LDM*. Yager pointed out in [64, 65] that one of the reasons is because linguistic information is so useful in these decision situations and because experience shows that:

> A realistic strategy for decision making under an environment with a great deal of uncertainty consists of describing the uncertain information by means of natural languages, because in many real decision situations the values to be used for the evaluation of the ratings and importance of alternatives/criteria of a decision making problem drawn from a linguistic scale facilitates the decision maker to provide the valuation.

Therefore, in this type of decision-making problem the use of linguistic descriptors is a useful, straightforward, and natural tool to represent preferences because of the nature of different aspects of the decision situation. To model and manage the inherent uncertainty and vagueness of linguistic descriptors, the fuzzy linguistic approach [4, 74] based on fuzzy set theory has been extensively used [32]. Hence LDM could use the fuzzy linguistic approach in its solving process whenever its fuzzy representation would be adequate for decision situations.

Consequently, a further detailed description of the fuzzy linguistic approach, its suitability for DM, and a general linguistic decision-solving process can be found below.

1.2.1 Fuzzy Linguistic Approach

One common approach to model linguistic information is the fuzzy linguistic approach [74] that uses fuzzy set theory [72] to manage the uncertainty and model linguistic information by using the concept of linguistic variable.

Zadeh [74] introduced the concept of linguistic variable as "a variable whose values are not numbers, but words or sentences in a natural or artificial language." A linguistic value is less precise than a number, but it is closer to human cognitive processes used successfully to solve problems dealing with uncertainty. Formally a linguistic variable is defined as follows.

Definition 1.1 ([75]). A linguistic variable is characterised by a quintuple $(H,T(H),U,G,M)$ in which H is the name of the variable; $T(H)$ (or simply T) denotes the term set of H, that is, the set of names of linguistic values of H, with each value being a fuzzy variable denoted generically by X and ranging across a universe of discourse U associated with the base variable u; G is a syntactic rule (*which usually takes the form of a grammar*) for generating the names of values of H; and M is a semantics rule for associating its meaning with each H, $M(X)$, which is a fuzzy subset of U.

The use of linguistic variables needs the selection of appropriate linguistic descriptors for the term set, including the analysis of their *granularity of uncertainty*, and their syntax and semantics. The former, commonly noted as $g + 1$, determines

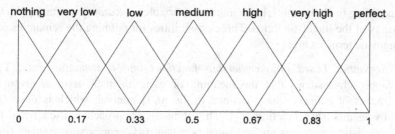

Fig. 1.2 A seven-term set with its semantics

the level of discrimination among different counts of uncertainty modelled by the linguistic descriptors in the linguistic term set, $S = \{s_0, \ldots, s_g\}$. A fine granule means a high level of discrimination, however, a coarse granule means a low-level one. This selection depends on the LDM problem. On the other hand, the selection of the syntax and suitable semantics is crucial to determine the validity of the fuzzy linguistic approach. There exist different approaches to choose the linguistic descriptors and different ways to define their linguistic semantics [38, 63, 74]

- The main approaches to select the linguistic descriptors are:

  1. *Ordered structure approach*: It defines the linguistic term set by means of an ordered structure providing the term set, S, distributed on a scale on which a total order is defined [63]. For example, a set of seven terms S, could be given as follows (graphically, Figure 1.2).

     $S = \{s_0 : nothing\ (n), s_1 : very\ low\ (vl), s_2 : low\ (l), s_3 : medium\ (m), s_4 : high\ (h), s_5 : very\ high\ (vh), s_6 : perfect\ (p)\}$

     Usually in these cases, the existence of the following operators is required.

     – A negation operator: $\text{Neg}(s_i) = s_j$ such that $j = g - i$ ($g + 1$ is the cardinality)
     – A maximisation operator: $\max(s_i, s_j) = s_i$ if $s_i \geq s_j$
     – A minimisation operator: $\min(s_i, s_j) = s_i$ if $s_i \leq s_j$

  2. *Context-free grammar approach*: It defines the linguistic term set by means of a context-free grammar, G, such that the linguistic terms are sentences generated by G [4, 47, 74]. A grammar G is a 4-tuple (V_N, V_T, I, P) being V_N the set of nonterminal symbols, V_T the set of terminal symbols, I the starting symbol, and P the production rules that may be defined in an extended Backus-Naur Form [7]. For example, between V_T and V_N primary terms such as $\{poor,\ fair\ good\}$, relationships such as $\{lower\ than,\ greater\ than\}$, and hedges such as $\{not,\ very\}$ can be found. Thus choosing I as any term and using P a linguistic term set such as $S = \{poor, very\_good, not\_good, \ldots\}$ could be generated.

- According to Definition 1.1, the linguistic variables associate a meaning with the syntax of the linguistic terms. Three possibilities for defining the semantics of a linguistic term set are:

  1. *Semantics based on membership functions and a semantics rule*: This approach assumes that the meaning of each linguistic term is given by means of a fuzzy subset defined in the $[0, 1]$ interval, which is described by membership functions [7]. This semantics approach is used when the linguistic descriptors are generated by means of a generative grammar. Thus, it is established by means of two elements [4, 74]:

     (i) The primary fuzzy sets associated with the primary linguistic terms.
     (ii) A semantics rule M for generating the fuzzy sets of the nonprimary fuzzy sets.

  2. *Semantics based on an ordered structure of the linguistic term set*: This alternative introduces the semantics from the structure defined over the linguistic term set. This happens when the users provide their assessments by using an ordered linguistic term set. Under this semantics approach the distribution of the linguistic terms on scale $[0, 1]$ can be equally informative *symmetrical* [63] or not *nonsymmetrical* [28, 55].

  3. *Mixed semantics*: All linguistic terms are considered primary terms. It assumes elements from the previous approaches, that is, an ordered structure of the primary linguistic terms and fuzzy sets for semantics of the linguistic terms. As in semantics based on ordered structure, ordered linguistic term sets are assumed that are distributed on a scale assuming that each linguistic term is equally informative. On the other hand, as in semantics based on the ordered structure of the linguistic term set, it defines the semantics of the primary linguistic terms by means of the fuzzy sets [18].

Therefore, the semantics of the terms is represented by fuzzy numbers, described by membership functions. The linguistic assessments given by users are just approximate ones. A way to characterise a fuzzy number is to use a representation based on parameters of its membership function [5]. Some authors consider that parametric membership functions (trapezoidal, triangular) are good enough to capture the vagueness of these linguistic assessments [20]. The trapezoidal representation is achieved by the 4-tuple (a, b, d, c), in which b and d indicate the interval in which the membership value is 1, with a and c indicating the left and right limits of the definition domain of the trapezoidal membership function. A particular case of this type of representation is the linguistic assessments whose membership functions are triangular, that is, $b = d$, therefore the representation of this type of membership function by 3-tuples (a, b, c).

Figure 1.2 shows a linguistic term set with the syntax and semantics of their terms.

1.2.2 Why Fuzzy Linguistic Modelling for LDM?

The fuzzy linguistic approach provides the basis to model information linguistically by using a fuzzy representation, but it is necessary to understand why fuzzy set theory can be useful to model and manage the uncertainty of preferences in DM. For this understanding it is convenient to review the different interpretations of the semantics of fuzzy sets introduced in [21] in which it is described how the semantics of fuzzy sets is exploited in terms of similarity, uncertainty, and preference such that graded membership plays a role in three different types of information-driven tasks: *classification and data analysis*, *approximate reasoning*, and *decision-making problems*.

Let $\mu_F(u)$ be the membership function of the fuzzy set F defined on referential U; the three interpretations of this degree of membership according to the previous paragraph are [21]:

1. *Degree of Similarity*: $\mu_F(u)$ is the degree of proximity of u to prototype elements of F. This is the most common and oldest interpretation of membership grades since Bellman et al. [2] proposed the interest of the fuzzy set concept in classification. This view has been very useful in clustering analysis, regression analysis, and so on.
2. *Degree of Uncertainty*: This type of interpretation of the membership function was introduced by Zadeh in [76] within possibility theory and later on developed in his theory of approximated reasoning [77]. In such an interpretation, $\mu_F(u)$ is the degree of possibility that a parameter x will have the value u taking into account that all the knowledge about it is that "x is F".
3. *Degree of Preference*: In this interpretation F represents either a set of objects more or less preferred or values of a decision variable x, and $\mu_F(u)$ represents either the intensity of preference regarding the object u, or the feasibility of selecting u as a value of x. Fuzzy sets then represent criteria or flexible constraints. This view was introduced by Bellman and Zadeh [3] and it was the starting point of the broad research on fuzzy optimisation, especially fuzzy linear programming and decision analysis.

Therefore, by using the interpretation of *degree of preference* for semantics of fuzzy sets, the use of fuzzy linguistic labels to express the intensity of preference for a given alternative in a decision-making problem seems natural and usual.

1.2.3 LDM Solving Scheme

Once the convenience and suitability of using linguistic information in decision-making problems that present vagueness and uncertainty have been clearly stated, it is necessary to analyse whether the resolution scheme for a LDM problem changes significantly from a classical decision-solving scheme without linguistic information.

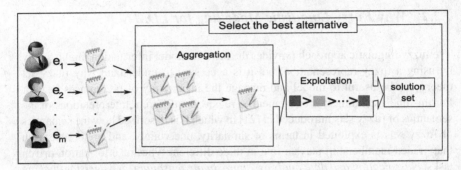

Fig. 1.3 Solving scheme of a decision-making problem

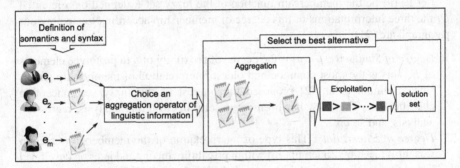

Fig. 1.4 Scheme of a linguistic decision-making problem

Starting from the decision process presented in Figure 1.1, a reduced basic decision resolution scheme consists of two main phases [48] (see Figure 1.3):

1. An *aggregation phase* that aggregates the values provided by the experts to obtain a collective assessment for the alternatives.
2. An *exploitation phase* of the collective assessments to rank, sort, or choose the best one(s) among the alternatives.

The use of linguistic information in decision making modifies the previous scheme by introducing two new steps [27] (see Figure 1.4):

1. *The choice of the linguistic term set with its semantics.* It establishes the linguistic expression domain in which experts provide their linguistic assessments about the alternatives according to their knowledge.
2. *The choice of the aggregation operator of linguistic information.* A proper linguistic aggregation operator is chosen for aggregating the linguistic assessments. The appropriateness of the operator depends on each single decision problem.
3. *Aggregation phase.* It obtains linguistic collective assessments by aggregating the linguistic assessments provided by the experts using the appropriate linguistic aggregation operator.
4. *Exploitation phase.* It obtains a ranking to choose the best alternative(s) starting from the linguistic collective assessments.

The previous linguistic resolution scheme shows the necessity of linguistic computing models to operate with linguistic information to achieve a solution for the LDM problem. Previously, the existence of different linguistic computational methodologies has been pointed out, taking into account the use of fuzzy linguistic modelling; the methodology that stands out over the others to work with linguistic information is the CW methodology.

1.3 Computing with Words in Decision Making

The concept of computing usually implies calculation processes either by mathematical means of numbers and symbols or by a computer. Paying attention to computing processes done by human beings, it is remarkable that they employ mostly words in computing and reasoning, arriving at results linguistically expressed from linguistic premises [78]. Hence, CW applies the same view to their computing processes aiming at obtaining linguistic outcomes from linguistic inputs.

Because words have fuzzy denotations when they are used by human beings, the paradigm of Computing with Words was clearly stated as a branch of fuzzy logic by Zadeh in [78] in which CW was defined as "A methodology in which words are used in place of numbers for computing and reasoning." Later on, Zadeh in [79] added that "CW is a methodology in which the objects of computation are words and propositions drawn from a natural language."

Even though it is clear what CW is for, it is also necessary to clarify why CW makes sense as a methodology for solving complex problems in which linguistic objects are the objects of computation. Zadeh in [46] provides his view about why CW is useful to solve these problems:

> Humans have many remarkable capabilities. Among them there are two that stand out in importance. First, the capability to converse, communicate, reason and make rational decisions in an environment of imprecision, uncertainty, incompleteness of information and partiality of truth. And second, the capability to perform a wide variety of physical and mental tasks without any measurements and any computations. In large measure, Computing with Words is inspired by these remarkable capabilities.

From previous paragraphs it can be inferred that CW rests on three main rationales [46]:

1. Much of human knowledge is linguistically described.
2. Words are less precise than numbers, therefore CW could be a powerful tool to deal with imprecise information.
3. Precision carries a cost. If there is a tolerance for imprecision, it can be exploited by using words in place of numbers.

It is remarkable that root foundations of CW were established much earlier than the proper methodology of CW, [73, 74] defined the concepts of *linguistic variable*, *granulation*, *fuzzy constraint*, and *fuzzy constraint propagation*, making the pivotal role of fuzzy logic in CW become even clearer. It is important to remark that CW involves wide-ranging ramifications and applications from learning to decision making, including programming, knowledge representation, and so on.

In spite of the different ramifications and applications of CW, this book focuses its interests on the use of CW in LDM. Because CW is based on the human ability to perform different tasks without needing any numerical precise measurement and such a capability is sustained by the brain's ability to manipulate different perceptions (usually imprecise, uncertain, or partial insight), it plays a key role in decision processes that need human knowledge or preferences to make a decision by means of computing and reasoning processes [24].

Previously a crucial aspect of CW was highlighted that consists of its processes, and aims at computing from linguistic inputs to provide understandable outcomes based on linguistic information; that is, CW carries out a computing process *from words to words* that is the basis of the CW methodology. This idea, shown in Figure 1.5, has been developed in DM since the early 1980s, when different researchers including Tong and Bonissone [54], Schmucker [50], and Yager [64] started to propose different computing schemes to work with linguistic information. Such schemes are quite similar and have a structure in which the input linguistic information should be mapped into fuzzy set models and the results should be expressed in linguistic information easily understandable by human beings.

Yager points out the importance of the processes of *translation* and *retranslation* in CW [66, 67]; see Figure 1.6. The former translates the linguistic inputs into a machine-manipulative format based on fuzzy tools in which the computations are carried out, and the latter consists of converting the computing results into linguistic information again to facilitate human comprehension (which is one of the main objectives of CW).

Consequently, different linguistic computing models have been developed and applied as the computational basis for CW in LDM [29, 35, 52, 57, 71]. Following, the classical linguistic computational models which have been widely used in LDM are briefly revised.

Fig. 1.5 Computing with Words scheme

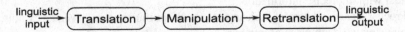

Fig. 1.6 Yager's Computing with Words scheme

1.4 Classical Linguistic Computational Models

Due to the relevance of LDM in real-world problems and the necessity of methodologies for CW, there exist different linguistic computational models. This section focuses on the classical ones.

1.4.1 Linguistic Computational Model Based on Membership Functions

This computational model is based on the fuzzy linguistic approach and represents the linguistic information according to Definition 1.1 (see Figure 1.2). And it makes the computations directly on the membership functions of the linguistic terms by using the Extension Principle [32]. Fuzzy arithmetic provides a result of a fuzzy computation on a set of n linguistic labels in the term set, $T(H)$, a fuzzy number, $F(\mathbb{R})$, that usually does not match any linguistic label in $T(H)$ (see Figure 1.7). This computational model has these characteristics:

1. In those problems where accuracy outweighs interpretability (ranking purposes), the results are expressed by the fuzzy numbers themselves using fuzzy ranking procedures to obtain a final order of the alternatives [1, 26].
2. If an interpretable and linguistic result is needed then an approximation function $app_1(\cdot)$ is applied to associate the fuzzy result $F(\mathbb{R})$ with a label in $T(H)$ [17, 40, 67]:

$$T(L)^n \xrightarrow{\tilde{F}} F(\mathbb{R}) \xrightarrow{app_1(\cdot)} T(L)$$

The approximation process implies a loss of information and lack of accuracy of the results as is clearly shown in Figure 1.7.

Another linguistic computational model based on membership functions makes use of type-2 fuzzy sets (see Figure 1.8, an interval type-2 fuzzy set representation) to model the linguistic assessments [44, 56, 57]. The use of type-2 fuzzy sets has been justified in different ways:

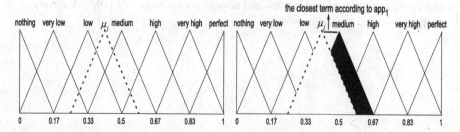

Fig. 1.7 Linguistic computational model based on membership functions

Fig. 1.8 Representation of
an interval type-2 fuzzy set

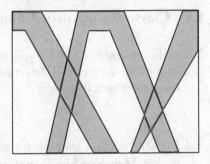

- In [56]: "Type-1 representation is a 'reductionist' approach for it discards the
  spread of membership values by averaging or curve fitting techniques and hence,
  camouflages the 'uncertainty' embedded in the spread of membership values."
- In [45] "Words mean different things to different people and so are uncertain.
  Therefore, it is necessary a fuzzy set model for a word that has the potential to
  capture its uncertainties, and an interval type-2 fuzzy set should be used as a
  fuzzy set model of a word."

Its computational model is mainly based on a particular kind of type-2
fuzzy set, interval type-2 fuzzy set which maintains the uncertainty modelling
properties of general type-2 fuzzy sets, interval type-2 fuzzy sets but reducing
the computational efforts that are needed to work with them. As in type-1 fuzzy
sets, the type-2 fuzzy sets based model needs to approximate the resulting type-2
fuzzy set from a linguistic operation by mapping the result into a linguistic
assessment producing a loss of information. Wu proposed a reconstruction
decoder that preserves the shape information of the CW engine output in a simple
form without sacrificing much accuracy [61]. Moreover, *it is equivalent to the
2-tuple representation* under certain conditions as mentioned by Wu.

1.4.2 Linguistic Symbolic Computational Models Based on Ordinal Scales

Symbolic models have been widely used in CW because of their simple computational processes and high interpretability. The initial proposal for a symbolic
model [64] uses max-min operators, and new symbolic proposals [19, 62] introduce
aggregation-based symbolic models.

1.4.2.1 Linguistic Symbolic Computational Model Based on Ordinal Scales and Max-Min Operators

This model introduced by Yager in [64] represents the information according to the fuzzy linguistic approach (see Figure 1.7), but imposes a linear ordering to the linguistic term set $S = \{s_1, s_2, \ldots, s_g\}$ such that $s_i \geq s_j \Leftrightarrow i \geq j$.

Using the ordered structure of the linguistic term set to accomplish symbolic computations in such ordered linguistic scales, the classical operators *max*, *min*, and *neg* are proposed:

- $max(s_i, s_j) = s_i$ if $s_i \geq s_j$,
- $min(s_i, s_j) = s_i$ if $s_i \leq s_j$ and
- $neg(s_i) = s_{g-i+1}$ where g is the cardinality of S.

This model obtains easily understandable linguistic results, but their accuracy is questionable because they provide results based on the maximum or minimum values ignoring the intermediate ones.

More operators have been proposed for this model; Yager [65, 68] studied several aggregation operators for ordinal information such as weighted norm operators, uninorm operators, and ordinal mean type operators. Buckley [9] proposed different variations of the median, max, and min operators to aggregate linguistic opinions and criteria.

1.4.2.2 Linguistic Symbolic Computational Model Based on Convex Combinations

It extends the previous one by providing a wider range of aggregation operators by using a convex combination of linguistic labels [19], that acts directly on the label indexes, $\{0, \ldots, g\}$, of the linguistic term set, $S = \{s_0, \ldots, s_g\}$, in a recursive way producing a real value on the granularity interval, $[0, g]$, of the linguistic term set S. Note that this model usually assumes that the cardinality of the linguistic term set is odd and that linguistic labels are symmetrically placed around a middle term. As the result of an aggregation based on convex combination usually does not match with a term of the label set S, it is also necessary to introduce an approximation function $app_2(\cdot)$ to obtain a solution in the linguistic term set S:

$$S^n \xrightarrow{C} [0, g] \xrightarrow{app_2(\cdot)} \{0, \ldots, g\} \to S$$

Similarly to the model presented in Section 1.4.1, the approximation process produces a loss of information in the final results.

1.4.3 Characterising Classical Linguistic Computational Models

Once the classical linguistic computational models have been reviewed, it is convenient to analyse and characterise in short some issues regarding their way of making operations and their accuracy in order to characterise both models and clarify the aims of this book.

- *Computations*: The computational models based on membership functions use fuzzy arithmetic to accomplish their operations obtaining fuzzy results, meanwhile the symbolic models do not operate on fuzzy values but finally obtain a fuzzy result. Therefore, the latter models deal with a simpler operational methodology than the former ones, facilitating the computations with linguistic information.
- *Accuracy*: The models based on membership functions obtain accurate fuzzy values as a result of the fuzzy arithmetic computations but they usually do not match with initial linguistic terms and an approximation process is necessary to provide linguistic outputs. However, the symbolic models need an approximation process or deal with extreme values to obtain linguistic outputs directly. Hence the former models can obtain more accurate results but they are not linguistically interpretable, therefore both models need an approximation process to obtain linguistic results.

According to the previous two issues, it is clear that symbolic models are simpler in their computations than those based on membership functions and both models provide loss of information in their results to obtain linguistic outputs as needed by CW. Consequently, the necessity of improving linguistic computational models to obtain more accurate results in CW processes is clear. Because of their features, it seems more adequate to pay more attention to the symbolic models due to their simplicity. Therefore this book is focused on symbolic models that improve the performance of classical linguistic computational models.

1.4.4 Other Linguistic Computational Models

As mentioned before, because of the high attention that CW has received in the last years, other new approaches and methodologies for CW (some considering not only the fuzzy approach) have been introduced in the specialised literature. Although the book does not focus on them it is important to keep the eye on them because they are complementary to the previous ones and could be useful in some decision situations:

- Lawry presents both an alternative approach to CW based on mass assignment theory and a new framework for linguistic modelling that avoid some of the complexity problems that arise through using the extension principle in Zadeh's CW methodology [33–35].

- Rubin defines CW as a symbolic generalisation of fuzzy logic [49].
- Ying et al. propose a new formal model for CW based on fuzzy automata whose inputs are strings of fuzzy subsets of the input alphabet [10, 71].
- Wang et al. extend Ying's work considering CW via a different computational model, in particular, Turing machines [60].
- Tang and Zheng present a new linguistic modelling that can be applied in CW that does not directly rely on fuzzy sets to model the meaning of natural language terms, but uses some fuzzy relations between the linguistic labels to model their semantics [52].
- Türkşen proposes the use of meta-linguistic axioms as a foundation for CW as an extension of fuzzy sets and logic theory [57].

1.5 Solving a Linguistic Decision Problem: Comparative Analysis

For concluding this chapter it is interesting to analyse the performance of the different classical linguistic computational models solving a LDM problem. Therefore this section first introduces a simple LDM problem and solves it by using different linguistic computational models within the paradigm of CW, shown in Figure 1.6. Afterwards it presents a performance analysis among the different classical linguistic computational models used to clarify the importance and necessity of using accurate symbolic models such as the 2-tuple linguistic model, which is the main object of interest of this book.

1.5.1 Solving a LDM Problem by Different Linguistic Computational Models

Let $E = \{e_1, e_2, e_3, e_4\}$ and $X = \{x_1, x_2, x_3, x_4\}$ be a set of experts and alternatives, respectively, in a LDM problem in which the information is provided by means of linguistic terms in $S = \{nothing\ (n), very\ low\ (vl), low\ (l), medium\ (m), high\ (h), very\ high\ (vh), perfect\ (p)\}$ (see Figure 1.2). Each expert provides his or her preferences by a preferences vector (see Table 1.1).

Table 1.1 Preferences provided by experts

	μ_{ij}	Alternatives			
		x_1	x_2	x_3	x_4
Experts	e_1	vl	m	m	l
	e_2	m	l	vl	h
	e_3	h	vl	m	m
	e_4	h	h	l	l

Table 1.2 Solution of the LDM problem with the classical linguistic computational models

	Collective values				Solution
	x_1	x_2	x_3	x_4	
MF	(0.33,0.5,0.67)	(0.25,0.42,0.58)	(0.21,0.38,0.54)	(0.29,0.46,0.63)	
MF with app_1	m	{l,m}	l	m	$x_1 = x_2 = x_4 > x_3$
CC	m	m	l	m	$x_1 = x_2 = x_4 > x_3$
Min	vl	vl	vl	l	$x_4 > x_1 = x_2 = x_3$
Max	h	h	m	h	$x_1 = x_2 = x_4 > x_3$

μ_{ij} is the degree of preference that the expert, e_i with $i \in \{1, \ldots, 4\}$, provides regarding the alternative, x_j with $j \in \{1, \ldots, 4\}$.

Using the linguistic resolution scheme presented in Figure 1.4 where the aggregation process is carried out without loss of generality by an arithmetic mean operator, some of the different linguistic computational models reviewed previously obtain the results shown in Table 1.2.

Remark 1.1. Note that MF stands for membership functions and CC stands for convex combination.

Remark 1.2. Note that for the linguistic computational model based on ordinal scales and max-min operators, the problem has been solved by using the maximum and minimum aggregation operators. The approximation function $app_1(\cdot)$, used for the linguistic computational model based on membership functions, is the *minimum Euclidean distance*.

1.5.2   Comparative Analysis

This analysis not only studies the issues pointed out in Section 1.4.3, but also to what extent the classical linguistic computational models applied to the previous LDM problem fulfil the CW paradigm. Therefore, different features of the classical linguistic computational models regarding their fuzzy representation, accuracy, and interpretability are analysed. Table 1.3 summarises such features of the different models based on the results obtained in the decision problem.

From the data presented in Table 1.3:

- The linguistic computational model based on membership functions provides a fuzzy number as the result, therefore it could be considered accurate, but the result is not a linguistic output and it is difficult to understand. In order to obtain an interpretable and linguistic result required by CW, it is necessary to apply an approximation process, in this case app_1, but this implies loss of information and lack of accuracy in its results.

Table 1.3 Comparative analysis of the linguistic computational models

	Representation	Accuracy	Comprehension
MF	Fuzzy	Accurate	Difficult to understand
MF with app_1	Fuzzy	Lack of accuracy	Easy to understand
CC	Fuzzy	Lack of accuracy	Easy to understand
Min	Fuzzy	Lack of accuracy	Easy to understand
Max	Fuzzy	Lack of accuracy	Easy to understand

- The linguistic computational model based on convex combination obtains a linguistic output as the result, but it uses an approximation function. Therefore, it also produces loss of information and lack of precision in the results.
- The linguistic computational model based on ordinal scales and max-min operators obtains as the result a linguistic value, but is not accurate because it obtains results based on maximum or minimum values without considering any value in between that could be more adequate.

Due to the lack of accuracy and loss of information in the computing processes of the previous computational models, there could be (as in this case) multiple alternatives that obtain the same linguistic term (see Table 1.2) and thus it is not possible to discern which is best one.

Keep in mind the paradigm of CW that aims at obtaining linguistic outputs, as a result of the CW processes, that are easy to understand by human beings. The reviewed models follow the CW paradigm, but all of them present either loss of information or lack of precision in their results. Consequently, Herrera and Martínez defined the 2-tuple linguistic model in order to provide a linguistic modelling which represents the discrete linguistic information as a continuous domain to avoid the loss of information and lack of accuracy in CW processes that presents the classical linguistic computational models. Chapter 2 provides a depth revision of this model and its characteristics. Additionally, the previous LDM problem is solved by using the 2-tuple linguistic model to show its advantages regarding the classical models.

References

1. K. Anagnostopoulos, H. Doukas, and J. Psarras. A linguistic multicriteria analysis system combining fuzzy sets theory, ideal and anti-ideal points for location site selection. *Expert Systems with Applications*, 35(4):2041–2048, 2008.
2. R. Bellman, L. Kalaba, and L.A. Zadeh. Abstraction and pattern classification. *Journal of Mathematical Analysis and Applications*, 13(1):1–7, 1966.
3. R.E. Bellman and L.A. Zadeh. Decision making in a fuzzy environment. *Management Science*, 4(17), 1970.
4. P.P. Bonissone. *A fuzzy sets based linguistic approach: Theory and applications*, pages 329–339. Approximate Reasoning in Decision Analysis, North-Holland, 1982.

5. P.P. Bonissone and K.S. Decker. *Selecting Uncertainty Calculi and Granularity: An Experiment in Trading-Off Precision and Complexity*. In L.H. Kanal and J.F. Lemmer, Editors., Uncertainty in Artificial Intelligence. North-Holland, 1986.
6. R.F. Bordley and C.W. Kirkwood. Multiattribute preference analysis with performance targets. *Operations Research*, 52(6):823–835, 2004.
7. G. Bordogna and G. Pasi. A fuzzy linguistic approach generalizing boolean information retrieval: A model and its evaluation. *Journal of the American Society for Information Science*, 44:70–82, 1993.
8. D. Bouyssou, T. Marchant, M. Pirlot, P. Perny, and A. Tsoukiàs. *Evaluation and Decision Models: A critical perspective*. Kluwer Academic Publishers, 2000.
9. J.J. Buckley. The multiple judge, multiple criteria ranking problem: A fuzzy set approach. *Fuzzy Sets and Systems*, 13:23–37, 1984.
10. Y. Cao, M. Ying, and G. Chen. Retraction and generalized extension of computing with words. *IEEE Transactions on Fuzzy Systems*, 15(6):1238–1250, 2007.
11. S.L. Chang, R.C. Wang, and S.Y. Wang. Applying a direct multi-granularity linguistic and strategy-oriented aggregation approach on the assessment of supply performance. *European Journal of Operational Research*, 177(2):1013–1025, 2007.
12. S.J. Chen and C.L. Hwang. *Fuzzy multiple attribute decision-making methods and applications*, volume 375. Springer Berlin Heidelberg, 1992.
13. Y. Chen, X. Zeng, M. Happiette, P. Bruniaux, R. Ng, and W. Yu. Optimisation of garment design using fuzzy logic and sensory evaluation techniques. *Engineering applications of artificial intelligence*, 22(2):272–282, 2009.
14. Y. Chen, X. Zeng, M. Happiette, P. Bruniaux, R. Ng, and W. Yu. Optimisation of garment design using fuzzy logic and sensory evaluation techniques. *Engineering Applications of Artificial Intelligence*, 22(2):272–282, 2009.
15. Z. Chen and D. Ben-Arieh. On the fusion of multi-granularity linguistic label sets in group decision making. *Computers and Industrial Engineering*, 51(3):526–541, 2006.
16. R.T. Clemen. *Making Hard Decisions. An Introduction to Decision Analysis*. Duxbury Press, 1995.
17. R. Degani and G. Bortolan. The problem of linguistic approximation in clinical decision making. *International Journal of Approximate Reasoning*, 2:143–162, 1988.
18. M. Delgado, F. Herrera, E. Herrera Viedma, and L. Martínez. Combining numerical and linguistic information in group decision making. *Information Sciences*, 107(1–4):177–194, 1998.
19. M. Delgado, J.L. Verdegay, and M.A Vila. On aggregation operations of linguistic labels. *International Journal of Intelligent Systems*, 8(3):351–370, 1993.
20. M. Delgado, M.A. Vila, and W. Voxman. On a canonical representation of fuzzy numbers. *Fuzzy Sets and Systems*, 94:125–135, 98.
21. D. Dubois and H. Prade. The three semantics of fuzzy sets. *Fuzzy Sets and Systems*, 90:141–150, 1997.
22. R. Duncan and H. Raiffa. *Games and Decision. Introduction and Critical Survey*. Dover Publications, 1985.
23. D. Ettema, T. Gärling, L. Eriksson, M. Friman, L.E. Olsson, and S. Fujii. Satisfaction with travel and subjective well-being: Development and test of a measurement tool. *Transportation Research Part F: Traffic Psychology and Behaviour*, 14(3):167–175, 2011.
24. T. Evangelos. *Multi-criteria decision making methods: a comparative study*. Kluwer Academic Publishers, Dordrecht, 2000.
25. C. Fletcher. Performance appraisal and management: The developing. *Journal of Occupational and Organization Psychology*, 74:473–487, 2001.
26. G. Fu. A fuzzy optimization method for multicriteria decision making: An application to reservoir flood control operation. *Expert Systems with Applications*, 34(1):145–149, 2008.
27. F. Herrera and E. Herrera-Viedma. Linguistic decision analysis: Steps for solving decision problems under linguistic information. *Fuzzy Sets and Systems*, 115(1):67–82, 2000.

28. F. Herrera, E. Herrera-Viedma, and L. Martínez. A fuzzy linguistic methodology to deal with unbalanced linguistic term sets. *IEEE Transactions on Fuzzy Systems*, 16(2):354–370, 2008.
29. F. Herrera and L. Martínez. A 2-tuple fuzzy linguistic representation model for computing with words. *IEEE Transactions on Fuzzy Systems*, 8(6):746–752, 2000.
30. Q. Zuo H.T. Nguyen, V. Kreinovich. Interval-valued degrees of belief: Applications of interval computations to expert systems and intelligent control. *International Journal of Uncertainty, Fuzziness and Knowledge-Based Systems*, 5(3):317–358, 1997.
31. V.N. Huynh and Y. Nakamori. A satisfactory-oriented approach to multiexpert decision-making with linguistic assessments. *IEEE Transactions on Systems, Man, and Cybernetics, Part B: Cybernetics*, 35(2):184–196, 2005.
32. G.J. Klir and B. Yuan. *Fuzzy sets and fuzzy logic: Theory and Applications*. Prentice-Hall PTR, 1995.
33. J. Lawry. An alternative approach to computing with words. *International Journal of Uncertainty, Fuzziness and Knowledge-Based Systems*, 9 (Suppl):3–16, 2001.
34. J. Lawry. A methodology for computing with words. *International Journal of Approximate Reasoning*, 28:51–89, 2001.
35. J. Lawry. A framework for linguistic modelling. *Artificial Intelligence*, 155(1–2):1–39, 2004.
36. J. Lawry. An overview of computing with words using label semantics. *Studies in Fuzziness and Soft Computing*, 220:65–87, 2008.
37. J. Lu, G. Zhang, D. Ruan, and F. Wu. *Multi-Objective Group Decision Making. Methods, Software and Applications with Fuzzy Set Techniques*. Imperial College Press, 2007.
38. L. Martínez. Sensory evaluation based on linguistic decision analysis. *International Journal of Approximate Reasoning*, 44(2):148–164, 2007.
39. L. Martínez and F. Herrera. An overview on the 2-tuple linguistic model for computing with words in decision making: Extensions, applications and challenges. *Information Sciences*, 207(1):1–18, 2012.
40. L. Martínez, J. Liu, and J. B. Yang. A fuzzy model for design evaluation based on multiple criteria analysis in engineering systems. *International Journal of Uncertainty, Fuzziness and Knowledge-Based Systems*, 14(3):317–336, 2006.
41. L. Martínez, J. Liu, J.B. Yang, and F. Herrera. A multigranular hierarchical linguistic model for design evaluation based on safety and cost analysis. *International Journal of Intelligent Systems*, 20(12):1161–1194, 2005.
42. L. Martínez, D. Ruan, and F. Herrera. Computing with words in decision support systems: An overview on models and applications. *International Journal of Computational Intelligence Systems*, 3(4):382–395, 2010.
43. L. Martínez, D. Ruan, F. Herrera, E. Herrera-Viedma, and P.P. Wang. Linguistic decision making: Tools and applications. *Information Sciences*, 179(14):2297–2298, 2009.
44. J.M. Mendel. An architecture for making judgement using computing with words. *International Journal of Applied Mathematics and Computer Sciences*, 12(3):325–335, 2002.
45. J.M. Mendel. Computing with words: Zadeh, turing, popper and occam. *IEEE Computational Intelligence Magazine*, 2(4):10–17, 2007.
46. J.M. Mendel, L.A. Zadeh, E. Trillas, R.R. Yager, J. Lawry, H. Hagras, and S. Guadarrama. What computing with words means to me: Discussion forum. *IEEE Computational Intelligence Magazine*, 5(1):20–26, 2010.
47. R.M. Rodríguez, L. Martínez, and F. Herrera. Hesitant fuzzy linguistic term sets for decision making. *IEEE Transactions on Fuzzy Systems*, 20(1):109–119, 2012.
48. M. Roubens. Fuzzy sets and decision analysis. *Fuzzy Sets and Systems*, 90:199–206, 1997.
49. S.H. Rubin. Computing with words. *IEEE Transactions on Systems, Man and Cybernetics, Part B: Cybernetics*, 29(4):518–524, 1999.
50. K.S. Schmucker. *Fuzzy Sets, Natural Language Computations, and Risk Analysis*. Computer Science Press, Rockville, MD, 1984.
51. J.S. Son, J.H. Hong, and K.O. Kim. Effects of interval length between tasting sessions and sweetener level on long-term acceptability of novel green tea drinks. *Food Quality and Preference*, 21(8):956–966, 2010.

52. Y. Tang and J. Zheng. Linguistic modelling based on semantic similarity relation among linguistic labels. *Fuzzy Sets and Systems*, 157(12):1662–1673, 2006.

53. J.F. Le Téno and B. Mareschal. An interval version of PROMETHEE for the comparison of building products' design with ill-defined data on environmental quality. *European Journal of Operational Research*, 109:522–529, 1998.

54. M. Tong and P.P. Bonissone. A linguistic approach to decision making with fuzzy sets. *IEEE Transactions on Systems, Man and Cybernetics*, 10:716–723, 1980.

55. V. Torra. Negation function based semantics for ordered linguistic labels. *International Journal of Intelligent Systems*, 11:975–988, 1996.

56. I.B. Türkşen. Type 2 representation and reasoning for CWW. *Fuzzy Sets and Systems*, 127:17–36, 2002.

57. I.B. Türkşen. Meta-linguistic axioms as a foundation for computing with words. *Information Sciences*, 177(2):332–359, 2007.

58. J. Wang, J.B. Yang, and P. Sen. Multi-person and multi-attribute design evaluations using evidential reasoning based on subjective safety and cost analyses. *Reliability Engineering and System Safety*, 52(2):113–128, 1996.

59. Y.M. Wang, J.B. Yang, and D.L. Xu. A preference aggregation method through the estimation of utility intervals. *Computers and Operations Research*, 32:2027–2049, 2005.

60. Y.S. Wang and T.I. Tang. Assessing customer perceptions of website service quality in digital marketing environments. *Journal of End User Computing*, 15(3):14–31, 2003.

61. D. Wu. A reconstruction decoder for computing with words. *Information Sciences*, 255:1–15, 2014.

62. Z. Xu. A method based on linguistic aggregation operators for group decision making with linguistic preference relations. *Information Sciences*, 166(1–4):19–30, 2004.

63. R. R. Yager. An approach to ordinal decision making. *International Journal of Approximate Reasoning*, 12(3):237–261, 1995.

64. R.R. Yager. A new methodology for ordinal multiobjective decision based on fuzzy sets. *Decision Science*, 12:589–600, 1981.

65. R.R. Yager. Non-numeric multi-criteria multi-person decision making. *Group Decision and Negotiation*, 2:81–93, 1993.

66. R.R. Yager. *Computing with words and information/intelligent systems 2:applications*, chapter Approximate reasoning as a basis for computing with words, pages 50–77. Physica Verlag, 1999.

67. R.R. Yager. On the retranslation process in Zadeh's paradigm of computing with words. *Systems, Man, and Cybernetics, Part B: Cybernetics, IEEE Transactions on*, 34(2):1184–1195, 2004.

68. R.R. Yager. Aggregation of ordinal information. *Fuzzy Optimization and Decision Making*, 6(3):199–219, 2007.

69. J. Yang and G. Mandan. An evidential reasoning approach for multiple attribute decision making with uncertainty. *IEEE Transactions on Systems, Man and Cybernetics*, 24(1):1–17, 1994.

70. J.B Yang, J. Liu, J.Wang, H.S. Sii, and H.W. Wang. Belief rule-base inference methodology using the evidential reasoning approach-RIMER. *IEEE Transactions on Systems, Man and Cybernetics, Part A: Systems and Humans*, 36(2):266–285, 2006.

71. M. Ying. A formal model of computing with words. *IEEE Transactions on Fuzzy Systems*, 10(5):640–652, 2002.

72. L.A. Zadeh. Fuzzy sets. *Information and Control*, 8:338–353, 1965.

73. L.A. Zadeh. Outline of a new approach to the analysis of complex systems and decision processes. *IEEE Transactions on Systems, Man and Cybernetics*, SMC-3(1):28–44, 1973.

74. L.A. Zadeh. The concept of a linguistic variable and its applications to approximate reasoning. *Information Sciences, Part I, II, III*, 8,8,9:199–249,301–357,43–80, 1975.

75. L.A. Zadeh. The concept of a linguistic variable and its applications to approximate reasoning. Part I. *Information Sciences*, 8:199–249, 1975.

76. L.A. Zadeh. Fuzzy sets as a basis for a theory of possibility. *Fuzzy Sets and Systems*, 1:3–28, 1978.
77. L.A. Zadeh. *A theory of approximate reasoning*, pages 149–194. In: Machine Intelligence. Elsevier, 1979.
78. L.A. Zadeh. Fuzzy logic = computing with words. *IEEE Transactions on Fuzzy Systems*, 4(2):103–111, 1996.
79. L.A. Zadeh. From computing with numbers to computing with words - from manipulation of measurements to manipulation of perceptions. *IEEE Transactions on Circuits and Systems I: Fundamental Theory and Applications*, 46(1):105–119, 1999.
80. C. Zopounidis and M.Doumpos. *Intelligent Decision Aiding Systems Based On Multiple Criteria For Financial Engineering*. Kluwer Academic Publishers, 2000.

Chapter 2
2-Tuple Linguistic Model

2.1 Improving Symbolic Computational Approaches

In Chapter 1 the necessity of Computing with Words (CW) in linguistic decision making (LDM) has been shown and the classical semantic and symbolic computational approaches to carry out such computing processes in the decision-solving scheme have been reviewed (see Figure 1.4).

The use of classical symbolic approaches provides several good features such as the simplicity of their computations and the understandability of the results because their fuzzy semantics representation and syntax perfectly match with the terms in the linguistic term set, S, of the inputs for the CW processes. However, the symbolic approaches both based on *max-min* operators (Section 1.4.2.1) and *convex combination* (Section 1.4.2.2) present a lack of accuracy in their results, because the linguistic terms are represented by discrete elements defined in a continuous universe making it necessary to have either the use of approximation processes or the use of operators with a limited computing capacity.

Therefore, it would be necessary to improve the symbolic approaches by means of a new approach able to keep the computational simplicity and understandability of the results. Additionally, it must be able to represent accurately linguistic results that do not match with the initial terms of the linguistic term set, S, both in the fuzzy semantics and in the syntax. Hence, it is clear that to achieve such a goal, the development of a new computational approach is not only necessary, but also a new representation that can show in a continuous way the discrete linguistic terms.

Taking into account the previous premises and the goal pursued, a new linguistic representation model was introduced, the so-called 2-tuple linguistic model, which provides a continuous fuzzy representation for linguistic values and is the basis for a new computational model that keeps the simplicity of symbolic computations and overcomes the accuracy limitations of the classical symbolic computational approaches pointed out in Section 1.5, obtaining accurate linguistic results according to the CW scheme (see Figure 1.6).

© Springer International Publishing Switzerland 2015
L. Martínez et al., *The 2-tuple Linguistic Model*, DOI 10.1007/978-3-319-24714-4_2

2.2 A 2-Tuple Fuzzy Linguistic Representation Model Based on Symbolic Translation

The need of a new linguistic model as the 2-tuple linguistic model that will be used for CW processes in LDM implies that it should keep a fuzzy representation of the linguistic information and an easy to understand syntax, that is, similar to the semantics and syntax used by the fuzzy linguistic approach (see Figure 1.2).

The rationale behind the 2-tuple linguistic model comes from the lack of accuracy in classical symbolic approaches, that is, when a result does not match perfectly with a term in the initial linguistic term set, S. In such approaches, it must be approximated to the closest one, losing some information in the approximation process. Consequently, the 2-tuple linguistic model should avoid such a loss by keeping not only the closest term as the classical symbolic approach, but also the information that previous approaches remove from the final result. To do so, it represents the *translation* of the linguistic term obtained from the symbolic computation to the closest term in the initial linguistic term set (see Figure 2.1).

Therefore, the 2-tuple fuzzy linguistic representation model consists of modelling the linguistic information by means of a pair of elements [5]:

1. Let $s_i \in S = \{s_0, \ldots, s_g\}$ be a linguistic term similar to the fuzzy linguistic approach whose semantics is provided by a fuzzy membership function and the syntax chosen according to the choices offered by the fuzzy linguistic approach (see Section 1.2.1).
2. α is a numerical value, *Symbolic Translation*, that indicates the translation of the fuzzy membership function which represents the closest term, $s_i \in \{s_0, \ldots, s_g\}$, if s_i does not match exactly the computed linguistic information. The value of α is then defined as

$$\alpha = \begin{cases} [-0.5, 0.5) & \text{if } s_i \in \{s_1, s_2, \ldots, s_{g-1}\} \\ [0, 0.5) & \text{if } s_i = s_0 \\ [-0.5, 0) & \text{if } s_i = s_g \end{cases} \qquad (2.1)$$

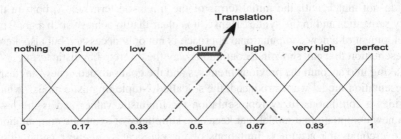

Fig. 2.1 Symbolic translation and 2-tuple fuzzy linguistic representation

Hence, the linguistic information expressed by this pair of elements is noted as (s_i, α), and the 2-tuple linguistic value. For a better understanding of this representation keep in mind that a symbolic computation on linguistic terms in S obtains a value $\beta \in [0, g]$ (see Section 1.4) that will be transformed into a equivalent 2-tuple linguistic value, (s_i, α) by means of the Δ_S function defined as follows.

Definition 2.1 ([5]). Let $S = \{s_0, \ldots, s_g\}$ be a set of linguistic terms and $\overline{S}$ the *2-tuple set associated with S* defined as $\overline{S} = S \times [-0.5, 0.5)$. The function Δ_S : $[0, g] \longrightarrow \overline{S}$ is given by

$$\Delta_S(\beta) = (s_i, \alpha), \quad \text{with} \quad \begin{cases} i = \text{round}\,(\beta), \\ \alpha = \beta - i, \end{cases} \tag{2.2}$$

with *round* the function that assigns to β the closest integer number $i \in \{0, 1, \ldots, g\}$ to β.

Therefore, a 2-tuple linguistic value $(s_i, \alpha) \in \overline{S}$ is identified with a numerical value in the interval of granularity of S, $[0, g]$.

Proposition 2.1. *Let $S = \{s_0, \ldots, s_g\}$ be a linguistic term set and $(s_i, \alpha) \in \overline{S}$ be a 2-tuple linguistic value. There is a function, Δ_S^{-1}:*

$$\Delta_S^{-1} : \overline{S} \longrightarrow [0, g]$$
$$\Delta_S^{-1}(s_i, \alpha) = i + \alpha.$$

Such that, from a 2-tuple linguistic value, it returns its equivalent numerical value $\beta \in [0, g]$.

Remark 2.1. From Definition 2.1 and Proposition 2.1, the transformation of a linguistic term in $s_i \in S$ into a 2-tuple linguistic value in $\overline{S}$ is carried out by adding a zero as a symbolic translation to the linguistic term:

$$s_i \in S \Rightarrow (s_i, 0) \in \overline{S}$$

Example 2.1. Let's suppose a symbolic aggregation operator, $\varphi(\cdot)$ whose input are different labels assessed in $S = \{nothing, very\ low, low, medium, high, very\ high, perfect\}$, obtaining the results:

$$\varphi(high, high, high, very\ low) = 3.25 = \beta_1$$
$$\varphi(low, nothing, medium, low) = 1.75 = \beta_2$$

with $\beta_1 = 3.25$ and $\beta_2 = 1.75$; then the 2-tuple linguistic values of these symbolic results that do not match with any linguistic term in S (see Figure 2.2) are:

$$\Delta_S(3.25) = (s_3, 0.25) = (\textbf{medium}, \textbf{0.25})$$
$$\Delta_S(1.75) = (s_2, -0.25) = (\textbf{low}, \textbf{-0.25})$$

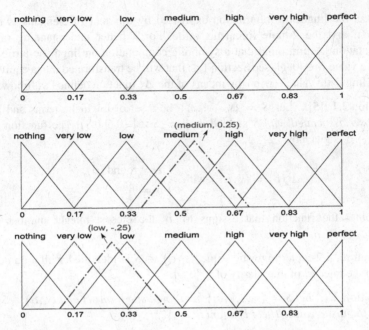

Fig. 2.2 A 2-tuple linguistic representation

In Figure 2.2 it can be seen that the 2-tuple fuzzy linguistic representation model keeps the fuzzy representation and syntax according to the fuzzy linguistic approach.

2.3 A 2-Tuple Fuzzy Linguistic Computational Model

Once the linguistic information was represented as a continuous value by means of the 2-tuple linguistic model, the next step was to develop a computing model to allow us to accomplish the processes of CW in LDM (see Figure 1.4).

Therefore, a linguistic computational approach based on the functions Δ_S and Δ_S^{-1} was defined to extend the basic operations defined for the classic symbolic approaches [20, 22], into the 2-tuple linguistic model [5]. Such initial 2-tuple basic operations are:

1. Ordering 2-tuple linguistic values
   The ordering of linguistic information represented by 2-tuple linguistic values is carried out according to an ordinary lexicographic order.
   Let (s_k, α_1) and (s_l, α_2) be two 2-tuple linguistic values, with each one representing an amount of linguistic information:

- if $k < l$ then $(s_k, \alpha_1) < (s_l, \alpha_2)$
- if $k = l$ then

  (a) if $\alpha_1 = \alpha_2$ then (s_k, α_1), (s_l, α_2) represents the same information
  (b) if $\alpha_1 < \alpha_2$ then $(s_k, \alpha_1) < (s_l, \alpha_2)$
  (c) if $\alpha_1 > \alpha_2$ then $(s_k, \alpha_1) > (s_l, \alpha_2)$

2. Negation operator of a 2-tuple linguistic value
   The notion of negation is a fundamental concept of linguistics, knowledge representation, logical systems, and so on. Hence, its definition is quite important for dealing with the 2-tuple linguistic model. It was defined as an extension of the classical negation operator for linguistic information in the fuzzy linguistic approach [21]:

   Definition 2.2 ([5]). Let $(s_i, \alpha) \in \bar{S}$, be a 2-tuple linguistic value and $S = \{s_0, \ldots, s_g\}$, the negation operator for a 2-tuple, defined as

   $$Neg((s_i, \alpha)) = \Delta(g - (\Delta^{-1}(s_i, \alpha)))$$ (2.3)

   with $g + 1$ the granularity of uncertainty of S.

3. 2-tuple aggregation operators
   The aggregation of information plays a key role in the decision-solving scheme for LDM problems (see Figure 1.4). The aggregation of a set of 2-tuple linguistic values must be a 2-tuple linguistic value that summarises such a set. Many 2-tuple linguistic aggregation operators have been defined in the literature [9, 14, 15, 25] to make the aggregation of linguistic information much more flexible. Section 2.5 is devoted to different 2-tuple linguistic aggregation operators that can be applied in different LDM problems according to their needs.

2.4 Computing with 2-Tuple Linguistic Values in Decision Making: Example

This section solves the LDM problem presented in Section 1.5.1 by using the 2-tuple linguistic model and compares the results obtained with those shown in Table 1.1.

In order to solve the decision problem, the linguistic resolution scheme depicted in Figure 1.4 is also used here, and without loss of generality the aggregation operator used to aggregate the preferences provided by experts is the 2-tuple arithmetic mean that is reviewed in the next section. Table 2.1 shows the results obtained.

The classical linguistic computational models used in Chapter 1, Section 1.5 to solve the LDM problem followed the CW paradigm, but due to the loss of information and lack of accuracy in their computational processes the results were not accurate enough to choose the best solution. However, analysing Table 2.1 with the results obtained by the 2-tuple linguistic model, it is easy to see that unlike

Table 2.1 Solution of the LDM problem with different linguistic computational models

	Collective values				Solution
	x_1	x_2	x_3	x_4	
MF	(0.33,0.5,0.67)	(0.25,0.42,0.58)	(0.21,0.38,0.54)	(0.29,0.46,0.63)	
MF with app_1	m	{l,m}	l	m	$x_1 = x_2 = x_4 > x_3$
CC	m	m	l	m	$x_1 = x_2 = x_4 > x_3$
Min	vl	vl	vl	l	$x_4 > x_1 = x_2 = x_3$
Max	h	h	m	h	$x_1 = x_2 = x_4 > x_3$
2-tuple	$(m, 0)$	$(m, -0.5)$	$(l, 0.25)$	$(m, -0.25)$	$x_1 > x_4 > x_2 > x_3$

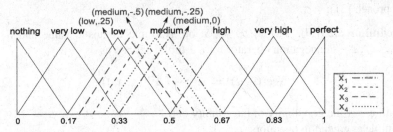

Fig. 2.3 Results of the 2-tuple linguistic model for the LDM problem

the classical models that obtain the same linguistic result in three alternatives, the 2-tuple linguistic model is able to uncover the best alternative among different alternatives, in spite of different alternatives for obtaining the same linguistic term, by means of the *symbolic translation*. Therefore, the 2-tuple linguistic model obtains more accurate results than the classical ones because it has a greater level of discrimination and hence, greater accuracy. A graphic representation of the results of the 2-tuple linguistic values for each alternative are shown in Figure 2.3.

From previous results it is clear that the 2-tuple linguistic model improves the accuracy of the CW processes regarding classical symbolic approaches because of its representation and additionally it keeps the basis of the fuzzy linguistic approach and follows the paradigm of CW. Thus, it seems more adequate to deal with linguistic information in decision making than with previous symbolic models.

2.5 2-Tuple Aggregation Operators

The aggregation of multiple values into a single one is an essential process for every discipline based on data processing, including of course decision making as pointed out previously. A key factor to determine the suitable aggregation function for a given problem depends on the relationship among the information to be aggregated. There have been defined and introduced a huge range of aggregation operators in the literature [2] that can be applied to different decision-making problems according to their requirements. Inasmuch as our interest in this book is focused on LDM and in the 2-tuple linguistic model, this section reviews some of the most common aggregation operators that have been defined for the 2-tuple linguistic model. They have been classified by operator families such as:

- Basic average aggregation operators
- Based on the geometric average
- Based on the harmonic average
- Based on the power average
- Based on Choquet integral
- Dynamic aggregation operators

2.5.1 Basic Average Aggregation Operators

This section introduces the simplest and most basic average aggregation operators extended for 2-tuple linguistic values such as the arithmetic mean, weighted average, linguistic ordered weighted aggregation, and the hybrid weighted arithmetic average.

The first aggregation operator defined for aggregating 2-tuple linguistic values was the arithmetic mean that extends the arithmetic mean for numerical values.

Definition 2.3 ([5]). Let $X = \{(s_1, \alpha_1), \ldots, (s_n, \alpha_n)\}$ be a set of 2-tuple linguistic values; the 2-tuple arithmetic mean, $\bar{x} : \overline{S}^n \mapsto \overline{S}$, is computed as

$$\bar{x}((s_1, \alpha_1), \ldots, (s_n, \alpha_n)) = \Delta \left(\frac{1}{n} \sum_{i=1}^{n} \Delta^{-1}(s_i, \alpha_i) \right) = \Delta \left(\frac{1}{n} \sum_{i=1}^{n} \beta_i \right) \quad (2.4)$$

The arithmetic mean for 2-tuple linguistic values allows us to compute the mean of a set of linguistic values in a linguistic and precise way without any approximation process.

Example 2.2. Let's suppose an example where the expert provides her assessments in the linguistic term set, $S = \{s_0 : nothing\ (n), s_1 : very\ low\ (vl), s_2 : low\ (l), s_3 : medium\ (m), s_4 : high\ (h), s_5 : very\ high\ (vh), s_6 : perfect\ (p)\}$, shown in Figure 2.1, providing the linguistic preference vector:

$$\{l, h, m, vl\}$$

The aggregation of these values by using the 2-tuple arithmetic mean as aggregation operator is:

- The preference vector is transformed into 2-tuple linguistic values:

$$\{(l, 0), (h, 0), (m, 0), (vl, 0)\}$$

- The result of the aggregation is:

$$\bar{x}((l,0),(h,0),(m,0),(vl,0)) =$$

$$= \Delta(\frac{1}{4}(\Delta^{-1}(l,0) + \Delta^{-1}(h,0) + \Delta^{-1}(m,0) + \Delta^{-1}(vl,0))) = \Delta(2.5) = (\mathbf{m}, -0.5)$$

Another usual aggregation operator is the weighted average operator that integrates the importance of each element in the aggregation process. This operator which deals with 2-tuple linguistic values is defined as

Definition 2.4 ([5]). Let $X = \{(s_1, \alpha_1), \ldots, (s_n, \alpha_n)\}$ be a set of 2-tuple linguistic values and $W = \{w_1, \ldots, w_n\}$ be their associated weights. The 2-tuple weighted average, $\bar{x}^w : \bar{S}^n \mapsto \bar{S}$, is:

$$x^w((s_1, \alpha_1), \ldots, (s_n, \alpha_n)) = \Delta\left(\frac{\sum_{i=1}^n \Delta^{-1}(s_i, \alpha_i) \cdot w_i}{\sum_{i=1}^n w_i}\right) = \Delta\left(\frac{\sum_{i=1}^n \beta_i \cdot w_i}{\sum_{i=1}^n w_i}\right)$$

Example 2.3. Keep using the data of Example 2.2; they are aggregated by using the weighted average operator. First, it is necessary to define the weighting vector $W = \{w_1, \ldots, w_n\}$; in this example we use:

$$W = \{0.2, 0.15, 0.5, 0.15\}$$

The aggregation outcome using the 2-tuple weighted average operator is computed as

$$\bar{x}^w((l,0),(h,0),(m,0),(vl,0)) =$$

$$= \Delta(0.2 * (\Delta^{-1}(l,0) + 0.15 * \Delta^{-1}(h,0) + 0.5 * \Delta^{-1}(m,0) + 0.15 * \Delta^{-1}(vl,0))) =$$

$$= \Delta(2.65) = (\mathbf{m}, -0.35)$$

The OWA (ordered weighted aggregation) operator introduced by Yager in [21], which weights the importance of the ordered elements, has been widely used in decision making. Its linguistic extension, L2TOWA, to deal with 2-tuple linguistic values is defined as

Definition 2.5 ([10]). A L2TOWA operator of dimension n is a mapping $L2TOWA : \bar{S}^n \mapsto \bar{S}$, which has an associated weighting vector $W = \{w_1, \ldots, w_n\}$ such that $w_j \in [0, 1]$ and $\sum_{j=1}^n w_j = 1$, then:

$$L2TOWA((s_1, \alpha_1), \ldots, (s_n, \alpha_n)) = \Delta(\sum_{j=1}^n w_j \cdot \beta_j) \qquad (2.5)$$

With β_j the jth largest value of the $\beta_i = \Delta^{-1}(s_i, \alpha_i)| \ i = \{1, \ldots, n\}$ values.

An important question in the definition of the OWA operator is how to obtain the associated weighting vector W. There are different methods to compute the OWA weights. An interesting proposal was presented in [23] which is based on nondecreasing linguistic quantifiers Q. Therefore, the weighting vector W is computed as

Definition 2.6 ([23]). A nondecreasing linguistic quantifier is a function Q : $[0, 1] \rightarrow [0, 1]$ defined by

$$
Q(x) = \begin{cases} 0 & \text{if } x \le a, \\ \frac{x-a}{b-a} & \text{if } a < x \le b, \\ 1 & \text{if } x > b. \end{cases} \tag{2.6}
$$

where $a, b \in [0, 1]$ and $a < b$. $Q(x) \ge Q(y)$ whenever $x \ge y$.

Yager proposed the following method to compute the OWA weights, w_i, upon $Q(x)$ [21, 23]:

$$
w_i = Q\left(\frac{i}{n}\right) - Q\left(\frac{i-1}{n}\right), \ i = \{1, \dots, n\} \tag{2.7}
$$

Some examples of nondecreasing linguistic quantifiers are:

- *Most* with $(a, b) = (0.3, 0.8)$
- *At least half* with $(a, b) = (0, 0.5)$
- *As many as possible* with $(a, b) = (0.5, 1)$

Example 2.4. This example again uses the same data of previous examples, but the weighting vector is obtained by applying the previous linguistic quantifier *most*. Therefore, the weights are obtained as

$$
w_1 = Q(1/4) - Q(0) = Q(0.25) = 0
$$
$$
w_2 = Q(2/4) - Q(1/4) = Q(0.5) - Q(0.25) = 0.4 - 0 = 0.4
$$
$$
w_3 = Q(3/4) - Q(2/4) = Q(0.75) - Q(0.5) = 0.9 - 0.4 = 0.5
$$
$$
w_4 = Q(1) - Q(3/4) = 1 - 0.9 = 0.1
$$

$$
W = \{0, 0.4, 0.5, 0.1\}
$$

The aggregation values obtained by using the L2TOWA operator are:

$L2TOWA((l, 0), (h, 0), (m, 0), (vl, 0)) =$

$= \Delta(0 * (\Delta^{-1}(h, 0) + 0.4 * \Delta^{-1}(m, 0) + 0.5 * \Delta^{-1}(l, 0) + 0.1 * \Delta^{-1}(vl, 0))) =$

$= \Delta(2.3) = (l, 0.3)$

It can be seen from Definitions 2.4 and 2.5 that the former weights are related to the 2-tuple linguistic arguments, although the latter weights are used according to the ordered position of such arguments. Therefore, the weighting vectors represent different aspects in both operators. An interesting issue is to combine both operators.

Definition 2.7 ([13]). Let $X = \{(s_1, \alpha_1), \ldots, (s_n, \alpha_n)\}$ be a set of 2-tuple linguistic values; the 2-tuple hybrid weighted arithmetic average (T2HWA) operator of dimension n is a mapping $T2HWA : \overline{S}^n \mapsto \overline{S}$,

$$T2HWA((s_1, \alpha_1), \ldots, (s_n, \alpha_n)) = \Delta \left(\sum_{j=1}^{n} (w_j \beta_j') \right) \qquad (2.8)$$

Let $W = \{w_1, \ldots, w_n\}$ be the weighting vector for the ordered arguments satisfying that $w_j \in [0, 1]$ and $\sum_{j=1}^{n} w_j = 1$; β_j' is the jth largest value of the (β_i') $(i = 1, \ldots, n)$ with $(\beta_i' = n\omega_i\beta_i)$ where $\omega = \{\omega_1, \ldots, \omega_n\}$ is the weighting vector associated with the arguments (β_i) $(i = 1, \ldots, n)$ satisfying that $\omega_i \in [0, 1]$ and $\sum_{i=1}^{n} \omega_i = 1$; n is the balancing coefficient.

Example 2.5. Let's suppose the previous set of 2-tuple linguistic values, the weighting vector for the arguments $\omega = \{0.2, 0.15, 0.5, 0.15\}$, and the weighting vector for the ordered arguments $W = \{0.1, 0.35, 0.4, 0.15\}$, the aggregation by using the T2HWA operator is:

$$(s_1', \alpha_1') = \Delta(4 * 0.2 * \Delta^{-1}(l, 0)) = (l, -.4),$$

$$(s_2', \alpha_2') = \Delta(4 * 0.15 * \Delta^{-1}(h, 0)) = (l, 0.4),$$

$$(s_3', \alpha_3') = \Delta(4 * 0.5 * \Delta^{-1}(m, 0) = (p, 0),$$

$$(s_4', \alpha_4') = \Delta(4 * 0.15 * \Delta^{-1}(vl, 0) = (vl, -.4)$$

$T2HWA((l, 0), (h, 0), (m, 0), (vl, 0)) =$

$= \Delta(0.1 * \Delta^{-1}(p, 0) + 0.35 * \Delta^{-1}(l, 0.4) + 0.4 * \Delta^{-1}(l, -.4) + 0.15 * \Delta^{-1}(vl, -.4)) =$

$= \Delta(2.17) = \mathbf{(l, 0.17)}$

More hybrid arithmetic averaging operators can be found in [13].

2.5.2 Operators Based on Geometric Average

The geometric average (GA) operator is a type of average that shows the typical value of a set of numbers by using the product of their values. It is often used to compare different items that have different numerical ranges. There are different extensions of this operator such as weighted geometric averaging (WGA) and ordered weighted geometric averaging (OWGA) operators. Both of them have been extended to deal with 2-tuple linguistic values.

Definition 2.8 ([17]). Let $X = \{(s_1, \alpha_1), \ldots, (s_n, \alpha_n)\}$ be a set of 2-tuple linguistic values; the 2-tuple geometric averaging (TGA) operator of dimension n is a mapping $TGA : \overline{S}^n \mapsto \overline{S}$,

$$TGA((s_1, \alpha_1), \ldots, (s_n, \alpha_n)) = \Delta((\prod_{i=1}^{n} \beta_i)^{1/n}), \quad \beta_i = \Delta^{-1}(s_i, \alpha_i) \tag{2.9}$$

Example 2.6. By using the data of Example 2.2, the result of the aggregation is:

$$TGA((l, 0), (h, 0), (m, 0), (vl, 0)) =$$

$$= \Delta((\Delta^{-1}(l, 0) \times \Delta^{-1}(h, 0) \times \Delta^{-1}(m, 0) \times \Delta^{-1}(vl, 0))^{1/4}) = \Delta(2.21) = (\mathbf{l}, \mathbf{0.21})$$

Definition 2.9 ([17]). The 2-tuple weighted geometric averaging operator of dimension n is a mapping $TWGA : \overline{S}^n \mapsto \overline{S}$, which has an exponential weighting vector $W = \{w_1, \ldots, w_n\}$ such that $w_i \in [0, 1]$ and $\sum_{i=1}^{n} w_i = 1$, then:

$$TWGA((s_1, \alpha_1), \ldots, (s_n, \alpha_n)) = \Delta(\prod_{i=1}^{n} \beta_i^{w_i}), \quad \beta_i = \Delta^{-1}(s_i, \alpha_i) \tag{2.10}$$

Remark 2.2. If the exponential weighting vector is $W = \{1/n, 1/n, \ldots, 1/n\}$, the TWGA is reduced to TGA.

Example 2.7. Let us suppose the exponential weighting vector $W = \{0.2, 0.15, 0.5, 0.15\}$ and the same set of 2-tuple linguistic values as in Example 2.2; the result of applying the TWGA operator is:

$$TWGA((l, 0), (h, 0), (m, 0), (vl, 0)) =$$

$$= \Delta(\Delta^{-1}(l, 0)^{0.2} \times \Delta^{-1}(h, 0)^{0.15} \times \Delta^{-1}(m, 0)^{0.5} \times \Delta^{-1}(vl, 0)^{0.15}) =$$

$$= \Delta(2.45) = (\mathbf{l}, \mathbf{0.45})$$

Definition 2.10 ([17]). The 2-tuple ordered weighted geometric averaging (TOWGA) operator of dimension n is a mapping $TOWGA : \overline{S}^n \mapsto \overline{S}$, which has an associated weighting vector W that satisfies $w_j \in [0, 1]$ and $\sum_{j=1}^{n} w_j = 1$:

$$TOWGA((s_1, \alpha_1), \ldots, (s_n, \alpha_n)) = \Delta(\prod_{j=1}^{n} \beta_j^{w_j}) \tag{2.11}$$

where β_j is the jth largest value of $\beta_i = \Delta^{-1}(s_i, \alpha_i) \mid i = \{1, \ldots, n\}$.

Example 2.8. Let us suppose the weighting vector $W = \{0.1, 0.35, 0.4, 0.15\}$ and the previous set of 2-tuple linguistic values; the result of applying the TOWGA operator is:

$$TOWGA = ((l, 0), (h, 0), (m, 0), (vl, 0)) =$$

$$= \Delta(\Delta^{-1}(h, 0)^{0.1} \times \Delta^{-1}(m, 0)^{0.35} \times \Delta^{-1}(l, 0)^{0.4} \times \Delta^{-1}(vl, 0)^{0.15})) =$$

$$= \Delta(2.23) = (l, 0.23)$$

From Definitions 2.9 and 2.10 it can be seen that the TWGA operator integrates the importance into the linguistic arguments, and the TOWGA operator weights the ordered positions of the linguistic arguments instead of weighting the arguments themselves. Therefore, the weighting vectors represent different aspects in both operators. Nevertheless, such operators only take into account one aspect. Hence, a new operator was proposed to combine both aspects.

Definition 2.11 ([17]). The 2-tuple hybrid geometric averaging (THGA) operator of dimension n is a mapping $THGA : \overline{S}^n \mapsto \overline{S}$, which has an associated weighting vector $W = \{w_1, \ldots, w_n\}$ that satisfies $w_j \in [0, 1]$ and $\sum_{j=1}^{n} w_j = 1$:

$$THGA((s_1, \alpha_1), \ldots, (s_n, \alpha_n)) = \Delta(\prod_{j=1}^{n} \beta_j'^{w_j}) \qquad (2.12)$$

where β_j' is the jth largest value of the 2-tuple linguistic weighted arguments $\beta_i' = \beta_i^{n\omega_i}$, $i = \{1, \ldots, n\}$ and ω is the exponential weighting vector of the β_i with $\omega_i \in [0, 1]$ and $\sum_{i=1}^{n} \omega_i = 1$ and n is the balancing coefficient.

Example 2.9. If we use the same data of Example 2.2 with $\omega = \{0.2, 0.15, 0.5, 0.15\}$, the weighting vector for the arguments and $W = \{0.1, 0.35, 0.4, 0.15, \}$ the weighting vector for the ordered arguments, the aggregation by using the THGA operator is:

$$\beta_1' = \Delta^{-1}(l, 0)^{(4*0.2)} = 1.74,$$

$$\beta_2' = \Delta^{-1}(h, 0)^{(4*0.15)6} = 2.3,$$

$$\beta_3' = \Delta^{-1}(m, 0)^{(4*0.5)} = 9,$$

$$\beta_4' = \Delta^{-1}(vl, 0)^{(4*0.15)} = 1$$

$$THGA((l, 0), (h, 0), (m, 0), (vl, 0)) = \Delta(9^{0.1} \times 2.3^{0.35} \times 1.74^{0.4} \times 1^{0.15}) = \Delta(2.08) =$$

$$= (l, 0.08)$$

More hybrid geometric averaging operators for 2-tuple can be found in [14].

2.5.3   Operators Based on Harmonic Average

Another well-known aggregation operator is the harmonic average. It is defined as the reciprocal of the arithmetic mean of the reciprocals, and is used to compute the average of values which vary across time. Wei defined several extensions of this operator to deal with 2-tuple linguistic values [16].

Definition 2.12 ([16]). The 2-tuple weighted harmonic average of dimension n is a mapping $TWHA : \overline{S}^n \mapsto \overline{S}$, which has a weighting vector $W = \{w_1, \ldots, w_n\}$ such that $w_i \in [0, 1]$ and $\sum_{i=1}^n w_i = 1$:

$$TWHA((s_1, \alpha_1), \ldots, (s_n, \alpha_n)) = \Delta\left(1 / \sum_{j=1}^n \frac{w_i}{\beta_i}\right), \quad \beta_i = \Delta^{-1}(s_i, \alpha_i) \qquad (2.13)$$

Example 2.10. By using the same set of 2-tuple linguistic values as in Example 2.2 and the weighted vector $W = \{0.2, 0.15, 0.5, 0.15\}$, the result of aggregating the values by TWHA operator is:

$$TWHA((l, 0), (h, 0), (m, 0), (vl, 0)) =$$

$$= \Delta\left(\frac{1}{\frac{0.2}{\Delta^{-1}(l,0)} + \frac{0.15}{\Delta^{-1}(h,0)} + \frac{0.5}{\Delta^{-1}(m,0)} + \frac{0.15}{\Delta^{-1}(vl,0)}}\right) = \Delta(2.2) = (\mathbf{1, 0.2})$$

Definition 2.13 ([16]). The 2-tuple ordered weighted harmonic average (TOWHA) of dimension n is a mapping $TWHA : \overline{S}^n \mapsto \overline{S}$, which has a weighting vector W associated with the order of the arguments (s_i, α_i) such that $w_j \in [0, 1]$ and $\sum_{j=1}^n w_j = 1$:

$$TOWHA((s_1, \alpha_1), (s_2, \alpha_2), \ldots, (s_n, \alpha_n)) = \Delta\left(1 / \sum_{j=1}^n \frac{w_j}{\beta_j},\right) \qquad (2.14)$$

where β_j is the jth largest value of $\beta_i = \Delta^{-1}(s_i, \alpha_i) \mid i = \{1, \ldots, n\}$ values.

Example 2.11. Let us suppose the weighted vector $W = \{0.1, 0.35, 0.4, 0.15\}$ and the previous set of 2-tuple linguistic values; the result of applying the TOWHA is the following one.

$$TOWHA((l, 0), (h, 0), (m, 0), (vl, 0)) =$$

$$= \Delta\left(\frac{1}{\frac{0.1}{\Delta^{-1}(h,0)} + \frac{0.35}{\Delta^{-1}(m,0)} + \frac{0.4}{\Delta^{-1}(l,0)} + \frac{0.15}{\Delta^{-1}(vl,0)}}\right) = \Delta(2.03) = (\mathbf{1, 0.3})$$

A combination of TWHA and TOWHA was proposed to take into account the importance of the arguments and also the weight related to the positions of the values to be aggregated.

Definition 2.14 ([16]). The 2-tuple combined weighted harmonic average (TCWHA) of dimension n is a mapping $TCWHA : \overline{S}^n \mapsto \overline{S}$, which has an associated weighting vector $W = \{w_1, \ldots, w_n\}$ such that $w_j \in [0, 1]$ and $\sum_{j=1}^n w_j = 1$:

$$TCWHA((s_1, \alpha_1), \ldots, (s_n, \alpha_n)) = \Delta \left(1 / \sum_{j=1}^n \frac{w_j}{\beta'_j} \right) \tag{2.15}$$

where β'_j is the jth largest of the 2-tuple linguistic values $\beta'_i = \beta_i / n\omega_i \mid i = \{1, \ldots, n\}\}$ and ω is the weighting vector of the 2-tuple linguistic values β_i with $\omega_i \in [0, 1]$ and $\sum_{i=1}^n \omega_i = 1$ and n is the balancing coefficient.

Example 2.12. By using the same set of 2-tuple linguistic values of the Example 2.2 with $\omega = \{0.2, 0.15, 0.5, 0.15\}$, the weighting vector for the arguments, and $W = \{0.1, 0.35, 0.4, 0.15, \}$, the weighting vector for the ordered arguments, the aggregation by using the TCWHA operator is:

$$\beta'_1 = \frac{\Delta^{-1}(l, 0)}{4 * 0.2} = 2.25,$$

$$\beta'_2 = \frac{\Delta^{-1}(h, 0)}{4 * 0.15} = 6.67,$$

$$\beta'_3 = \frac{\Delta^{-1}(m, 0)}{4 * 0.5} = 1.5,$$

$$\beta'_4 = \frac{\Delta^{-1}(vl, 0)}{4 * 0.15} = 1.67$$

$$TCWHA((l, 0), (h, 0), (m, 0), (vl, 0)) =$$

$$= \Delta \left(\frac{1}{\frac{0.1}{6.67} + \frac{0.35}{2.25} + \frac{0.4}{1.67} + \frac{0.15}{1.5}} \right) = \Delta(2.02) = (l, 0.02)$$

2.5.4 Operators Based on Power Average

The power average was defined by Yager [24] to consider the relationship among the argument values to be aggregated. This operator has been extended to aggregate 2-tuple linguistic values.

Definition 2.15 ([18]). Let $X = \{(s_1, \alpha_1), \ldots, (s_n, \alpha_n)\}$ be a set of 2-tuple linguistic values, the 2-tuple linguistic power average operator (2TLPA) is defined as

$$2TLPA((s_1, \alpha_1), \ldots, (s_n, \alpha_n)) = \Delta \left(\frac{\sum_{j=1}^{n}(1 + T(s_j, \alpha_j))\beta_j}{\sum_{j=1}^{n}(1 + T(s_j, \alpha_j))} \right) \qquad (2.16)$$

where $T(s_j, \alpha_j)$ is computed as

$$T(s_j, \alpha_j) = \sum_{i=1, i \neq j}^{n} Supp((s_j, \alpha_j), (s_i, \alpha_i)) \qquad (2.17)$$

and $Supp((s_j, \alpha_j), (s_i, \alpha_i))$ is a function (a similarity measure) that must satisfy three properties which can be found in [18].

If each argument has a weight to reflect its importance, the previous operator is then defined as

Definition 2.16 ([18]). Let $X = \{(s_1, \alpha_1), \ldots, (s_n, \alpha_n)\}$ be a set of 2-tuple linguistic values and $W = \{w_1, \ldots, w_n\}$, the weighting vector, which satisfies $w_j \in [0, 1]$ and $\sum_{j=1}^{n} w_j = 1$. The 2-tuple linguistic weighted power average operator (2TLWPA) is defined as

$$2TLWPA((s_1, \alpha_1), \ldots, (s_n, \alpha_n)) = \Delta \left(\frac{\sum_{j=1}^{n} w_j(1 + T(s_j, \alpha_j))\beta_j}{\sum_{j=1}^{n} w_j(1 + T(s_j, \alpha_j))} \right) \qquad (2.18)$$

By using the OWA and the 2TLPA operators, Xu and Wang [19] introduced the 2-tuple linguistic power ordered weighted average operator.

Definition 2.17 ([18]). Let $X = \{(s_1, \alpha_1), \ldots, (s_n, \alpha_n)\}$ be a set of 2-tuple linguistic values, the 2-tuple linguistic power ordered weighted average (2TLPOWA) operator is defined as

$$2TLPOWA((s_1, \alpha_1), \ldots, (s_n, \alpha_n)) = \Delta \left(\sum_{j=1}^{n} u_j \beta_j \right) \qquad (2.19)$$

where β_j is the jth largest value of the β_i and

$$u_j = g\left(\frac{B_j}{TV}\right) - g\left(\frac{B_{j-1}}{TV}\right), \quad B_j = \sum_{i=1}^{j} V_{\sigma(i)},$$

$$TV = \sum_{j=1}^{n} V_{\sigma(j)}, \quad V_{\sigma(j)} = 1 + T(s_{\sigma(j)}, \alpha_{\sigma(j)})$$

where $g : [0, 1] \rightarrow [0, 1]$ is a basic unit-interval monotonic function having the properties: (i) $g(0) = 0$; (ii) $g(1) = 1$; (iii) $g(x) \geq g(y)$ if $x > y$, and $T(r_{\sigma(j)}, \alpha_{\sigma(j)})$ is the support of the jth largest argument; that is,

$$T(s_{\sigma(j)}, \alpha_{\sigma(j)}) = \sum_{i=1, i \neq j}^{n} Supp((s_{\sigma(j)}, \alpha_{\sigma(j)}), (s_{\sigma(i)}, \alpha_{\sigma(i)})) \qquad (2.20)$$

where $Supp((s_{\sigma(j)}, \alpha_{\sigma(j)}), (s_{\sigma(i)}, \alpha_{\sigma(i)}))$ indicates the support of ith largest argument for the jth largest argument.

2.5.5 Operators Based on Choquet Integral

The Choquet integral [3, 4] is an important tool for decision making under uncertainty. It allows us to model the interdependence or correlation among different elements. The Choquet integral has been used as the basis to define new aggregation operators, among them 2-tuple correlated averaging, 2-tuple correlated geometric, and the generalised 2-tuple correlated averaging operators.

Definition 2.18 ([26]). Let $\{(s_1, \alpha_1), \ldots, (s_n, \alpha_n)\}$ be a set of 2-tuple linguistic values, X be the set of attributes, and μ be a fuzzy measure on X; the 2-tuple correlated averaging (2TCA) operator is then defined as

$$2TCA_{\mu}((s_1, \alpha_1), \ldots, (s_n, \alpha_n))$$

$$= \Delta \left(\sum_{i=1}^{n} (\mu(H_{\sigma(i)}) - \mu(H_{\sigma(i-1)})) \Delta^{-1}(s_{\sigma(i)}, \alpha_{\sigma(i)}) \right) \qquad (2.21)$$

being $(\sigma(1), \sigma(2), \ldots, \sigma(n))$ a permutation of $(1, \ldots, n)$ such that, $(s_{\sigma(1)}, \alpha_{\sigma(1)}) \geq (s_{\sigma(2)}, \alpha_{\sigma(2)}) \geq, \ldots, \geq (s_{\sigma(n)}, \alpha_{\sigma(n)})$, $x_{\sigma(i)}$ is the corresponding attribute to $(s_{\sigma(i)}, \alpha_{\sigma(i)})$, $H_{\sigma(i)} = \{x_{\sigma(k)} | k \leq i\}$ for $i \geq 1$, $H_{\sigma(0)} = \phi$.

Definition 2.19 ([26]). Let $\{(s_1, \alpha_1), \ldots, (s_n, \alpha_n)\}$ be a set of 2-tuple linguistic values, X be the set of attributes, and μ be a fuzzy measure on X; the 2-tuple correlated geometric (2TCG) operator is defined as

$$2TCG_{\mu}((s_1, \alpha_1), \ldots, (s_n, \alpha_n))$$

$$= \Delta \left(\prod_{i=1}^{n} \Delta^{-1}(s_{\sigma(i)}, \alpha_{\sigma(i)})^{(\mu(H_{\sigma(i)}) - \mu(H_{\sigma(i-1)}))} \right) \qquad (2.22)$$

Definition 2.20 ([26]). Let $\{(s_1, \alpha_1), \ldots, (s_n, \alpha_n)\}$ be a set of 2-tuple linguistic values, X be the set of attributes, μ be a fuzzy measure on X, and $\lambda > 0$; the generalised 2-tuple correlated averaging (G2TCA) operator is defined as

$$G2TCA_{\mu,\lambda}((s_1,\alpha_1),\ldots,(s_n,\alpha_n))$$

$$= \Delta \left(\sum_{i=1}^{n} (\mu(H_{\sigma(i)}) - \mu(H_{\sigma(i-1)}))(\Delta^{-1}(s_{\sigma(i)},\alpha_{\sigma(i)}))^{\lambda} \right)^{1/\lambda} \tag{2.23}$$

More aggregation operators which take into account correlation of information can be found in [25].

2.5.6 Dynamic Operators

Some decision problems take place in an environment that changes over time, for instance, environmental evaluations, investment decisions, medical diagnoses, and so on. In such cases, it is necessary to consider the time to solve the problems. Different dynamic aggregation operators have been introduced in the literature [7]. Liu et al. [8] extended the 2-tuple weighted average operator to deal with dynamic information.

Definition 2.21 ([8]). Let $X = \{(s(t_1),\alpha(t_1)),\ldots,(s(t_p),\alpha(t_p))\}$ be a set of 2-tuple linguistic values at p different periods of time $t_k(k = 1,2,\ldots,p)$, and $\lambda(t) = (\lambda(t_1),\ldots,\lambda(t_p))$ be the weighting vector of t_k; the dynamic 2-tuple weighted averaging (D2TWA) operator is:

$$D2TWA((s(t_1),\alpha(t_1)),\ldots,(s(t_p),\alpha(t_p))) = \tag{2.24}$$

$$\Delta \left(\sum_{k=1}^{p} \lambda(t_k)\Delta^{-1}(s(t_k),\alpha(t_k)) \right) = \Delta \left(\sum_{k=1}^{p} \lambda(t_k)\beta(t_k) \right)$$

where $\lambda(t_k) \geq 0$, $\sum_{k=1}^{p} \lambda(t_k) = 1$ and $\Delta^{-1}(r(t_k),\alpha(t_k)) = \beta(t_k)$.

The weighting vector $\lambda(t_k)$ can be calculated subjectively by experts involved in the problem according to difference importance over time or it can also be computed by other methods.

2.5.7 More Operators

Merigó and Lafuente presented in [11] the induced 2-tuple linguistic generalised OWA operator that is a generalisation of a wide range of 2-tuple linguistic aggregation operators. Wei and Zhao [15] defined dependent operators for 2-tuple linguistic values. More operators can be found in [1, 6, 12].

A deep review of the literature will provide the reader a wide range of aggregation operators for 2-tuple linguistic values which can be used in different decision situations according to the requirements to be satisfied by the aggregation process.

2.6   Illustrative Example

Once the main concepts and tools related to the 2-tuple linguistic model have been introduced in this chapter, the LDM problem presented in Section 1.5.1 is solved by following the LDM scheme shown in Figure 1.4, but applying some of the aggregation operators for 2-tuple defined previously.

In this problem, there is a set of experts, $E = \{e_1, \ldots, e_4\}$, and alternatives, $X = \{x_1, \ldots, x_4\}$, respectively. Experts provide their assessments by the linguistic term set $S = \{nothing, very\ low, low, medium, high, very\ high, perfect\}$ (see Figure 2.2).

- The performance vectors elicited by the experts and transformed into 2-tuple linguistic values are shown in Table 2.2.
- The 2-tuple linguistic values are aggregated by using different aggregation operators which have been introduced in Section 2.5. The weighting vector associated with the arguments is $\omega = (0.15, 0.3, 0.45, 0.1)$ and the weighting vector associated with the positions is $W = (0.2, 0.15, 0.4, 0.25)$. Table 2.3 shows the collective performance values for each alternative and the solution.

Table 2.3 shows the accuracy of the 2-tuple linguistic model disregarding the operator used, because it represents the results of the computing processes keeping the symbolic translation when the linguistic result does not exactly match with any initial linguistic term in S. Unlike the results obtained by using the classical symbolic models (see Table 1.2) were not accurate because of the approximation process. The linguistic results based on the 2-tuple linguistic model are also easy to understand by human beings. Consequently, the 2-tuple linguistic model has been widely used in LDM and even though it is a quite recent model, some important extensions have been developed to generalise and extend the 2-tuple linguistic model. The next chapter is focused on such extensions.

			Alternatives			
			x_1	x_2	x_3	x_4
Experts		p_1	$(vl, 0)$	$(m, 0)$	$(m, 0)$	$(l, 0)$
		p_2	$(m, 0)$	$(l, 0)$	$(vl, 0)$	$(h, 0)$
		p_3	$(h, 0)$	$(vl, 0)$	$(m, 0)$	$(m, 0)$
		p_4	$(h, 0)$	$(h, 0)$	$(l, 0)$	$(l, 0)$

Table 2.2 Assessments provided by experts transformed into 2-tuple linguistic values

Table 2.3 Results using different aggregation operators for 2-tuple linguistic values

	Collective values				
	x_1	x_2	x_3	x_4	Solution
$\bar{x}$	(m,0)	(m,−0.5)	(l,0.25)	(m,−0.25)	$x_1 > x_4 > x_2 > x_3$
$\bar{x}^w$	(m,0.25)	(l,−0.1)	(vl,0.45)	(n,0.2)	$x_1 > x_2 > x_3 > x_4$
L2TOWA	(m,−0.15)	(l,0.3)	(l,−0.05)	(vl,0)	$x_1 > x_2 > x_3 > x_4$
T2HWA	(m,−0.33)	(l,−0.13)	(l,0.03)	(l,0.48)	$x_1 > x_4 > x_3 > x_2$
TGA	(m,−0.37)	(l,0.21)	(l, 0.06)	(m,−0.37)	$x_1 > x_4 > x_2 > x_3$
TGWA	(h,−0.26)	(m,0.4)	(m,0)	(h,−0.17)	$x_4 > x_1 > x_3 > x_2$
TGOWA	(m,−0.48)	(l,0.05)	(l, −0.06)	(l,0.44)	$x_1 > x_4 > x_2 > x_3$
THGA	(m,−0.49)	(l,−0.37)	(l,−0.17)	(l,0.42)	$x_1 > x_4 > x_3 > x_2$
TWHA	(m,−0.42)	(vl,0.48)	(l,−0.18)	(m,−0.14)	$x_4 > x_1 > x_3 > x_2$
TOWHA	(l,0.12)	(l,−0.18)	(l,−0.24)	(l,0.35)	$x_4 > x_1 > x_2 > x_3$
TCWHA	(l, 0.44)	(vl,0.36)	(l,−0.36)	(m,−0.18)	$x_4 > x_1 > x_3 > x_2$
2TLPA	(m,0.1)	(m,−0.5)	(l,0.26)	(m,−0.28)	$x_1 > x_4 > x_2 > x_3$
2TLWPA	(m,0.32)	(l,−0.08)	(l,0.28)	(m,0.02)	$x_1 > x_4 > x_3 > x_2$

References

1. D. Ben-Arieh and Z. Chen. Linguistic group decision-making: Opinion aggregation and measures of consensus. *Fuzzy Optimisation and Decision Making*, 5(4):371–386, 2006.
2. T. Calvo, G. Mayor, and R. Mesiar, editors. *Aggregation operators. New trends and applications*, volume 97 of *Studies in Fuzziness and Soft Computing*. Physica-Verlag, New York, 2002.
3. G. Choquet. *Theory of capacities*, volume 5, pages 131–295. Annales de l'institut Fourier, 1953.
4. M. Grabisch. The application of fuzzy integrals in multicriteria decision making. *European Journal of Operational Research*, 89(3):445–456, 1996.
5. F. Herrera and L. Martínez. A 2-tuple fuzzy linguistic representation model for computing with words. *IEEE Transactions on Fuzzy Systems*, 8(6):746–752, 2000.
6. Y.P. Jiang and Z.P & Fan. Property analysis of the aggregation operators for 2-tuple linguistic information. *Control and Decision*, 18(6):754–757, 2003.
7. Y.H. Lin, P.C. Lee, and H.I. Ting. Dynamic multi-attribute decision making model with grey number evaluations. *Expert Systems with Applications*, 35(4):1638–1644, 2008.
8. X. Liu and W. Yang. A new multi-period linguistic aggregation operator and its application to financial product selection, 2013.
9. L. Martínez and F. Herrera. An overview on the 2-tuple linguistic model for computing with words in decision making: Extensions, applications and challenges. *Information Sciences*, 207(1):1–18, 2012.
10. J.M. Merigó, M. Casanovas, and L. Martínez. Linguistic aggregation operators for linguistic decision making based on the dempster-shafer theory of evidence. *International Journal of Uncertainty, Fuzziness and Knowledge-Based Systems*, 18(3):287–304, 2010.
11. J.M. Merigó and A.M. Gil-Lafuente. Induced 2-tuple linguistic generalized aggregation operators and their application in decision-making. *Information Sciences*, 236:1–16, 2013.
12. J.I. Peláez and J.M. Doña. LAMA: A linguistic aggregation of majority additive operator. *International Journal of Intelligent Systems*, 18(7):809–820, 2003.
13. S.P. Wan. 2-tuple linguistic hybrid arithmetic aggregation operators and application to multi-attribute group decision making. *Knowledge-Based Systems*, 45:31–40, 2013.

14. S.P. Wan. Some hybrid geometric aggregation operators with 2-tuple linguistic information and their applications to multi-attribute group decision making. *International Journal of Computational Intelligence Systems*, 6(4):750–763, 2013.
15. G. Wei and X. Zhao. Some dependent aggregation operators with 2-tuple linguistic information and their application to multiple attribute group decision making. *Expert Systems with Applications*, 39(5):5881–5886, 2012.
16. G.W. Wei. Some harmonic aggregation operators with 2-tuple linguistic assessment information and their application to multiple attribute group decision making. *International Journal of Uncertainty, Fuzziness and Knowledge-Based Systems*, 19(6):977–998, 2011.
17. Y. Xu and H. Ling. An approach to group decision making problems based on 2-tuple linguistic aggregation operators. In F. Yu, Y. Chen, and Q. Zhou, editors, *ISECS International Colloquium on Computing, Communication, Control, and Management*, volume 3, pages 73–77, Guangzhou, China, 2008. IEEE.
18. Y. Xu and H. Wang. Approaches based on 2-tuple linguistic power aggregation operators for multiple attribute group decision making under linguistic environment. *Applied Soft Computing Journal*, 11(5):3988–3997, 2011.
19. Z.S. Xu and M.M. Xia. Distance and similarity measures for hesitant fuzzy sets. *Information Sciences*, 181(11):2128–2138, 2011.
20. R.R. Yager. A new methodology for ordinal multiobjective decision based on fuzzy sets. *Decision Science*, 12:589–600, 1981.
21. R.R. Yager. On ordered weighted averaging aggregation operators in multicriteria decision making. *IEEE Transactions on Systems, Man, and Cybernetics*, 18:183–190, 1988.
22. R.R. Yager. Non-numeric multi-criteria multi-person decision making. *Group Decision and Negotiation*, 2:81–93, 1993.
23. R.R. Yager. Quantifier guided aggregation using OWA operators. *International Journal Intelligent Systems*, 11:49–73, 1996.
24. R.R. Yager. The power average operator. *IEEE Transactions on Systems, Man and Cybernetics, Part A: Systems and Humans*, 31(6):724–731, 2001.
25. W. Yang. Induced choquet integrals of 2-tuple linguistic information. *International Journal of Uncertainty, Fuzziness and Knowledge-Based Systems*, 21(2):175–200, 2013.
26. W. Yang and Z. Chen. New aggregation operators based on the Choquet integral and 2-tuple linguistic information. *Expert Systems with Applications*, 39(3):2662–2668, 2012.

Chapter 3
Linguistic Approaches Based on the 2-Tuple Fuzzy Linguistic Representation Model

3.1 Extending the 2-Tuple Linguistic Model

The importance of linguistic information for modelling uncertainty and accomplishing Computing with Words (CW) processes in decision making can be seen in the scientific literature of the topic in which many proposals have been developed since the 1980s [6, 8, 11, 16] not only to solve such problems with such type of information, but also to improve the accuracy of the results. However, if attention is only focused on the linguistic symbolic approaches, it is easy to see the relevance of the 2-tuple fuzzy linguistic representation model that is reflected in the strong interest shown by researchers both to apply it in many different real-world applications and to develop new symbolic representation models to improve different aspects of the 2-tuple linguistic model in CW [12]. The former have found that many decision-based applications have been solved by using the 2-tuple linguistic model (see Chapter 7 of this book) and the latter have provoked the development of some novel linguistic symbolic approaches in recent years:

1. Xu in [15] introduced the extended linguistic variable based on the concept of virtual linguistic terms to improve the operational laws of symbolic operations.
2. Wang and Hao developed a new way to represent linguistic information that is a generalisation and extension of the 2-tuple linguistic model [13] which was later extended again by Guo et al. in [4] by using a third parameter to deal with incomplete linguistic preferences.
3. Dong et al. [2] introduced the concept of numerical scale with the aim of completing the 2-tuple linguistic model and proportional 2-tuple models for CW and making the elicitation of information more consistent in different decision situations.
4. An extended 2-tuple linguistic model was introduced by Li [7] that fuses the use of virtual linguistic terms and 2-tuple linguistic values.

© Springer International Publishing Switzerland 2015
L. Martínez et al., *The 2-tuple Linguistic Model*, DOI 10.1007/978-3-319-24714-4_3

5. Yang [17] proposed for representing and aggregating linguistic information the counted linguistic variable with the aim of providing better results and being easier to understand.

It is clear that previous approaches except for Xu [15] and Yang [17] have been developed either as an extension of the 2-tuple linguistic model or make heavy use of its concepts and ideas. This chapter reviews those models that either are based or extend the 2-tuple linguistic model [2, 7, 13] that may be useful in problems in which the 2-tuple linguistic model is limited because of specific issues of the problem or its stakeholders.

3.2   Linguistic Proportional 2-Tuple Model

The use of symbolic translation in the 2-tuple linguistic model to complement the linguistic information of the linguistic terms and increase the accuracy of the CW processes is the basis of the linguistic proportional 2-tuple model [13] introduced by Wang and Hao, in which they replace the *symbolic translation* by a *symbolic proportion* of the linguistic term and allow the assessment of linguistic variables by pairs of consecutive linguistic terms with their corresponding proportions. This approach generalises the 2-tuple linguistic model and may provide more accurate results than this model when the semantics of the linguistic terms are trapezoidal membership functions.

This linguistic proportional 2-tuple represents linguistic information by means of a pair of successive linguistic terms, $s_i, s_{i+1} \in S = \{s_0, \ldots, s_g\}$ with their respective proportions, $\alpha, \beta \in [0, 1]$, such as $(\alpha s_i, \beta s_{i+1})$, e.g.:

$$(0.15A, 0.85B)$$

It can be interpreted as 15 % of linguistic term A and 85 % of linguistic term B. It is remarkable that if B were used as the approximative grade then some performance information would be lost.

Therefore, the linguistic proportional 2-tuple model is based on the concept of *symbolic proportion* [13].

Definition 3.1 ([13]). Let $S = \{s_0, s_1, \ldots, s_g\}$ be an ordinal term set, $I = [0, 1]$ and

$$IS \equiv I \times S = \{(\alpha, s_i) : \alpha \in [0, 1] \ and \ i = \{0, 1, \ldots, g\}\} \tag{3.1}$$

where S is the ordered set of $g + 1$ ordinal terms $\{s_0, \ldots, s_g\}$. Given a pair (s_i, s_{i+1}) of two successive ordinal terms of S, any two elements (α, s_i), (β, s_{i+1}) of IS is a so-called symbolic proportion pair and α, β is a pair of symbolic proportions of the pair (s_i, s_{i+1}) if $\alpha + \beta = 1$.

A symbolic proportion pair (α, s_i), $(1 - \alpha, s_{i+1})$ is denoted by $(\alpha s_i, (1-\alpha)s_{i+1})$ and the set of all the symbolic proportion pairs are denoted by $\overline{\overline{S}}$; that is, $\overline{\overline{S}} = \{(\alpha s_i, (1 - \alpha)s_{i+1}) : \alpha \in [0, 1] \text{ and } i = \{0, 1, \dots, g - 1\}\}$.

$\overline{\overline{S}}$ is called the *ordinal proportional 2-tuple set* generated by S and the members of $\overline{\overline{S}}$, *ordinal proportional 2-tuples*, which are used to represent the ordinal information for CW.

In a similar way to the 2-tuple linguistic model, Wang and Hao introduced functions in order to facilitate the computations with this type of representation.

Definition 3.2 ([13]). Let $S = \{s_0, s_1, \dots, s_g\}$ be an ordinal term set and $\overline{\overline{S}}$ be the ordinal proportional 2-tuple set generated by S. The function $\pi : \overline{\overline{S}} \to [0, g]$ was defined by

$$\pi((\alpha s_i, (1 - \alpha)s_{i+1})) = i + (1 - \alpha), \tag{3.2}$$

where $i = \{0, 1, \dots, g - 1\}, \alpha \in [0, 1]$ and π is called the position index function of ordinal proportional 2-tuples.

Note that, under the identification convention which was remarked after Equation (3.1), the position index function π becomes a bijective mapping from $\overline{\overline{S}}$ to $[0, g]$ and its inverse $\pi^{-1} : [0, g] \to \overline{\overline{S}}$ is defined by

$$\pi^{-1}(x) = ((1 - \beta)s_i, \beta s_{i+1}), x \in [0, g] \tag{3.3}$$

where $i = E(x)$, E is the integer part function, $\beta = x - i$.

Wang and Hao claimed that this model can operate in a precise way beyond uniformly and symmetrically distributed triangular membership labels as the 2-tuple linguistic model. To do so, they proposed the use of symmetrical trapezoidal fuzzy numbers $s_i = (a_i, b_i, c_i, d_i)$ and the use of their *canonical characteristic values*, $CCV(s_i) = (b_i + c_i)/2$ that were extended for proportional 2-tuples in [14] as

Definition 3.3 ([14]). Let S and $\overline{\overline{S}}$ and CCV on S as previously; the CCV for a proportional 2-tuple, $(\alpha s_i, (1 - \alpha)s_{i+1}) \in \overline{\overline{S}}$, is defined:

$$CCV((\alpha s_i, (1 - \alpha)s_{i+1})) = \alpha CCV(s_i), (1 - \alpha)CCV(s_{i+1}). \tag{3.4}$$

To operate with linguistic information under proportional 2-tuple contexts, Wang and Hao expanded the computational techniques for symbolic information to proportional 2-tuples and underlying definitions of linguistic labels and linguistic variables are taken into account in the process of aggregating linguistic information by assigning CCV of the corresponding linguistic labels [13, 14]. They presented an interesting transformation function between $\overline{S}$ and $\overline{\overline{S}}$:

Proposition 3.1 ([13]). *Let S, $\overline{S}$ and $\overline{\overline{S}}$ be as before. The transformation function $h : \overline{\overline{S}} \to \overline{S}$ is defined as*

$$h((\alpha s_i, (1 - \alpha)s_{i+1})) = \begin{cases} (s_{i+1}, -\alpha), & 0 \le \alpha \le 1/2 \\ (s_i, 1 - \alpha), & 1/2 \le \alpha \le 1 \end{cases} \tag{3.5}$$

h is a bijective mapping.

With such a mapping the proportional 2-tuples can be transformed into 2-tuple linguistic values and the computational model developed for the latter can be used to obtain the computational results and later on transformed into proportional 2-tuples by h^{-1}.

Recently Guo et al. [4] extended the linguistic proportional 2-tuple model into the proportional 3-tuple by adding a new parameter that will be useful to deal with in incomplete assessments where the linguistic proportional 2-tuple model cannot deal with them because the former does not consider incompleteness or the latter because the premise $\alpha + \beta = 1$ makes the assessments provide complete linguistic information.

The proportional 3-tuple aims at representing linguistic assessments from human beings' view when incomplete information arises regarding uncertain subjective judgments that are usual in complex problems. Therefore, a linguistic proportional 3-tuple consists of a linguistic proportional 2-tuple and a numerical parameter, ε, that represents the extent of ignoring information which human beings cannot provide because of the uncertainty or lack of information, such that:

$$\begin{cases} (\alpha, s_i, \beta, s_{i+1}, 0) \ if \ \alpha + \beta = 1 \\ (\alpha, s_i, \beta, s_{i+1}, \varepsilon) \ if \ \alpha + \beta < 1 \end{cases} \tag{3.6}$$

In this case, the set of all symbolic proportion pairs $\overline{\overline{S'}} = \{(\alpha s_i, (\beta)s_{i+1}) : \alpha, \beta \in [0, 1], \varepsilon = 1 - \alpha - \beta \ and \ i = \{0, 1, \ldots, g - 1\}$ is called the proportional 3-tuple set generated by S. Therefore a proportional 3-tuple assessment is denoted as

$$\begin{cases} Complete : & (\alpha, s_i, \beta, s_{i+1}, 0) \ if \ \alpha + \beta = 1 \\ Incomplete : & (\alpha, s_i, \beta, s_{i+1}, \varepsilon) \ if \ \alpha + \beta < 1 \end{cases} \tag{3.7}$$

To accomplish CW processes with proportional 3-tuples, the CCV introduced by Wang and Hao [13, 14] is extended to deal with this new representation:

Definition 3.4 ([4]). Let S and $\overline{\overline{S'}}$ and CCV on S as previously; the canonical characteristic value function, CCV, for a proportional 3-tuple, $(\alpha s_i, (\beta)s_{i+1}, \varepsilon) \in \overline{\overline{S'}}$, is defined:

$$\begin{aligned} CCV((\alpha s_i, (\beta)s_{i+1}, \varepsilon)) &= (\alpha CCV(s_i) + (\beta CCV(s_{i+1})), \varepsilon) = \\ &= ((\alpha c_i) + (1 - \alpha - \varepsilon)c_{i+1}, \varepsilon) = (l, \varepsilon), \ with \ l \in (0, 1], \end{aligned} \tag{3.8}$$

with c_i the CCV of s_i, $i = \{0, 1, \ldots, g - 1\}$.

Proposition 3.2 ([4]). *There is always a CCV^{-1} function such that from any (l, ε) it returns a proportional 3-tuple $(\alpha s_i, (\beta)s_{i+1}, \varepsilon) \in \overline{\overline{S'}}$ such that $CCV((\alpha s_i, (\beta)s_{i+1}, \varepsilon)) = (l, \varepsilon)$.*

3.3   The Numerical Scale to Extend the 2-Tuple Linguistic Model

The 2-tuple linguistic model and the linguistic proportional 2-tuple model [5, 13] manage the CW processes by transformation functions between the linguistic and numerical domains that support the *translation* and *retranslation* processes of the CW. Dong et al. [2] considered that the crucial task for accomplishing computational processes with linguistic information assessed by using these 2-tuple based models is to set a *numerical scale* function that establishes a mapping between the linguistic information and numerical values that facilitate the computations with linguistic information.

Even though the 2-tuple linguistic models [5, 13] use different representation formats for modelling linguistic information, Dong et al. aim at extending such representations to unify their computational process by formally defining the concept of *numerical scale*.

Definition 3.5 ([2]). Let $S = \{s_i | i = 0, \ldots, g\}$ be a linguistic term set and $\mathbb{R}$ be the real number set. The function $NS : S \to \mathbb{R}$ is defined as a *numerical scale* of S and $NS(s_i)$ is called the numerical index of s_i.

Definition 3.6 ([2]). Let S, $\overline{S}$, and NS on S be the set of linguistic terms, the set of 2-tuple linguistic values, and the numerical scale respectively. The numerical scale NS for a 2-tuple linguistic value $(s_i, \alpha) \in \overline{S}$ is defined by:

$$NS(s_i, \alpha) = \begin{cases} NS(s_i) + \alpha \times (NS(s_{i+1}) - NS(s_i)), \alpha \geq 0 \\ NS(s_i) + \alpha \times (NS(s_i) - NS(s_{i-1})), \alpha < 0 \end{cases} \tag{3.9}$$

From such a definition,

Proposition 3.3 ([2]). *If the setting for the numerical scale is $NS(s_i) = i$, for $i = \{0, 1, \ldots, g\}$ then:*

$$NS(s_j, \alpha_j) = \Delta^{-1}(s_j, \alpha_j) \text{ for any } (s_i, \alpha_i) \in \overline{S}.$$

Remark 3.1. Proposition 3.3 is only valid with triangular membership functions. But if the semantics is represented by other membership functions such as trapezoidal membership functions as indicated in the linguistic proportional 2-tuple model, the proposition should be reconsidered.

Proposition 3.4 ([2]). *If the setting for the numerical scale is* $NS(s_i) = CCV(s_i)$, *for* $i = \{1, \ldots, g\}$ *then:*

$$NS(s_j, \alpha_j) = CCV(h^{-1}((s_j, \alpha_j)) = (\alpha s_i, (\beta)s_{i+1}) \in \bar{\bar{S}} \text{ for any}(s_i, \alpha_i) \in \bar{S}.$$

Therefore, according to Proposition 3.3 the 2-tuple linguistic model is obtained when setting $NS(s_i) = i$ and according to Proposition 3.4 the linguistic proportional 2-tuple model is obtained when setting $NS(s_i) = CCV(s_i)$.

Dong et al. introduced in [2] different concepts and models such as the transitive calibration matrix, its consistent index, and an optimisation model, in order to compute the numerical scale of a linguistic term set with the aim to complete the 2-tuple based models for CW and make the information of the experts more consistent in different decision situations.

Eventually in [1] Dong et al. present different scale functions to deal with 2-tuple linguistic values in the well-known multicriteria decision-making model, analytic hierarchy process (AHP) [10]. Finally, in [3] Dong et al. introduce an interval version of the 2-tuple fuzzy linguistic representation model for CW.

3.4   Extended 2-Tuple Fuzzy Linguistic Variables

Xu introduced [15] a linguistic symbolic approach that uses the extended linguistic variables with the aim of increasing the linguistic operational laws and the precision of the linguistic computations.

Definition 3.7 ([15]). Let $S = \{s_{-\frac{g}{2}}, \ldots, s_0, \ldots, s_{\frac{g}{2}}\}$, be a linguistic discrete term set, with $g + 1$ being the cardinality of S that is extended into a continuous term set $\hat{S} = \{s_\alpha | \alpha \in [-t, t]\}$, where t ($t >> g/2$) is a sufficiently large positive integer. $\hat{S}$ is called a set of extended linguistic variables associated with S. If $s_\alpha \in S$, then s_α is called an *original linguistic term*; otherwise, s_α is called a *virtual linguistic term*.

By using extended linguistic variables Xu introduced the following operational laws [15]. Let $s_\alpha, s_\beta \in \hat{S}$, be any two linguistic terms and $\mu, \mu_1, \mu_2 \in [0, 1]$:

1. $(s_\alpha)^\mu = s_{\alpha^\mu}$
2. $(s_\alpha)^{\mu_1} \otimes (s_\alpha)^{\mu_2} = (s_\alpha)^{\mu_1 + \mu_2}$
3. $(s_\alpha \otimes s_\beta)^\mu = (s_\alpha)^\mu \otimes (s_\beta)^\mu$
4. $s_\alpha \otimes s_\beta = s_\beta \otimes s_\alpha = s_{\alpha\beta}$
5. $s_\alpha \oplus s_\beta = s_{\alpha+\beta}$
6. $s_\alpha \oplus s_\beta = s_\beta \oplus s_\alpha$
7. $\mu s_\alpha = s_{\mu\alpha}$
8. $(\mu_1 + \mu_2)s_\alpha = \mu_1 s_\alpha \oplus \mu_2 s_\alpha$
9. $\mu(s_\alpha \oplus s_\beta) = \mu s_\alpha \oplus \mu s_\beta$

In Section 3.1 it was indicated that the extended linguistic variables do not follow the ideas of the 2-tuple linguistic model. In [9] it was pointed out that the extended linguistic variables are not either within the fuzzy linguistic approach or the CW paradigm. Because of its wide use and easy extension to a 2-tuple fuzzy linguistic representation, in [7] Li introduced an extended 2-tuple fuzzy linguistic representation.

The extended 2-tuple fuzzy linguistic representation assumes that $s_a \in \hat{S}$ is a symbolic result of operating with terms in the linguistic term set $S = \{s_\alpha | \alpha = -t, -t+1, \ldots, t-1, t\}$, being $\hat{S} = \{s_\alpha | \alpha \in [-t, t]\}$, the extended linguistic term set associated with S.

Definition 3.8 ([7]). Let $\varphi : \hat{S} \rightarrow S \times [-0.5, 0.5)$ be a mapping such that for any $s_a \in \hat{S}$, $\varphi(s_a) = (s_{i_a}, a - i_a)$ with $s_{i_a} \in S$ and $i_a \in \{-t, -t+1, \ldots, t-1, t\}$ that satisfies the relation:

$$|a - i_a| = min\{|a - i|/i \in \{-t, -t+1, \ldots, t-1, t\}\}$$

Therefore, $\varphi(s_a) \cdot = (s_{i_a}, a - i_a)$ is called the extended 2-tuple fuzzy linguistic representation of $s_a \in \hat{S}$, which can be interpreted as equivalent information.

In the extended 2-tuple fuzzy linguistic representation $(s_{i_a}, a - i_a)$, i_a is the closest integer to value a; that is, s_{i_a} is the closest linguistic term to the extended linguistic variable $s_a \in \hat{S}$ and $a - i_a \in [-0.5, 0.5)$ is the symbolic translation which expresses the difference between $s_a \in \hat{S}$ and $s_{i_a} \in S$.

Once the extended linguistic information is transformed into extended 2-tuple fuzzy linguistic information the computing processes can be carried out by the 2-tuple fuzzy linguistic computational model and the results are obtained by means of 2-tuple linguistic values.

References

1. Y. Dong, W.C. Hong, Y. Xu, and S. Yu. Selecting the individual numerical scale and prioritization method in the analytic hierarchy process: A 2-tuple fuzzy linguistic approach. *IEEE Transactions on Fuzzy Sets*, 19(1):13–25, 2011.
2. Y. Dong, Y. Xu, and S. Yu. Computing the numerical scale of the linguistic term set for the 2-tuple fuzzy linguistic representation model. *IEEE Transactions on Fuzzy Systems*, 17(6): 1366–1378, 2009.
3. Y. Dong, G. Zhang, W.C. Hong, and S. Yu. Linguistic computational model based on 2-tuples and intervals. *IEEE Transactions on Fuzzy Systems*, 21(6):1006–1018, 2013.
4. W.T. Guo, V.N. Huynh, and Y. Nakamori. A proportional 3-tuple fuzzy linguistic representation model for screening new product projects. *Journal of Systems Science and Systems Engineering*, DOI:10.1007/s11518-015-5269-x:1--22, 2015.
5. F. Herrera and L. Martínez. A 2-tuple fuzzy linguistic representation model for computing with words. *IEEE Transactions on Fuzzy Systems*, 8(6):746–752, 2000.
6. J. Lawry. A framework for linguistic modelling. *Artificial Intelligence*, 155(1–2):1–39, 2004.

7. D.F. Li. Multiattribute group decision making method using extended linguistic variables. *International Journal of Uncertainty, Fuzziness and Knowledge-Based Systems*, 17(6): 793–806, 2009.
8. C.H. Nguyen, V.N. Huynh, and W. Pedrycz. A construction of sound semantic linguistic scales using 4-tuple representation of term semantics. *International Journal of Approximate Reasoning*, 55(3):763–786, 2014.
9. R.M. Rodríguez and L. Martínez. An analysis of symbolic linguistic computing models in decision making. *International Journal of General Systems*, 42(1):121–136, 2013.
10. T.L. Saaty. *The Analytic Hierarchy Process*. McGraw-Hill, New York, 1980.
11. Y. Tang and J. Zheng. Linguistic modelling based on semantic similarity relation among linguistic labels. *Fuzzy Sets and Systems*, 157(12):1662–1673, 2006.
12. I. Truck. Comparison and links between two 2-tuple linguistic models for decision making. *Knowledge-Based Systems*, 87:61–68, 2015.
13. J.H. Wang and J. Hao. A new version of 2-tuple fuzzy linguistic representation model for computing with words. *IEEE Transactions on Fuzzy Systems*, 14(3):435–445, 2006.
14. J.H. Wang and J. Hao. An approach to computing with words based on canonical characteristic values of linguistic labels. *IEEE Transactions on Fuzzy Systems*, 15(4):593–604, 2007.
15. Z. Xu. A method based on linguistic aggregation operators for group decision making with linguistic preference relations. *Information Sciences*, 166(1–4):19–30, 2004.
16. R.R. Yager. Non-numeric multi-criteria multi-person decision making. *Group Decision and Negotiation*, 2:81–93, 1993.
17. W.E. Yang, X.F. Wang, and J.Q. Wang. Counted linguistic variable in decision-making. *International Journal of Fuzzy Systems*, 16(2):196–203, 2014.

Chapter 4
Decision Making in Heterogeneous Context: 2-Tuple Linguistic Based Approaches

4.1 Heterogeneous Contexts

Real-world decision-making problems usually imply uncertainty in their context of definition. It has already been shown how linguistic information can be very useful to model such uncertainty when it is nonprobabilistic in nature. Such a modelling and its computational models facilitate by means of Computing with Words (CW) processes, robust, accurate, and easily understandable results.

The 2-tuple linguistic model has been shown and applied in Chapter 2 to decision-making problems defined in decision frameworks in which all decision makers agreed on the linguistic scale and its meanings. However, this situation does not always happen, because often hard decision problems imply the need for more complex decision definition contexts in which the management of heterogeneous information is necessary. Under the *heterogeneous information* concept this chapter considers two type of contexts:

1. *Multigranular Linguistic Information context*: The information can be elicited by means of linguistic information, but the linguistic terms can belong to different linguistic term sets with either different semantics or granularity.
2. *Nonhomogeneous Information context*: The elicitation of information can be assessed in different expression domains both qualitative (linguistic information) or quantitative (numerical, interval-valued).

Therefore, the need for dealing with heterogeneous contexts, both multiple linguistic scales and different expression domains, might be because of one or several of the reasons below:

1. Words mean different things to different people [19], also this situation may occur because of different situations:

© Springer International Publishing Switzerland 2015
L. Martínez et al., *The 2-tuple Linguistic Model*, DOI 10.1007/978-3-319-24714-4_4

(a) Stakeholders, experts, and decision makers who take part in the decision-making problem can have different degrees of knowledge about the alternatives, criteria, and indicators involved in the decision situation. Therefore, the meaning of the words is highly dependent on the degree of distinction that they can provide, that is, the granularity of uncertainty of the linguistic term set used to express their knowledge. A fine granule means a high degree of distinction whereas a coarse granule means a low degree of distinction.

(b) Inherent uncertainty of linguistic information causes different people to have different perceptions about the meaning of words. In these situations, the semantics is usually slightly different for them. In these situations, the use of type-2 fuzzy sets [18, 21] is quite useful, but the interest of this book is rather focused on the management of multigranular linguistic information that appears when there are different degrees of knowledge in the definition context.

2. The alternatives, criteria, indicators, and other aspects that must be assessed in a decision problem can have different nature or involve different types of uncertainty and then different types of information modelling are necessary.

3. Stakeholders, experts, and decision makers involved in decision-making problems may come from different knowledge areas, and because of their expertise might prefer the use of different expression domains to elicit or manage their knowledge about the problem.

The first situation usually implies the use of multiple linguistic scales with different granularity; the second and third situations imply the use of nonhomogeneous information assessed in different domains, including numerical, interval-valued, linguistic, and so on.

In decision making both heterogeneous contexts either multigranular linguistic or nonhomogeneous information need a proper framework to manage and make computations with such heterogeneous information that includes linguistic information. Moreover, whenever it is necessary to obtain ease in understanding results (linguistic output according to the CW scheme), in both cases the use of the 2-tuple linguistic model can provide accurate and linguistic results. Hence, this chapter introduces several 2-tuple linguistic based approaches to deal with heterogeneous information that follow the general solving scheme shown in Figure 4.1 disregarding the type of heterogeneous information managed.

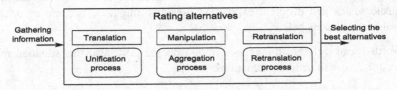

Fig. 4.1 General decision scheme dealing with heterogeneous contexts in decision making

The coming sections show three different 2-tuple linguistic based approaches for CW dealing with multiple linguistic scales, and one 2-tuple linguistic based method able to integrate information assessed in a nonhomogeneous context into a linguistic domain in order to operate linguistically with the nonhomogeneous information. Additionally, different illustrative examples of decision-making problems solved by the previous approaches are described.

4.2   Multigranular Linguistic Information: 2-Tuple Linguistic Based Approaches

In decision-making problems that present multiple experts or multiple criteria it may be necessary to model the linguistic information by means of multiple scales with different granularity [4, 15, 17]. This necessity may come because the use of linguistic information implies the choice of appropriate linguistic descriptors and their semantics [9] in which its *granularity of uncertainty* should consider the more granularity the more the level of discrimination, and because the distinct experts or criteria might need a different degree of discrimination according to their knowledge or nature. In this context, it is still necessary to accomplish CW processes with this type of information, and different approaches have been introduced in the specialised literature [1, 2, 14]. However, such approaches present some limitations of either inaccuracy or lack of interpretability.

The 2-tuple linguistic model has facilitated the processes of CW with multiple linguistic scales of distinct granularity overcoming previous limitations. This section shows three 2-tuple linguistic based approaches [8, 10, 12] to deal with multigranular linguistic information in decision making that provide accurate and easily understandable linguistic results. Such approaches are:

1. *Fusion Approach for Managing Multigranular Linguistic Information* [10]: This approach deals initially with the fuzzy semantics of the linguistic terms and obtains results expressed by 2-tuple linguistic values.
2. *Linguistic Hierarchies* [12]: It defines a linguistic structure to deal with different linguistic scales in a symbolic way and obtains accurate results that can be expressed in any linguistic scale of the structure.
3. *Extended Linguistic Hierarchies* [8]: It extends the previous one to facilitate the use of any linguistic scale.

All these 2-tuple linguistic based models for computing with multiple linguistic scales perform according to the scheme shown in Figure 4.2 that follows the general scheme of Figure 4.1 and consists of the following steps which are further detailed in each model.

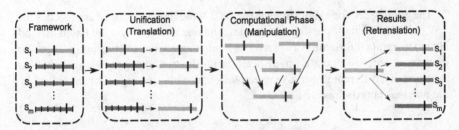

Fig. 4.2 A CW scheme for multigranular linguistic information

(a) A multigranular linguistic **framework** is defined to fix all the linguistic term sets in which the linguistic information will be elicited by the experts.
(b) **Unification** of the multigranular linguistic information that consists in a translation process which conducts the multigranular linguistic information into a unique linguistic domain.
(c) A **computational** phase in which the processes of CW that manipulate the linguistic information are carried out by using 2-tuple linguistic values.
(d) A **retranslation** process is needed to fulfil the CW scheme and express the results by 2-tuple linguistic values in the initial expression domains.

The coming sections show in further detail each of the previous 2-tuple linguistic based approaches to deal with multigranular linguistic information together with illustrative examples of their performance in decision making.

4.2.1 Fusion Approach for Managing Multigranular Linguistic Information

This approach, introduced in [10, 13], deals with decision frameworks in which the linguistic information would be assessed in multiple linguistic scales without any constraint. It uses the extension principle, the 2-tuple linguistic model, and its computing model. Figure 4.3 shows how the fusion approach adapts the general scheme shown in Figure 4.2.

4.2.1.1 Framework

The different approaches presented in Section 4.2 deal with frameworks, F_{MS}, that can have different linguistic term sets (scales). This approach does not impose any limitation to the linguistic term sets that can be used to assess the linguistic information in the multigranular context.

$$F_{MS} = \{S_i\}, \; S_i = \{s_0^i, \ldots, s_{g_i}^i\}, \; i = \{1, \ldots, n\}$$

Therefore in any linguistic term set of the framework, each linguistic term $s_j^i \in S_i$ has its own semantics, $\mu_{s_i}(x)$, and granularity, g_i.

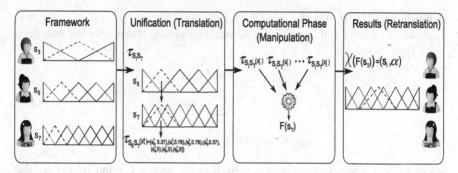

Fig. 4.3 A 2-tuple fusion scheme for multigranular linguistic information

4.2.1.2 Unification Phase

The information that conforms the decision framework, F_{MS}, belongs to different linguistic scales, thereby before carrying out any computational process and similarly to the quantitative processes dealing with multiple numerical scales, that normalise the information, usually $[0, 1]$. This approach, firstly, unifies the multigranular linguistic information into a unique linguistic term set, called the basic linguistic term set (BLTS) by means of fuzzy sets. This unification process consists of two steps:

- *Selection of the BLTS, noted as S_T*: It must be a linguistic term set which allows maintaining the uncertainty degrees associated with each purpose and the ability of discrimination to express the knowledge. With this goal in mind, the BLTS ought to have maximum granularity but also fulfil Miller's observation [20] regarding the capability of distinction levels of human beings. There are two possibilities:

  1. When there is only one term set with the maximum granularity, it is then chosen as S_T.
  2. If there are two or more linguistic term sets with maximum granularity then S_T is chosen depending on the semantics of these linguistic term sets, having again two possible situations for choosing S_T:

     (a) All the linguistic term sets have the same semantics; then S_T is any of them.
     (b) There are some linguistic term sets with different semantics. S_T is then a BLTS with a number of terms greater than the number of terms that a person is able to discriminate (see [20]).

- *Unification process*: Once the BLTS has been chosen the multigranular linguistic information can be transformed into the BLTS by using a transformation function $\tau_{S_i S_T}(\cdot)$ which can express any linguistic term $s_j^i \in S_i$ as a fuzzy set defined in S_T, $F(S_T)$, defined as

Definition 4.1 ([10]). Let $S_i = \{s_0^i, \ldots, s_{g_i}^i\}$ and $S_T = \{s_0^T, \ldots, s_{g_T}^T\}$ be two linguistic term sets and, $g_T > g_i$. A multigranularity transformation function, $\tau_{S_i S_T}(\cdot)$ is:

$$\tau_{S_i S_T} : S_i \longrightarrow F(S_T)$$

$$\tau_{S_i S_T}(s_j^i) = \sum_{k=0}^{g_T} s_k^T / \gamma_k^j, \tag{4.1}$$

$$\gamma_k^j = \max_y \min\{\mu_{s_j^i}(y), \mu_{s_k^T}(y)\}$$

where $F(S_T)$ is the set of fuzzy sets defined in S_T, and $\mu_{s_j^i}(y)$ and $\mu_{s_k^T}(y)$ are the membership functions of the fuzzy sets associated with the linguistic terms s_j^i and s_k^T, respectively.

An example to illustrate this transformation process could be the following one.

Example 4.1. Let $S_i = \{s_0^i, s_1^i, \ldots, s_4^i\}$ and $S_T = \{s_0^T, s_1^T, \ldots, s_6^T\}$ be two linguistic term sets that define the framework F_{MS}, with $g_i = 4$ and $g_T = 6$, respectively, whose BLTS would be S_T according to its selection process. Their associated semantics are (see Figure 4.4):

$$
\begin{array}{ll}
s_0^i \ (0, 0, 0.25) & s_0^T \ (0, 0, 0.16) \\
s_1^i \ (0, 0.25, 0.5) & s_1^T \ (0, 0.16, 0.34) \\
s_2^i \ (0.25, 0.5, 0.75) & s_2^T \ (0.16, 0.34, 0.5) \\
s_3^i \ (0.5, 0.75, 0.1) & s_3^T \ (0.34, 0.5, 0.66) \\
s_4^i \ (0.75, 1, 1) & s_4^T \ (0.5, 0.66, 0.84) \\
& s_5^T \ (0.66, 0.84, 1) \\
& s_6^T \ (0.84, 1, 1)
\end{array}
$$

The fuzzy sets obtained by applying $\tau_{S_i S_T}$ for s_0^i and s_1^i are:

$$s_0^i = \{(s_0^T, 1), (s_1^T, 0.58), (s_2^T, 0.18), (s_3^T, 0), (s_4^T, 0), (s_5^T, 0), (s_6^T, 0)\}$$

$$s_1^i = \{(s_0^T, 0.39), (s_1^T, 0.85), (s_2^T, 0.85), (s_3^T, 0.39), (s_4^T, 0), (s_5^T, 0), (s_6^T, 0)\}$$

In Figure 4.4 the transformation process for both linguistic terms can be seen graphically.

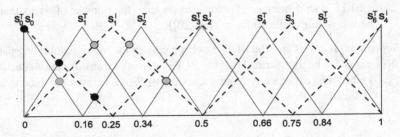

Fig. 4.4 Term sets S_i and S_T

4.2.1.3 Computational Phase

Once the multigranular linguistic information has been unified into fuzzy sets in S_T, it is time to carry out the CW processes. There are two different ways to accomplish such computing processes:

- Fuzzy arithmetic can be used [6, 10] to operate directly on the fuzzy sets obtaining fuzzy sets as results that must be translated into linguistic information in the retranslation process.
- The fuzzy sets in S_T could also be transformed into 2-tuple linguistic values by using the function χ defined as

Definition 4.2 ([13]). Let $F(S_T)$ be a fuzzy set in the BLTS; S_T; χ is a function that transforms such a fuzzy set into a 2-tuple linguistic value as

$$\chi : F(S_T) \to \overline{S_T}$$

$$\chi(F(S_T)) = \Delta \left(\frac{\sum_{j=0}^{g} j \gamma_j}{\sum_{j=0}^{g} \gamma_j} \right) = \Delta(\beta) = (s, \alpha) \qquad (4.2)$$

Afterwards, the CW processes are carried out by using 2-tuple linguistic values.

4.2.1.4 Retranslation Phase: Results

Consequently to obtain linguistic results, the process depends on the way that computing processes have been carried out:

- If the results come from the use of fuzzy arithmetic, such fuzzy sets must be transformed into linguistic ones by using the function $\chi(\cdot)$ (see Definition 4.2), whose outcome will be a 2-tuple linguistic value in the BLTS, S_T. Keep in mind that fuzzy arithmetic decreases the accuracy of the final results.

$$\chi : F(S_T) \to \overline{S_T}$$

- However, if the computations have been accomplished on linguistic information represented by 2-tuple linguistic values, the results obtained will be directly linguistic and accurate ones.

4.2.1.5 Illustrative Decision-Making Problem Example: Fusion Approach

Let's suppose that Paul wants to buy a new car. He has selected four different models {car1, car2, car3, and car4} and he does not know which option is the best one, therefore, he will provide his assessments over the four alternatives taking into account four criteria {comfort, design, price, and safety}.

A. Framework

Paul has a different degree of knowledge about the criteria, therefore he will use different linguistic term sets to express opinions over the criteria such as

- Comfort $\rightarrow S^5$
- Design $\rightarrow S^7$
- Price $\rightarrow S^9$
- Safety $\rightarrow S^5$

which are S^5, S^7, and S^9 linguistic term sets with five, seven, and nine linguistic terms that conform the framework, F_{MS}. Figure 4.5 shows the syntax and semantics of such linguistic term sets.

Once the framework has been defined, Paul expresses his assessments r_{ij}, with i the alternatives and j the criteria (see Table 4.1).

A multicriteria decision-making process which follows the scheme shown in Figure 4.3 is used to solve the decision problem.

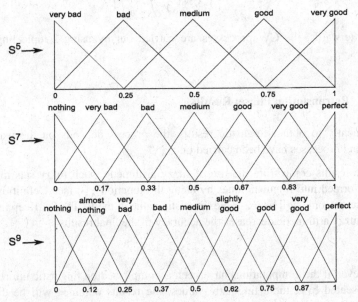

Fig. 4.5 Syntax and semantics of the linguistic term sets S^5, S^7, and S^9

Table 4.1 Paul's assessments			Criteria			
			Comfort	Design	Price	Safety
Alternatives	Car$_1$		s_3^5	s_3^7	s_4^9	s_2^5
	Car$_2$		s_3^5	s_4^7	s_6^9	s_3^5
	Car$_3$		s_4^5	s_3^7	s_3^9	s_3^5
	Car$_4$		s_4^5	s_5^7	s_5^9	s_4^5

Table 4.2 Assessments represented by fuzzy sets in S^9

r_{ij}^T	Fuzzy sets defined in S^9
r_{11}^9	$\{(s_0,0),(s_1,0),(s_2,0),(s_3,0),(s_4,0.33),(s_5,0.66),(s_6,1),(s_7,0.66),(s_8,0.33)\}$
r_{12}^9	$\{(s_0,0),(s_1,0),(s_2,0.14),(s_3,0.57),(s_4,1),(s_5,0.57),(s_6,0.14),(s_7,0),(s_8,0)\}$
r_{13}^9	$\{(s_0,0),(s_1,0),(s_2,0),(s_3,0.5),(s_4,1),(s_5,0.5),(s_6,0),(s_7,0),(s_8,0)\}$
r_{14}^9	$\{(s_0,0),(s_1,0),(s_2,0.33),(s_3,0.66),(s_4,1),(s_5,0.66),(s_6,0.33),(s_7,0),(s_8,0)\}$
r_{21}^9	$\{(s_0,0),(s_1,0),(s_2,0),(s_3,0),(s_4,0.33),(s_5,0.66),(s_6,1),(s_7,0.66),(s_8,0.33)\}$
r_{22}^9	$\{(s_0,0),(s_1,0),(s_2,0),(s_3,0),(s_4,0.43),(s_5,0.86),(s_6,0.71),(s_7,0.28),(s_8,0)\}$
r_{23}^9	$\{(s_0,0),(s_1,0),(s_2,0),(s_3,0),(s_4,0),(s_5,0.5),(s_6,1),(s_7,0.5),(s_8,0)\}$
r_{24}^9	$\{(s_0,0),(s_1,0),(s_2,0),(s_3,0),(s_4,0.33),(s_5,0.66),(s_6,1),(s_7,0.66),(s_8,0.33)\}$
r_{31}^9	$\{(s_0,0),(s_1,0),(s_2,0),(s_3,0),(s_4,0),(s_5,0),(s_6,0.33),(s_7,0.66),(s_8,1)\}$
r_{32}^9	$\{(s_0,0),(s_1,0),(s_2,0.14),(s_3,0.57),(s_4,1),(s_5,0.57),(s_6,0.14),(s_7,0),(s_8,0)\}$
r_{33}^9	$\{(s_0,0),(s_1,0),(s_2,0.5),(s_3,1),(s_4,0.5),(s_5,0),(s_6,0),(s_7,0),(s_8,0)\}$
r_{34}^9	$\{(s_0,0),(s_1,0),(s_2,0),(s_3,0),(s_4,0.33),(s_5,0.66),(s_6,1),(s_7,0.66),(s_8,0.33)\}$
r_{41}^9	$\{(s_0,0),(s_1,0),(s_2,0),(s_3,0),(s_4,0),(s_5,0),(s_6,0.33),(s_7,0.66),(s_8,1)\}$
r_{42}^9	$\{(s_0,0),(s_1,0),(s_2,0),(s_3,0),(s_4,0),(s_5,0.28),(s_6,0.71),(s_7,0.86),(s_8,0.43)\}$
r_{43}^9	$\{(s_0,0),(s_1,0),(s_2,0),(s_3,0),(s_4,0.5),(s_5,1),(s_6,0.5),(s_7,0),(s_8,0)\}$
r_{44}^9	$\{(s_0,0),(s_1,0),(s_2,0),(s_3,0),(s_4,0),(s_5,0),(s_6,0.33),(S_7,0.66),(s_8,1)\}$

Table 4.3 Assessments unified in S^9 transformed into 2-tuple linguistic values

		Criteria			
		Comfort	Design	Price	Safety
Alternatives	Car$_1$	(Good,0)	(Medium,0)	(Medium,0)	(Medium,0)
	Car$_2$	(Good,0)	(Slightly good,0.37)	(Good,0)	(Good,0)
	Car$_3$	(Very good, 0.33)	(Medium,0)	(Bad,0)	(Good,0)
	Car$_4$	(Very good, 0.33)	(Very good,−0.37)	(Slightly good,0)	(Very good,0.33)

B. Unification Phase

1. *Selection of the BLTS, S_T:* There is only one linguistic term set with the maximum granularity, therefore, S_T will be S^9.
2. *Unification process:* Applying the transformation function $\tau_{S_i S_j}(\cdot)$ (see Definition 4.1), all the assessments r_{ij}^T, represented as fuzzy sets defined in S^9, are obtained (see Table 4.2).

C. Computational Phase

Once all the assessments are expressed by means of fuzzy sets defined in the BLTS, S^9, for the sake of simplicity they are transformed into 2-tuple linguistic values by the function $\chi(\cdot)$ (see Definition 4.2). The results of the transformation are shown in Table 4.3.

According to Paul, each criterion has different importance, therefore the 2-tuple weighted average aggregation operator (see Definition 2.4) with the weighting vector $W = \{0.2, 0.1, 0.4, 0.3\}$ is applied to obtain the collective values for such alternatives (see Table 4.4).

Table 4.4 Collective values of the alternatives

Collective values			
Car1	Car2	Car3	Car4
(Medium,0.4)	(Good,−0.06)	(Slightly good,−0.13)	(Good,0.32)

D. Retranslation Phase

Because the aggregation has been carried out using 2-tuple linguistic values, the results obtained are linguistic, therefore, it is not necessary to transform them.

E. Exploitation Phase

The exploitation phase generates a solution set of alternative(s) (the best one(s)) for the decision problem. In this example the ranking obtained is:

$$car4 > car2 > car3 > car1$$

Therefore, the best option considering the criteria {comfort, design, price, and safety} is to buy **{car4=(good,0.32)}**.

4.2.2 Linguistic Hierarchies

Even though the previous approach provides a way to deal with multigranular linguistic information, obtaining linguistic results which are easy to understand, still presents a lack of accuracy in the transformation from fuzzy sets to linguistic values in the unification phase. In order to overcome this drawback, another 2-tuple linguistic based approach was introduced based on linguistic hierarchies (LH) to deal with multigranular linguistic information in a symbolic and precise way [3, 12]. This approach also follows the scheme shown in Figure 4.2 to accomplish the CW processes, but it introduces some slight modifications to deal with multiple linguistic scales in a symbolic way and without loss of accuracy (see Figure 4.6).

4.2.2.1 Framework

This approach builds a structure, the linguistic hierarchy (LH), that will be the framework, F_{MS}, for the decision problem, and over it a computational symbolic model based on the 2-tuple linguistic model is defined.

$$F_{MS} = LH$$

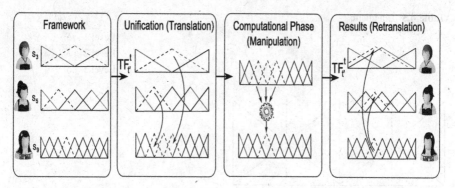

Fig. 4.6 A CW scheme for linguistic hierarchies

A LH is the union of all levels t: $LH = \bigcup_t S^n(t), t \in \{1, \ldots, m\}$. Each level t of a LH corresponds to a linguistic term set symmetrically distributed with an odd granularity of uncertainty, $n(t)$, denoted as

$$S^{n(t)} = \{s_0^{n(t)}, \ldots, s_{n(t)-1}^{n(t)}\}$$

The construction of a LH must satisfy two rules, called *linguistic hierarchy basic rules* [12], based on the following lemma.

Lemma 4.1. *Let* $S^{n(t)} = \{s_0^{n(t)}, \ldots, s_{n(t)-1}^{n(t)}\}$ *be an ordered linguistic term set in LH of a linguistic variable. The set of former modal points of the level t is defined as*

$$FP_t = \{fp_t^0, \ldots, fp_t^i, \ldots, fp_t^{2 \cdot \delta_t}\},$$

where each former modal point $fp_t^i \in [0, 1]$ *is located at*

$$fp_t^i = \frac{i}{2 \cdot \delta_t} \in [0, 1],$$

where $\delta_t = n(t) - 1 \in \mathbb{N}$.

- **Rule 1:** To preserve all *former modal points* of the membership functions of each linguistic term from one level to the following one.
- **Rule 2:** To make *smooth transitions between successive levels*. The aim is to add a new linguistic term set, $S^{n(t+1)}$, in the hierarchy such that a new linguistic term will be added between each pair of terms belonging to the term set of the previous level t. To carry out this insertion, it is necessary to reduce the support of the linguistic labels in order to keep a place for the new one located in the middle of them.

Table 4.5 shows the granularity for each linguistic term set of a LH according to the rules (shown graphically in Figure 4.7).

Table 4.5 Linguistic hierarchies

	$S^{n(t)}$	$S^{n(t)}$
Level 1	S^3	S^7
Level 2	S^5	S^{13}
Level 3	S^9	

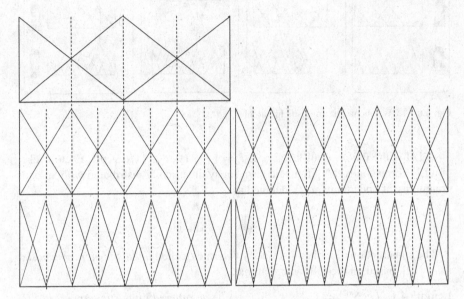

Fig. 4.7 Linguistic hierarchies of 3, 5, and 9 labels, and 7 and 13 labels

Remark 4.1. These rules induce a limitation regarding the linguistic term sets that can be used in a *LH*, because a linguistic term set of level $t + 1$ is obtained from its predecessor as

$$S^{n(t)} \rightarrow S^{n(2 \cdot n(t) - 1)} \tag{4.3}$$

4.2.2.2   Unification Phase

The multigranular linguistic information must be conducted in a unique domain before carrying out the CW processes. Thus, the multigranular linguistic informa-tion assessed in a linguistic hierarchy can be unified in any linguistic term set, $S^{n(t)}$ with $t = \{1, 2, \ldots, m\}$ of the LH by using a transformation function, $TF_{t'}^t$, between any two linguistic levels t and t', defined as

Definition 4.3 ([12]). Let $LH = \bigcup_t S^{n(t)}$ be a LH whose linguistic term sets are denoted as $S^{n(t)} = \{s_0^{n(t)}, \ldots, s_{n(t)-1}^{n(t)}\}$, and let us consider the 2-tuple fuzzy linguistic representation. The transformation function, $TF_{t'}^t : \overline{S^{n(t)}} \rightarrow \overline{S^{n(t')}}$, from a 2-tuple linguistic value in the level t to its correspondent 2-tuple linguistic value in the level t', in the LH is:

$$TF_{t'}^{t}(s_i^{n(t)}, \alpha^{n(t)}) = \Delta\left(\frac{\Delta^{-1}(s_i^{n(t)}, \alpha^{n(t)}) \cdot (n(t') - 1)}{n(t) - 1}\right) \tag{4.4}$$

Proposition 4.1. *The transformation function between linguistic terms in different levels of the linguistic hierarchy is a bijective function:*

$$TF_t^{t'}(TF_{t'}^{t}(s_i^{n(t)}, \alpha^{n(t)})) = (s_i^{n(t)}, \alpha^{n(t)})$$

Proof.

$$TF_{t'}^{t}(s_i^{n(t)}, \alpha^{n(t)}) = \Delta\left(\frac{\Delta^{-1}(s_i^{n(t)}, \alpha^{n(t)}) \cdot (n(t') - 1)}{n(t) - 1}\right),$$

therefore,

$$TF_t^{t'}\left(\Delta\left(\frac{\Delta^{-1}(s_i^{n(t)}, \alpha^{n(t)}) \cdot (n(t') - 1)}{n(t) - 1}\right)\right) =$$

$$= \Delta\left(\frac{\Delta^{-1}\left(\Delta\left(\frac{\Delta^{-1}(s_i^{n(t)}, \alpha^{n(t)}) \cdot (n(t')-1)}{n(t)-1}\right)\right) \cdot (n(t) - 1)}{n(t') - 1}\right) =$$

$$= \Delta\left(\frac{\Delta^{-1}(s_i^{n(t)}, \alpha^{n(t)}) \cdot (n(t') - 1) \cdot (n(t) - 1)}{(n(t) - 1) \cdot (n(t') - 1)}\right) =$$

$$= (s_i^{n(t)}, \alpha^{n(t)})$$

This result guarantees that the transformations between levels of a linguistic hierarchy are carried out without loss of information. □

Example 4.2. Let $LH = \bigcup_t S^{n(t)}$ be the linguistic hierarchy of the left side in Figure 4.7, whose levels are:

$$S^{n(1)} \{s_0^3, s_1^3, s_2^3\}$$
$$S^{n(2)} \{s_0^5, s_1^5, s_2^5, s_3^5, s_4^5\}$$
$$S^{n(3)} \{s_0^9, s_1^9, s_2^9, s_3^9, s_4^9, s_5^9, s_6^9, s_7^9, s_8^9\}$$

An example of the performance of the transformation function $TF_{t'}^{t}(s_i^{n(t)}, \alpha^{n(t)})$ between its different levels on linguistic terms of the LH would be:

$$TF_1^3(s_5^9, 0) = \Delta^{-1}\left(\frac{\Delta(s_5^9, 0) \cdot (3-1)}{9-1}\right) = \Delta^{-1}(1, 25) = (s_1^3, .25)$$

$$TF_3^1(s_1^3, .25) = \Delta^{-1}\left(\frac{\Delta(s_1^3, .25) \cdot (9-1)}{3-1}\right) = \Delta^{-1}(5) = (s_5^9, .0)$$

$$TF_2^3(s_5^9, 0) = \Delta^{-1}\left(\frac{\Delta(s_5^9, 0) \cdot (5-1)}{9-1}\right) = \Delta^{-1}(2.5) = (s_3^5, -.5)$$

$$TF_1^2(s_3^5, -.5) = \Delta^{-1}\left(\frac{\Delta(s_3^5, -.5) \cdot (3-1)}{5-1}\right) = \Delta^{-1}(1.25) = (s_1^3, .25)$$

4.2.2.3   Computational Phase

Inasmuch as the representation model used by LH and the results of the unification process are 2-tuple linguistic values, its computational model is based on the one presented in Chapter 2 for the 2-tuple linguistic model. It follows the linguistic decision scheme depicted in Figure 1.4 whose main phases are:

- *Aggregation* phase: In this case the conducted linguistic information by 2-tuple linguistic values in a level of the LH (usually the level with greatest granularity) will be aggregated to obtain a collective 2-tuple linguistic value in the level of unification.
- *Exploitation* phase: Different choice degree functions can be applied to obtain the final solution set of alternatives for the LDM problem. This phase can be either performed in the unification level in which the information has been conducted during the unification process or in any of the levels of the LH according to the retranslation phase because the final results will remain unchanged.

4.2.2.4   Retranslation Phase: Results

The proposition 4.1 proved that the transformation function, $TF_{t'}^t$, between linguistic terms in different levels, t and t', of the linguistic hierarchy is a bijective function, which guarantees that the transformations between levels of a linguistic hierarchy are carried out without loss of information.

It is then remarkable that the final results of any computational process, dealing with linguistic information assessed in a LH, can be expressed in any linguistic term set of the LH by means of a retranslation process accomplished by $TF_{t'}^t$ without loss of information (see Figure 4.6).

4.2.2.5 Illustrative Decision-Making Problem Example: Linguistic Hierarchies

A company needs to select the most suitable material for the automobile bumper. After some preliminary studies three different materials have been selected to evaluate {polycarbonate, polypropylene, and acrylonitrile butadiene styrene (ABS)}. The evaluation committee consists of three experts $\{e_1, e_2, e_3\}$ who are the heads of the economics, environment, and engineering departments, respectively. They consider four critical criteria {cost, heat resistance, tensile, and toxicity level} for the evaluation. Because each expert has a different degree of knowledge about the materials and criteria, they use different linguistic term sets in a LH according to their knowledge.

A. Framework

In this case the multigranular linguistic framework is defined by a LH. The LH is conformed by the linguistic term sets S^3, S^5, and S^9 with three, five, and nine linguistic terms (see Figure 4.8) which fulfil the linguistic hierarchy basic rules.

- Head of economics $(e_1) \rightarrow S^3$
- Head of environment $(e_2) \rightarrow S^5$
- Head of engineering $(e_3) \rightarrow S^9$

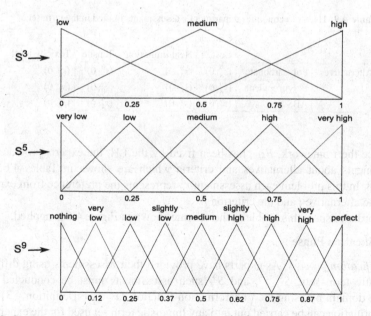

Fig. 4.8 Syntax and semantics of the linguistic term sets S^3, S^5, and S^9

Table 4.6 Head of economics department's assessments, (e_1)

		Criteria			
		Cost	Heat resistance	Tensile	Toxicity level
Alternatives	Polycarbonate	s_2^3	s_1^3	s_1^3	s_1^3
	Polypropylene	s_2^3	s_2^3	s_0^3	s_2^3
	ABS	s_1^3	s_1^3	s_1^3	s_0^3

Table 4.7 Head of environment department's assessments, (e_2)

		Criteria			
		Cost	Heat resistance	Tensile	Toxicity level
Alternatives	Polycarbonate	s_4^5	s_3^5	s_2^5	s_0^5
	Polypropylene	s_4^5	s_4^5	s_3^5	s_3^5
	ABS	s_3^5	s_3^5	s_4^5	s_2^5

Table 4.8 Head of engineering department's assessments, (e_3)

		Criteria			
		Cost	Heat resistance	Tensile	Toxicity level
Alternatives	Polycarbonate	s_6^9	s_0^9	s_6^9	s_5^9
	Polypropylene	s_5^9	s_7^9	s_7^9	s_5^9
	ABS	s_6^9	s_5^9	s_7^9	s_6^9

Table 4.9 Head of economics department's assessments unified in the term set S^9

		Criteria			
		Cost	Heat limitation	Tensile	Toxicity level
Alternatives	Polycarbonate	$(s_8^9, 0)$	$(s_4^9, 0)$	$(s_4^9, 0)$	$(s_4^9, 0)$
	Polypropylene	$(s_8^9, 0)$	$(s_8^9, 0)$	$(s_0^9, 0)$	$(s_8^9, 0)$
	ABS	$(s_4^9, 0)$	$(s_4^9, 0)$	$(s_4^9, 0)$	$(s_0^9, 0)$

Once the framework, F_{MS}, has been fixed by the LH, the experts provide their assessments about alternatives and criteria which are shown in Tables 4.6, 4.7, and 4.8. In this problem each assessment r_{ij}^k represents the preference from expert k over the alternative i and the criterion j.

In order to solve this problem, the scheme shown in Figure 4.6 is applied.

B. Unification Phase

Unification process: As experts have provided their assessments using different linguistic term sets, S^3, S^5, and S^9, such assessments must be conducted in a unique domain by using the transformation function $TF_{t'}^t$ (see Definition 4.3). The transformation can be carried out into any linguistic term set used for the experts. In this problem, it is used as unification domain S^9, because it is the linguistic term set with the highest granularity. Tables 4.9, 4.10, and 4.11 show the assessments unified into S^9.

Table 4.10 Head of environment department's assessments unified in the term set S^9

		Criteria			
		Cost	Heat limitation	Tensile	Toxicity level
Alternatives	Polycarbonate	$(s_8^9,0)$	$(s_6^9,0)$	$(s_4^9,0)$	$(s_0^9,0)$
	Polypropylene	$(s_8^9,0)$	$(s_8^9,0)$	$(s_6^9,0)$	$(s_6^9,0)$
	ABS	$(s_6^9,0)$	$(s_6^9,0)$	$(s_8^9,0)$	$(s_4^9,0)$

Table 4.11 Head of engineering department's assessments unified in the term set S^9

		Criteria			
		Cost	Heat limitation	Tensile	Toxicity level
Alternatives	Polycarbonate	$(s_6^9,0)$	$(s_0^9,0)$	$(s_6^9,0)$	$(s_5^9,0)$
	Polypropylene	$(s_5^9,0)$	$(s_7^9,0)$	$(s_7^9,0)$	$(s_5^9,0)$
	ABS	$(s_6^9,0)$	$(s_5^9,0)$	$(s_7^9,0)$	$(s_6^9,0)$

Table 4.12 Assessments obtained by aggregating experts' assessments

		Criteria			
		Cost	Heat limitation	Tensile	Toxicity level
Alternatives	Polycarbonate	$(s_7^9,0.47)$	$(s_3^9,0.07)$	$(s_4^9,0.13)$	$(s_3^9,0)$
	Polypropylene	$(s_7^9,0.2)$	$(s_8^9,-0.27)$	$(s_4^9,0.47)$	$(s_6^9,-0.13)$
	ABS	$(s_5^9,0.47)$	$(s_5^9,-0.2)$	$(s_6^9,0.27)$	$(s_3^9,0.07)$

C. Computational Phase

Once all the assessments have been unified into the linguistic term set S^9, they are aggregated to obtain a collective value for each alternative. In this example the aggregation process is a two-step process.

- *Aggregation of experts' assessments*: Firstly, the assessments r_{ij}^k, are aggregated by using the L2TOWA operator (see Definition 2.5), whose weighting vector W is obtained by applying the linguistic quantifier *most* (see Equations (2.6) and (2.7) to obtain the OWA weights). The weighting vector obtained is $W = \{0.07, 0.66, 0.27\}$ and the assessments r_{ij}, obtained from the aggregation are shown in Table 4.12.
- *Aggregation of criteria values*: Afterwards, the criteria for each alternative are aggregated. In this case the aggregation operator used is the 2-tuple weighted average operator (see Definition 2.4), because the criteria have different importance. The weighting vector is $W = \{0.3, 0.2, 0.25, 0.25\}$. Table 4.13 shows the collective values r_i, for each alternative.

D. Retranslation Phase

The collective values represented in the linguistic term set S^9 can be transformed into any original linguistic term set by using the Definition 4.3 without loss of

Table 4.13 Collective values of the alternatives

Collective values		
Polycarbonate	Polypropylene	ABS
(Slightly high,−0.36)	(High,0.29)	(Slightly high,−0.06)

Table 4.14 Retranslation of the collective values

		Collectives values		
		S^9	S^5	S^3
Alternatives	Polycarbonate	(Slightly high,−0.36)	(Medium,0.31)	(Medium,0.15)
	Polypropylene	(High,0.29)	(High,0.14)	(High,−0.42)
	ABS	(Slightly high,−0.06)	(Medium,0.46)	(Medium,0.23)

information (see Table 4.14). This way, experts can understand the final result better, because it is expressed in the same linguistic term set that they used to provide their preferences.

E. Exploitation Phase

In order to obtain the ranking of alternatives, the collective values represented in any linguistic term set of the LH can be used because the results remain unchanged. In this case, the linguistic term set S^9 has been used.

$$Polypropylene > ABS > Polycarbonate$$

Therefore, the most suitable material for the automobile bumper is
   {**Polypropylene=(high,0.29)**}.

4.2.3 *Extended Linguistic Hierarchies*

LH has provided accuracy for computing with multigranular linguistic information, however, it still presents an important limitation regarding the linguistic term sets that can be used in the framework that the fusion approach did not present. For example, the linguistic term sets with 5 and 7 labels are incompatible in LH, but sometimes both are necessary in a specific problem. In order to overcome such a limitation, an extended model has been proposed that builds a structure, the extended linguistic hierarchy (ELH) [8].

The computational scheme for ELH is similar to the previous one shown in Figure 4.6 but with some slight difference in the unification process (see Figure 4.9), because a new linguistic term set is added in the last level of the hierarchy, and all the assessments provided for experts by using different linguistic term sets are unified in the new linguistic term set as can be seen in Section 4.2.3.2.

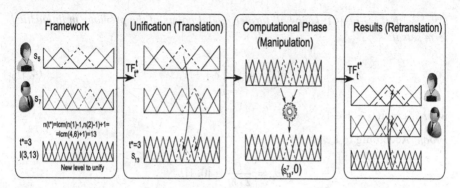

Fig. 4.9 A CW scheme for extended linguistic hierarchies

4.2.3.1 Framework

Similarly to the linguistic hierarchies, the extended linguistic hierarchies consist of a set of linguistic term sets that corresponds to a level, with each level, $S^{n(t)}$, a linguistic term set with different granularity, $n(t)$, from the remaining levels of the ELH. Thus, ELH will be the framework, F_{MS}, for the decision problem. However, unlike LH, the ELH can manage *any term set without any limitation*, because its construction process *redefines the linguistic hierarchical rules* to build the ELH and over it, the computational symbolic model based on the 2-tuple is used to accomplish the processes of CW in an accurate way.

$$F_{MS} = ELH$$

Because ELH must deal with any scale in the multigranular linguistic framework, the building of an ELH will consist in replacing the linguistic hierarchical basic rules that obligate us to keep the former modal points from one level, t, to the next one, t', by the following *extended hierarchical rules*.

- **Extended Rule 1:** To include a finite number of levels, $S^{n(t)}$, with $t = \{1, \ldots, m\}$, that define the multigranular linguistic context. There is no restriction about the granularity of these m linguistic term sets.
- **Extended Rule 2:** To add a final level, $S^{n(t^*)}$, such that $t^* = m + 1$ keeps all the former modal points of the previous m levels.

Therefore, in order to construct an ELH, first the m linguistic term sets that define the decision framework are added; in those m linguistic term sets the experts can elicit their information. Afterwards, a new linguistic term set, $S^{n(t^*)}$ with $t^* = m+1$, will be added according to the following theorem.

Theorem 4.1. *Let* $\{S^{n(1)}, \ldots, S^{n(m)}\}$ *be the set of m linguistic term sets, whose granularity* $n(t)$, *with* $t = \{1, \ldots, m\}$, *is an odd value. A new linguistic term set*

$S^{n(t^*)}$, with $t^* = m + 1$, *keeps all former modal points of the previous m linguistic term sets if:*

$$n(t^*) = (\prod_{t=1}^{m} \delta_t) + 1, \tag{4.5}$$

where $\delta_t = n(t) - 1 \in \mathbb{N}$.

Proof. According to Lemma 4.1:

$$fp_t^i = \frac{i}{2 \cdot \delta_t} \in [0, 1],$$

and

$$fp_{t^*}^j = \frac{j}{2 \cdot \delta_{t^*}} \in [0, 1],$$

Notice that according to Theorem 4.1:

$$\delta_t = n(t) - 1 \text{ and } \delta_{t^*} = n(t^*) - 1 = \prod_{t=1}^{m} \delta_t$$

Hence δ_t is a multiplier of δ_{t^*}.

Therefore, $\forall fp_t^i \in FP_t$, $t \in \{1, \dots, m\}$, there always exists $fp_{t^*}^j \in FP_{t^*}$, $t^* = m + 1$ such at $fp_t^i = fp_{t^*}^j$, i.e.,

$$\frac{i}{2 \cdot \delta_t} = \frac{j}{2 \cdot \delta_{t^*}}.$$

It then proves that $FP_t \subset FP_{t^*}$ $\forall t \in \{1, \dots, m\}$. $\qquad\qquad\square$

Example 4.3. The granularity of the level $t^* = 4$ for an ELH with $m = 3$ linguistic term sets whose granularities are 3, 5, and 7 is computed by:

$$(\prod_{t=1}^{m} \delta_t) + 1,$$

with $\delta_1 = 2$, $\delta_2 = 4$, and $\delta_3 = 6$. The granularity $n(t^*)$ is:

$$n(4) = (2 \cdot 4 \cdot 6) + 1 = 48 + 1 = 49.$$

However, the granularity of t^* determined by using Theorem 4.1 would be too high and might make the computational model more complex.

In order to make the use and construction of an ELH simpler there is an alternative way to minimise the granularity of t^* which can still keep all the former modal points of the previous levels, by using the least common multiple (LCM).

Definition 4.4. The LCM of m nonzero integer $\{a_1, \ldots, a_m\}$ is the smallest number designated by $LCM(a_1, \ldots, a_m)$ that is divisible by the m nonzero integer $\{a_1, \ldots, a_m\}$. It is defined as

$$LCM(a_1, \ldots, a_m) = min\ \{n \in \mathbb{N} : n \mid a_i \in \mathbb{N}\ for\ i = 1, \ldots, m\} \qquad (4.6)$$

Therefore, a new theorem to compute the granularity of the level t^* is proposed.

Theorem 4.2. Let $\{S^{n(1)}, \ldots, S^{n(m)}\}$ be the set of linguistic scales with any odd value of granularity. A new level, $S^{n(t^*)}$ with $t^* = m + 1$, that keeps the former modal points of the previous m levels:

$$n(t^*) = (LCM(\delta_1, \ldots, \delta_m)) + 1,\ t = \{1, \ldots, m\} \qquad (4.7)$$

Proof. Similar to the proof of Theorem 4.1, in this case, it is still truth that δ_t is a multiplier of δ_{t^*}. Hence,

$$j = \frac{(i \cdot \delta_t^*)}{\delta_t} \Rightarrow FP_t \subset FP_{t^*}, \forall t \in \{1, \ldots, m\}$$

□

Therefore, the way to compute the granularity of the linguistic term set, $t^* = m + 1$, in ELH will be:

$$n(t^*) = \big(LCM(n(1) - 1, \ldots, n(m) - 1)\big) + 1 \qquad (4.8)$$

Example 4.4. By using the framework of Example 4.3 with the linguistic term sets with granularities 3, 5, and 7, the granularity of the last level in the ELH according to Theorem 4.2 is:

$$(LCM(\delta_1, \delta_2, \delta_3)) + 1 = LCM(2, 4, 6) + 1 = 12 + 1 = 13$$

4.2.3.2 Unification Phase

The ELH also shares the computational scheme shown in Figure 4.6, therefore to deal with the multigranular linguistic information in ELH, its unification (see Figure 4.9), based on the transformation function $TF_{t'}^t$, is necessary [see Equation (4.4)] for LH. However, in the *ELH* these transformations do not guarantee the accuracy of the transformation between any two linguistic term sets because the linguistic term set cannot keep the former modal points with the next one. Therefore, in ELH the information is *always* conducted in the level t^* that keeps all the former modal points by using the transformation function, $TF_{t^*}^t$, t being any level in $\{1, \ldots, m\}$ and $t^* = m + 1$.

Definition 4.5. Let $S^{n(t)} = \{s_0^{n(t)}, s_1^{n(t)}, \ldots, s_{n(t)-1}^{n(t)}\}$ and $S^{n(t^*)} = \{s_0^{n(t^*)}, s_1^{n(t^*)}, \ldots, s_{n(t^*)-1}^{n(t^*)}\}$ be two linguistic term sets, with $t < t^*$. The linguistic transformation function $TF_{t^*}^t : \overline{S^{n(t)}} \longrightarrow \overline{S^{n(t^*)}}$ is defined by:

$$
TF_{t^*}^t(s_j^{n(t)}, \alpha_j) = \Delta_S \left(\frac{\Delta_S^{-1}(s_j^{n(t)}, \alpha_j^{n(t)}) \cdot (n(t^*) - 1)}{n(t) - 1} \right) = (s_k^{n(t^*)}, \alpha_k). \tag{4.9}
$$

4.2.3.3 Computational Phase

Similarly to the computational phase of LH introduced in Section 4.2.2.3, in the ELH the linguistic information conducted into the level t^* and represented by 2-tuple linguistic values has a computational model which is also based on the one presented in Chapter 2 for the 2-tuple linguistic model whose main phases are:

- *Aggregation* phase: In this case the conducted linguistic information by 2-tuple linguistic values in the level t^* of the LH will be aggregated to obtain a collective 2-tuple linguistic value in the level t^*.
- *Exploitation* phase: Different choice degree functions can be applied to obtain the final solution set of alternatives for the LDM problem. Such choice degree functions can be directly applied either to the results obtained in the aggregation phase or to the results expressed in other levels of the ELH after the retranslation phase because the results do not change.

4.2.3.4 Retranslation Phase: Results

Again as in the LH model, the results obtained in the computational phase are already 2-tuple linguistic values. But by using the transformation function $TF_{t'}^t$ [see Equation (4.4)] and keeping in mind that the unified information is expressed in the level t^* that can have a high granularity which is difficult to understand, a new transformation function $TF_{t'}^{t^*} : \overline{S^{n(t^*)}} \to \overline{S^{n(t')}}$, that transforms the linguistic terms at $S^{n(t^*)}$ in ELH into any level $S^{n(t')}$, $t' \in \{1, \ldots, m\})$ is defined. This transformation function obtains accurate results, because the linguistic term set of the level t^* keeps the former modal points of the other m levels of the ELH. This way, experts can obtain the results represented in the same linguistic term set that they used to express their assessments.

$$
TF_{t'}^{t^*} : \overline{S^{n(t^*)}} \longrightarrow \overline{S^{n(t')}}
$$

4.2.3.5 Illustrative Decision-Making Problem Example: Extended Linguistic Hierarchies

A software development company wants to hire a programmer. The human resources section has selected five candidates $\{x_1, x_2, x_3, x_4, x_5\}$ according to their curriculum vitae, but they only need one person. Therefore, they have to provide their opinions to decide who is the most suitable candidate. There are four people working in the human resources department $\{e_1, e_2, e_3, e_4\}$ and they have different experience in this department, thus they will use different linguistic term sets to express their preferences according to their knowledge.

A. Framework

The linguistic term sets used by people who work in human resources department are S^5, S^7, and S^9 with three, seven, and nine linguistic terms (see Figure 4.10).

- $e_1 \rightarrow S^5$
- $e_2 \rightarrow S^7$
- $e_3 \rightarrow S^9$
- $e_4 \rightarrow S^7$

In this problem, the LH model cannot be applied because of its limitation regarding the linguistic term sets that can be used in the framework. Therefore, the ELH model is used to solve this problem (see Figure 4.9). In order to build the

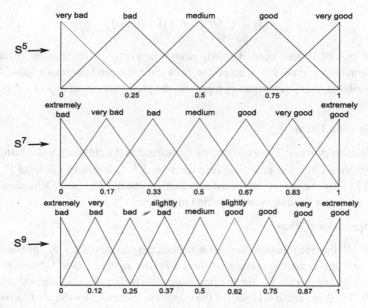

Fig. 4.10 Syntax and semantics of the linguistic term sets S^5, S^7, and S^9

Table 4.15 Assessments provided by experts

		Candidates				
		x_1	x_2	x_3	x_4	x_5
Experts	e_1	(s_3^5)	(s_2^5)	(s_1^5)	(s_4^5)	(s_4^5)
	e_2	(s_3^7)	(s_4^7)	(s_3^7)	(s_6^7)	(s_3^7)
	e_3	(s_3^9)	(s_5^9)	(s_5^9)	(s_7^9)	(s_6^9)
	e_4	(s_2^7)	(s_4^7)	(s_3^7)	(s_5^7)	(s_6^7)

Table 4.16 Assessments unified in the level t^*

		Candidates				
		x_1	x_2	x_3	x_4	x_5
Experts	e_1	$(s_{18}^{25},0)$	$(s_{12}^{25},0)$	$(s_6^{25},0)$	$(s_{24}^{25},0)$	$(s_{24}^{25},0)$
	e_2	$(s_{12}^{25},0)$	$(s_{16}^{25},0)$	$(s_{12}^{25},0)$	$(s_{24}^{25},0)$	$(s_{12}^{25},0)$
	e_3	$(s_9^{25},0)$	$(s_{15}^{25},0)$	$(s_{15}^{25},0)$	$(s_{21}^{25},0)$	$(s_{18}^{25},0)$
	e_4	$(s_8^{25},0)$	$(s_{16}^{25},0)$	$(s_{12}^{25},0)$	$(s_{20}^{25},0)$	$(s_{24}^{25},0)$

Table 4.17 Collective values of the candidates

Collective values				
x_1	x_2	x_3	x_4	x_5
$(s_9^{25},-0.5)$	$(s_{14}^{25},-0.5)$	$(s_9^{25},0)$	$(s_{21}^{25},-0.5)$	$(s_{15}^{25},0)$

ELH used as F_{MS}, the linguistic term sets, S^5, S^7, and S^9, are included as the basis and a new linguistic term set $(S^{n(t^*)})$ with $t^* = 4$ is added. The granularity of $n(4)$ is obtained according to Theorem 4.2.

$$n(4) = (LMC(4, 6, 8)) + 1 = 25$$

Once the ELH has been defined, people working in the human resources department (experts) provide their preferences about the candidates (see Table 4.15). In this problem, the assessments r_i^k represent the preference from expert k about the candidate i.

B. Unification Phase

Unification process: The assessments r_i^k, defined in different linguistic term sets, are transformed into the new linguistic term set $S^{n(t^*)}$, added in the level $t^* = 4$ of the ELH by means of the transformation function TF_{t*}^t (see Definition 4.5). Table 4.16 shows the assessments unified in the level t^*.

C. Computational Phase

Once all the information has been unified, the assessments r_i^k, provided by experts are aggregated by means of the L2TOWA operator (see Definition 2.5), whose weighting vector W, for the linguistic quantifier *"as many as possible"*, is $W=\{0, 0, 0.5, 0.5\}$. Table 4.17 shows the collective values r_i, for the alternatives.

Table 4.18 Collective values of the candidates transformed into S^7

Collective values				
x_1	x_2	x_3	x_4	x_5
(Bad,0.12)	(Medium,0.37)	(Bad,0.25)	(Very good,0.12)	(Good,−0.25)

D. Retranslation Phase

The collective values obtained in the level t^* might be transformed into any level of the original linguistic term sets $S^{n(t)}$ used in ELH. In this problem, S^7 is used in ELH, because experts can understand the final results more easily (Table 4.18).

E. Exploitation Phase

The collective values represented in S^7 are ordered to get the ranking of candidates.

$$x_4 > x_5 > x_2 > x_3 > x_1$$

Therefore, the best candidate for the programmer position is the candidate $\{x_4 = (\text{very good}, 0.12)\}$.

4.3 2-Tuple Linguistic Based Model to Deal with Nonhomogeneous Information

In Section 4.1 it was pointed out that apart from the multigranular linguistic information, another type of heterogeneous context in decision making may occur when experts elicit their knowledge with nonhomogeneous information such as numerical, linguistic, interval-valued, and so on. In decision problems with multiple experts or criteria this is not a rare situation [5, 7]. For this type of framework a 2-tuple linguistic based model was introduced in [13] to manage and operate with such type of information that performs a computing scheme (see Figure 4.11) with similar phases to the scheme for multigranular linguistic information shown in Figure 4.2.

4.3.1 Framework

In this approach the framework, F_{MS}, is defined by different expression domains, D, such as

- Numerical: Assessments represented as values in [0,1]
- Interval-valued: Assessments represented as intervals, $I([0,1])$
- Linguistic: Assessments represented as linguistic terms $s_i \in S = \{s_0, \ldots, s_g\}$

which will be used by experts to elicit their preferences and opinions.

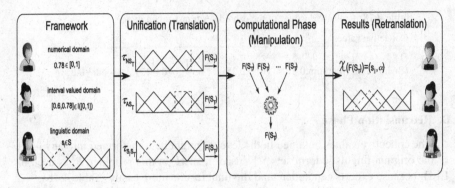

Fig. 4.11 CW scheme for nonhomogeneous information

4.3.2   *Unification Phase*

This phase consists of conducting the nonhomogeneous information into a common expression domain. There are different choices to conduct the information into a unique domain, but obviously such an expression domain in this book is a linguistic domain based on the 2-tuple linguistic model because of its features that facilitate the resolution of decision problems obtaining accurate and easy to understand results. The selection of a linguistic domain to conduct all the information aims at producing easily understood results by all the experts involved in the decision problem and able to represent the uncertainty of the nonhomogeneous information.

The unification phase is divided into two different steps:

- *Selection of the BLTS* S_T: the nonhomogeneous information is unified in a unique linguistic expression domain, called BLTS, whose selection follows the suggestions provided in Section 4.2.1.
- *Unification process*: once the BLTS, $S_T = \{s_0, \ldots, s_g\}$, has been chosen, the nonhomogeneous information is unified into fuzzy sets in the BLTS by means of transformation functions according to the nature of the information:

  1. Transforming numerical values in $[0, 1]$ into $F(S_T)$.
  2. Transforming linguistic terms into $F(S_T)$.
  3. Transforming interval-valued into $F(S_T)$.

Following, the transformation functions for each type of expression domain that could be integrated in the decision framework (numerical, linguistic, interval-valued) are shown.

1. *Numerical Values*

   Let $F(S_T)$ be the set of fuzzy sets in $S_T = s_0, \ldots s_g$, and ϑ a numerical value in $[0, 1]$. ϑ is transformed into a fuzzy set in $F(S_T)$ by computing the membership value of ϑ in the fuzzy number associated with the linguistic terms of S_T.

Definition 4.6 ([11]). The function τ_{NS_T} transforms a numerical value into a fuzzy set in S_T :

$$\tau_{NS_T} : [0, 1] \rightarrow F(S_T)$$

$$\tau_{NS_T}(\vartheta) = \sum_{i=0}^{g} s_i/\gamma_i, \tag{4.10}$$

$$\gamma_i = \mu_{s_i}(\vartheta) = \begin{cases} 0, & \text{if } \vartheta \notin Support(\mu_{s_i}(x)) \\ \frac{\vartheta - a_i}{b_i - a_i}, & \text{if } a_i \leq \vartheta \leq b_i \\ 1, & \text{if } b_i \leq \vartheta \leq d_i \\ \frac{c_i - \vartheta}{c_i - d_i}, & \text{if } d_i \leq \vartheta \leq c_i \end{cases}$$

Remark 4.2. For this definition membership functions $\mu_{s_i}(\cdot)$ are considered for linguistic labels, $s_i \in S_T$, represented by a parametric function (a_i, b_i, d_i, c_i). A particular case is the linguistic assessments whose membership functions are triangulars; that is, $b_i = d_i$.

Example 4.5. Let $\vartheta = 0.78$ be a numerical value to be transformed into a fuzzy set in $S_T = \{s_0, \ldots, s_4\}$. The semantics of this linguistic term set is:

$$s_0 = (0, 0, 0.25) \quad s_1 = (0, 0.25, 0.5) \quad s_2 = (0.25, 0.5, 0.75)$$

$$s_3 = (0.5, 0.75, 1) \quad s_4 = (0.75, 1, 1)$$

Therefore, the fuzzy set obtained is (see Figure 4.12):

$$\tau_{NS_T}(0.78) = \{(s_0, 0), (s_1, 0), (s_2, 0), (s_3, 0.88), (s_4, 0.12)\}$$

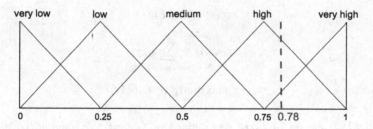

Fig. 4.12 Transforming a numerical value into a fuzzy set in S_T

Fig. 4.13 Membership
function of $A = [\underline{a}, \overline{a}]$

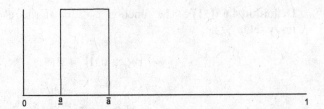

2. *Linguistic Terms*

   For linguistic information the transformation function utilised to transform the linguistic terms into fuzzy sets in the BLTS S_T, is the same as that introduced in Definition 4.1 in Section 4.2.1.

3. *Interval-Valued*

   Let $A = [\underline{a}, \overline{a}]$ be an interval-valued in $I([0, 1])$; to unify this type of information it is assumed that the interval-valued presents a representation inspired in the membership function of fuzzy sets [16], as follows.

$$\mu_A(\vartheta) = \begin{cases} 0, \text{ if } \vartheta < \underline{a} \\ 1, \text{ if } \underline{a} \le \vartheta \le \overline{a} \\ 0, \text{ if } \overline{a} < \vartheta \end{cases}$$

with ϑ a value in $[0, 1]$. The previous representation of an interval-value can be observed graphically in Figure 4.13.

Therefore, the transformation function of the interval-valued into a fuzzy set in the BLTS, S_T, is computed as

Definition 4.7 ([13]). Let $S_T = \{s_0, \dots, s_g\}$ be a BLTS, the function τ_{AS_T} transforms an interval-valued A in $I([0, 1])$ into a fuzzy set in S_T.

$$\tau_{AS_T} : A \to F(S_T)$$

$$\tau_{AS_T}(A) = \sum_{i=0}^{g} s_i/\gamma_i, \qquad (4.11)$$

$$\gamma_k^i = \max_y \min\{\mu_A(y), \mu_{s_k}(y)\}$$

with $F(S_T)$ the set of fuzzy sets defined in S_T, and $\mu_A(\cdot)$ and $\mu_{s_k}(\cdot)$ are the membership functions associated with the interval-valued A and the linguistic terms $s_k \in S_T$, respectively.

Example 4.6. Let $I = [0.6, 0.78]$ be an interval-valued to be transformed into a fuzzy set in S_T with five terms symmetrically distributed. The fuzzy set obtained after applying τ_{AS_T} is (see Figure 4.14):

$$\tau_{AS_T}([0.6, 0.78]) = \{(s_0, 0), (s_1, 0), (s_2, 0.6), (s_3, 1), (s_4, 0.2)\}$$

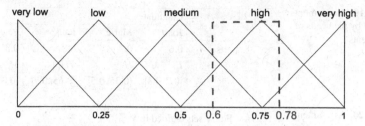

Fig. 4.14 Transforming an interval-valued into a fuzzy set in S_T

4.3.3 Computational Phase

Once the information has been conducted into just one expression domain, the computations are directly operated on fuzzy sets by using fuzzy arithmetic [6] similarly to the fusion approach for multigranular linguistic information (see Section 4.2.1)

4.3.4 Retranslation Phase: Results

Hence, similarly to the fusion approach in Section 4.2.1, to express the results by 2-tuple linguistic values, a retranslation process that uses the function $\chi(\cdot)$ [see Equation (4.2)] is performed.

4.3.5 Illustrative Decision-Making Problem Example: Nonhomogeneous Information

Let us suppose that a company with 50 employees and three departments {economic, production, engineering} must choose a worker representative. There are four candidates, {John, Marie, Paul, and Peter} and the director of the company has decided that only the head of each department will provide his or her assessment. They have different backgrounds, so they feel more comfortable using different types of information.

In order to solve this problem defined in a heterogeneous context, the scheme shown in Figure 4.11 is used.

A. Framework

- Head of economic department (e_1) → Numerical values: [0, 1]
- Head of production department (e_2) → Linguistic terms: {*nothing (N), very low (VL), low (L), medium (M), high (H), very high (VH), absolute (A)*}
- Head of engineering department (e_3) → Interval-valued: $I([0, 1])$

Table 4.19 Assessments provided by the heads of departments

		Candidates			
		John	Marie	Paul	Peter
Experts	e_1	0.6	0.7	0.8	0.8
	e_2	L	H	VH	M
	e_3	[0.7, 0.8]	[0.35, 0.5]	[0.65, 0.7]	[0.8, 0.9]

Table 4.20 Assessments represented by fuzzy sets in S^T

r_{ij}^T	Fuzzy sets defined in S^T
r_1^1	$\{(N, 0), (VL, 0), (L, 0), (M, 0.4), (H, 0.6), (VH, 0), (A, 0)\}$
r_2^1	$\{(N, 0), (VL, 0), (L, 0), (M, 0), (H, 0.8), (VH, 0.2), (A, 0)\}$
r_3^1	$\{(N, 0), (VL, 0), (L, 0), (M, 0), (H, 0.2), (VH, 0.8), (A, 0)\}$
r_4^1	$\{(N, 0), (VL, 0), (L, 0), (M, 0), (H, 0.2), (VH, 0.8), (A, 0)\}$
r_1^2	$\{(N, 0), (VL, 0.5), (L, 1), (M, 0.5), (H, 0), (VH, 0), (A, 0)\}$
r_2^2	$\{(N, 0), (VL, 0), (L, 0), (M, 0.5), (H, 1), (VH, 0.5), (A, 0)\}$
r_3^2	$\{(N, 0), (VL, 0), (L, 0), (M, 0), (H, 0.5), (VH, 1), (A, 0.5)\}$
r_4^2	$\{(N, 0), (VL, 0), (L, 0.5), (M, 1), (H, 0.5), (VH, 0), (A, 0)\}$
r_1^3	$\{(N, 0), (VL, 0), (L, 0), (M, 0), (H, 0.8), (VH, 0.8), (A, 0)\}$
r_2^3	$\{(N, 0), (VL, 0), (L, 0.9), (M, 1), (H, 0), (VH, 0), (A, 0)\}$
r_3^3	$\{(N, 0), (VL, 0), (L, 0), (M, 0.1), (H, 1), (VH, 0.2), (A, 0)\}$
r_4^3	$\{(N, 0), (VL, 0), (L, 0), (M, 0), (H, 0.2), (VH, 1), (A, 0.4)\}$

Table 4.21 Assessments transformed into 2-tuple linguistic values

		Candidates			
		John	Maria	Paul	Peter
Experts	e_1	$(H, -0.4)$	$(H, 0.19)$	$(VH, -0.19)$	$(VH, -0.19)$
	e_2	$(L, 0)$	$(H, 0)$	$(VH, 0)$	$(M, 0)$
	e_3	$(VH, -0.5)$	$(M, -0.47)$	$(H, 0.07)$	$(VH, 0.12)$

The three heads of departments provide their assessments over the four candidates (see Table 4.19) and they attempt to reach a collective decision. In this problem each assessment, r_i^k, represents the assessment by expert k over the alternative i.

B. Unification Phase

1. *Selection of the BLTS S_T*: It will be S, because it satisfies the conditions shown in Section 4.2.1.
2. *Unification process*: The assessments, r_i^k, are unified into $F(S_T)$ by means of the transformation functions from Definitions 4.1, 4.6 and 4.7 (see Table 4.20).

C. Computational Phase

Once all the assessments are expressed by means of fuzzy sets defined in the BLTS, S, for the sake of simplicity they are transformed into 2-tuple linguistic values by the function $\chi(\cdot)$ (see Definition 4.2). The results of the transformation are shown in Table 4.21.

Table 4.22 Collective values of the candidates

Collective values			
John	Maria	Paul	Peter
(Medium,0.36)	(High,-0.42)	(Very high,-0.37)	(High,0.3)

Afterwards, an aggregation operator is used to combine it. In this example it is used as an aggregation operator, the 2-tuple arithmetic mean (see Definition 2.3) obtaining the collective values shown in Table 4.22.

D. Retranslation Phase

Because the collective values obtained from the aggregation are represented by 2-tuple linguistic values, it is not necessary to transform them.

E. Exploitation Phase

The collective values represented by 2-tuple linguistic values in the linguistic term set S are ordered to obtain a ranking of the candidates.

$$Paul > Peter > Maria > John$$

Finally, the director of the company chooses the best candidate to represent the workers, in this case, $\{\textbf{Paul} = (\textbf{very high}, -\textbf{0.37})\}$.

References

1. S.L. Chang, R.C. Wang, and S.Y. Wang. Applying a direct multi-granularity linguistic and strategy-oriented aggregation approach on the assessment of supply performance. *European Journal of Operational Research*, 177(2):1013–1025, 2007.
2. Z. Chen and D. Ben-Arieh. On the fusion of multi-granularity linguistic label sets in group decision making. *Computers and Industrial Engineering*, 51(3):526–541, 2006.
3. O. Cordón, F. Herrera, and I. Zwir. Linguistic modeling by hierarchical systems of linguistic rules. *IEEE Transactions on Fuzzy Systems*, 10(1):2–20, 2001.
4. R. de Andrés, J.L. García-Lapresta, and L Martínez. A multi-granular linguistic model for management decision-making in performance appraisal. *Soft Computing*, 14(1):21–34, 2010.
5. D. Dhouib and S. Elloumi. A new multi-criteria approach dealing with dependent and heterogeneous criteria for end-of-life product strategy. *Applied Mathematics and Computation*, 218(5):1668–1681, 2011.
6. D. Dubois and H. Prade. *Fuzzy Sets and Systems: Theory and Applications*. Kluwer Academic., New York, 1980.
7. M. Espinilla, R. de Andrés, F.J. Martínez, and L. Martínez. A 360-degree performance appraisal model dealing with heterogeneous information and dependent criteria. *Information Sciences*, 222:459–471, 2013.
8. M. Espinilla, J. Liu, and L. Martínez. An extended hierarchical linguistic model for decision-making problems. *Computational Intelligence*, 27(3):489–512, 2011.
9. F. Herrera and E. Herrera-Viedma. Linguistic decision analysis: Steps for solving decision problems under linguistic information. *Fuzzy Sets and Systems*, 115(1):67–82, 2000.

10. F. Herrera, E. Herrera-Viedma, and L. Martínez. A fusion approach for managing multi-granularity linguistic terms sets in decision making. *Fuzzy Sets and Systems*, 114(1):43–58, 2000.
11. F. Herrera and L. Martínez. An approach for combining linguistic and numerical information based on 2-tuple fuzzy representation model in decision-making. *International Journal of Uncertainty, Fuzziness and Knowledge-Based Systems*, 8(5):539–562, 2000.
12. F. Herrera and L. Martínez. A model based on linguistic 2-tuples for dealing with multigranular hierarchical linguistic context in multi-expert decision making. *IEEE Transactions on Systems, Man, And Cybernetics - Part B: Cybernetics*, 31(2):227–234, 2001.
13. F. Herrera, L. Martínez, and P.J. Sánchez. Managing non-homogeneous information in group decision making. *European Journal of Operational Research*, 166(1):115–132, 2005.
14. V.N. Huynh and Y. Nakamori. A satisfactory-oriented approach to multiexpert decision-making with linguistic assessments. *IEEE Transactions on Systems, Man, and Cybernetics, Part B: Cybernetics*, 35(2):184–196, 2005.
15. Y.P. Jiang, Z.P. Fan, and J. Ma. A method for group decision making with multi-granularity linguistic assessment information. *Information Sciences*, 178(4):1098–1109, 2008.
16. D. Kuchta. Fuzzy capital budgeting. *Fuzzy Sets and Systems*, 111:367–385, 2000.
17. D.F. Li, Z.G. Huang, and G.H. Chen. A systematic approach to heterogeneous multiattribute group decision making. *Computers & Industrial Engineering*, 59(4):561–572, 2010.
18. J.M. Mendel. An architecture for making judgement using computing with words. *International Journal of Applied Mathematics and Computer Sciences*, 12(3):325–335, 2002.
19. J.M. Mendel, L.A. Zadeh, E. Trillas, R.R. Yager, J. Lawry, H. Hagras, and S. Guadarrama. What computing with words means to me: Discussion forum. *IEEE Computational Intelligence Magazine*, 5(1):20–26, 2010.
20. G.A. Miller. The magical number seven plus or minus two: Some limits on our capacity of processing information. *Psychological Review*, 63:81–97, 1956.
21. D. Wu and J.M. Mendel. Computing with words for hierarchical decision making applied to evaluating a weapon system. *IEEE Transactions on Fuzzy Systems*, 18:441–460, June 2010.

Chapter 5
Decision Making with Unbalanced Linguistic Information

5.1 Unbalanced Linguistic Information

Most linguistic decision problems model information with linguistic variables assessed in linguistic term sets whose terms are uniform and symmetrically distributed [3, 4, 8], because it is enough to obtain satisfactory results. It might raise the necessity in linguistic decision problems of modelling linguistic assessments by means of *linguistic information not uniformly distributed* which belongs to linguistic term sets that are not uniform or symmetrically distributed, that is, *unbalanced linguistic term sets* [7, 9, 10, 12]. This necessity may be due to the nature of the linguistic variables that participate in the problem, or because the preferences need a greater granularity on one side of the scale than on the other (see Figure 5.1).

The modelling of unbalanced linguistic information was initially proposed in [5] using the 2-tuple linguistic based approach based on linguistic hierarchies. Different researchers have paid attention to this approach and have proposed extensions, such as that presented by Abchir and Truck [1].

This chapter describes a new methodology to deal with unbalanced linguistic information; such a methodology not only develops a fuzzy representation method for unbalanced linguistic term sets, but also introduces a computational model to accomplish processes of Computing with Words (CW) without loss of information by using the 2-tuple linguistic model. This methodology is based on the proposal presented in [5], with the aim of making the computational process clearer and simpler. It consists of two different elements:

- First, it develops an unbalanced linguistic representation algorithm which assigns fuzzy semantics to the unbalanced linguistic terms by means of triangular membership functions from a *linguistic hierarchy* structure (introduced in Chapter 4, Section 4.2.2). Together the fuzzy representation, some additional information about the structure, and the semantics are provided to facilitate the computations with them.

© Springer International Publishing Switzerland 2015
L. Martínez et al., *The 2-tuple Linguistic Model*, DOI 10.1007/978-3-319-24714-4_5

Fig. 5.1 Unbalanced linguistic term set of five labels

- Second, a computational model is described for unbalanced linguistic term sets based on the 2-tuple linguistic model and on the previous representation to accomplish the CW processes without loss of information.

5.2 Representing Unbalanced Linguistic Information

Before starting to show the process of building a fuzzy representation for an unbalanced linguistic term set, it is convenient to fix some requirements that must achieve this representation:

- It should be a fuzzy representation which facilitates accurate and linguistic results by using the 2-tuple linguistic model. Therefore, it should fulfil the following points [6]:
  1. The semantics of the linguistic terms must be given by fuzzy numbers defined in the interval [0,1], which are usually described by membership functions. The membership functions considered are triangular ones whose representation is a three tuple (a,b,c), where b indicates the point in which the membership value is one, and a and c are the left and right limits of the membership function associated with the linguistic term [2].
  2. The semantics of all terms of the unbalanced linguistic term set must be a fuzzy partition.
- The fuzzy semantics must belong to the terms of a linguistic hierarchy, LH.

For the sake of simplicity, this section is divided into two parts. The first one presents the general ideas to achieve the representation for the unbalanced linguistic term sets and later on, a formal method and an algorithm that defines such a representation are described.

5.2.1 Basics for Representing Unbalanced Linguistic Information

Starting from a unbalanced linguistic term set similar to Figure 5.1, the general idea to obtain a fuzzy representation that fulfils the previous requirements consists of splitting the unbalanced linguistic term set, $\mathscr{S} = \{s_0, \ldots, s_g\}$, with an odd granularity $g + 1$, whose labels are nonuniformly and nonsymmetrically distributed around the central one, $s_c = s_{g/2}$, into three subsets: $\mathscr{S} = \mathscr{S}_L \bigcup \mathscr{S}_C \bigcup \mathscr{S}_R$:

- *Left lateral set*, $\mathscr{S}_L = \{s_0, \dots, s_{g/2-1}\}$: It contains all the labels less than the central label.
- *Central set*, $\mathscr{S}_C = \{s_c\}$: It just contains the central label.
- *Right lateral set*, $\mathscr{S}_R = \{s_{g/2+1}, \dots, s_g\}$: It contains all the labels greater than the central label.

Example 5.1. These subsets for the unbalanced linguistic term set of Figure 5.1 are:

- $\mathscr{S}_L = \{F\}$,
- $\mathscr{S}_C = \{D\}$,
- $\mathscr{S}_R = \{C, B, A\}$.

The methodology uses a linguistic hierarchy $LH = \bigcup_t S^{n(t)}$ to build the fuzzy representation of the terms in the unbalanced linguistic term set $\mathscr{S}$. How to represent the terms of the three term subsets, $\mathscr{S}_L$, $\mathscr{S}_C$, and $\mathscr{S}_R$ is analysed by using the different levels of the LH. Both $\mathscr{S}_L$ and $\mathscr{S}_R$ may be represented according to their granularity by using one or two levels of the LH (see Sections 5.2.1.1 and 5.2.1.2) and finally the subset $\mathscr{S}_C$ should be represented in a different way (see Section 5.2.1.3).

5.2.1.1 Representation Using One Level of the Linguistic Hierarchy

Initially, the granularity of $\mathscr{S}_L$ and $\mathscr{S}_R$, #($\mathscr{S}_R$), #($\mathscr{S}_L$), respectively, is analyzed according to the following condition.

$$\exists t \in LH \; / \; \frac{n(t) - 1}{2} = \#(\mathscr{S}_R) \; or \; \#(\mathscr{S}_L) \tag{5.1}$$

Equation (5.1) is satisfied, that is, if there exists one level t in the LH, $S_R^{n(t)}(/S_L^{n(t)})$, whose granularity of the subset is equal to the granularity of the $\mathscr{S}$ lateral subset, $\mathscr{S}_R(/\mathscr{S}_L)$. The basic representation procedure to assign the semantics to the labels of the lateral subset $\mathscr{S}_R(/\mathscr{S}_L)$ is:

$$\mathscr{S}_R \leftarrow S_R^{n(t)} \; (/ \; \mathscr{S}_L \leftarrow S_L^{n(t)}).$$

$s_i \leftarrow s_i^{n(t)}, s_i \in \mathscr{S}_R \; and \; s_i^{n(t)} \in S_R^{n(t)}$ analogously for $\mathscr{S}_L$

5.2.1.2 Representation Using Two Levels

However, if Equation (5.1) is not satisfied, the granularity of $\mathscr{S}_R(/\mathscr{S}_L)$ is not enough for their representation. Therefore, $\mathscr{S}$ is described in further detail by a set of five values:

$$\{(\#(\mathscr{S}_L), density_{\mathscr{S}_L}), \#(\mathscr{S}_C), (\#(\mathscr{S}_R), density_{\mathscr{S}_R})\}, \tag{5.2}$$

with $density_{\mathscr{S}_L}$ and $density_{\mathscr{S}_R}$ symbolic variables assessed in the set {*middle*, *extreme*}, that indicates if the higher granularity of the right(/left) lateral set of $\mathscr{S}$ is close to the central label or to the maximum(/minimum) label.

Example 5.2. This description for the grading system term set, $\mathscr{S} = \{F, D, C, B, A\}$ (see Figure 5.1), would be:

$$\{(1, extreme), 1, (3, extreme)\}$$

Assuming the description of $\mathscr{S}$, according to Equation (5.2) the procedure to represent the lateral set $\mathscr{S}_R(/\mathscr{S}_L)$ follows the next steps:

(a) *Selecting hierarchical levels of LH and assignable sets to assign the semantics*
(b) *Assigning semantics to the labels of the lateral set*

Remark 5.1. For the sake of clarity, these steps are focused just on the lateral set $\mathscr{S}_R$, although the procedure for $\mathscr{S}_L$ is symmetrically analogous.

(a) *Selecting Hierarchical Levels and Assignable Sets*

If Equation (5.1) is not satisfied, then two levels t and $t+1$ in LH must exist, such that

$$\frac{n(t) - 1}{2} < \#(\mathscr{S}_R) < \frac{n(t + 1) - 1}{2} \tag{5.3}$$

The terms of $\mathscr{S}_R$ will be then represented by means of semantics of terms belonging to $S_R^{n(t)}$ and $S_R^{n(t+1)}$, called assignable sets and noted as $AS_R^{n(t)}$ and $AS_R^{n(t+1)}$, respectively. These assignable label subsets are composed of:

$$AS_R^{n(t)} = S_R^{n(t)} = \{s_{\frac{n(t)-1}{2}+1}^{n(t)}, \dots, s_{n(t)-1}^{n(t)}\},$$
$$AS_R^{n(t+1)} = S_R^{n(t+1)} = \{s_{\frac{n(t+1)-1}{2}+1}^{n(t+1)}, \dots, s_{n(t+1)-1}^{n(t+1)}\}$$

Example 5.3. Given the LH with 3, 5, and 9 linguistic terms shown in Figure 4.7 to represent the labels of the linguistic term set, $\mathscr{S} = \{F, D, C, B, A\}$ shown in Figure 5.1, the assignable sets for the right lateral set $\mathscr{S}_R = \{C, B, A\}$ are those dashed-rectangles in Figure 5.2.

Once the assignable sets have been selected, it is necessary to decide how to assign the semantics of the linguistic terms in the assignable subsets $AS_R^{n(t)}$ and $AS_R^{n(t+1)}$ to represent the labels of $\mathscr{S}_R$.

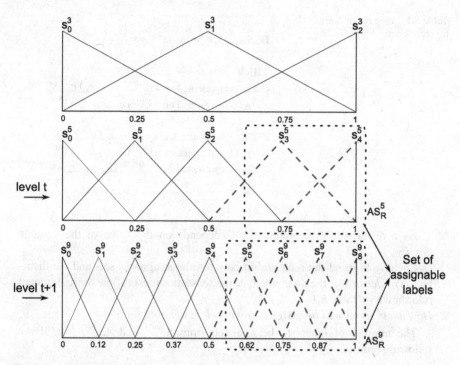

Fig. 5.2 Assignable term subsets

(b) *Assigning Semantics to the Labels of the Lateral Set*

The assignment of the semantics from $AS_R^{n(t)}$ and $AS_R^{n(t+1)}$ to $\mathscr{S}_R$ is based on the answer to the three questions:

1. Which is the distribution of labels in the lateral set?
2. How many terms will be assigned from each assignable set?
3. How should the semantics be assigned?

These answers are shown in further detail below:

1. *Which is the distribution of labels in the lateral set?*

The assignment of the semantics to the labels in $\mathscr{S}_R$ depends on their distribution, taking into account that the semantics for the labels in the area with higher density will be assigned from $AS_R^{n(t+1)}$, and the semantics for the labels with less density will be from $AS_R^{n(t)}$. Hence, it is necessary to distinguish in $\mathscr{S}_R$ two label subsets:

$$\mathscr{S}_R = \mathscr{S}_{RC} \bigcup \mathscr{S}_{RE},$$

with $\mathscr{S}_{RC}$ the subset that contains the labels close to the central label of $s_c \in \mathscr{S}$ and $\mathscr{S}_{RE}$ the subset that contains the labels close to the extreme $s_g \in \mathscr{S}$.

Table 5.1 Assignment rule
for representing $\mathscr{S}_R$

IF $density_{\mathscr{S}_R}=$ "extreme"
THEN
$\quad\mathscr{S}_{RE}$ is represented on $AS_R^{n(t+1)}$, i.e., $\mathscr{S}_{RE} \subset AS_R^{n(t+1)}$
$\quad\mathscr{S}_{RC}$ is represented on $AS_R^{n(t)}$, i.e., $\mathscr{S}_{RC} \subset AS_R^{n(t)}$
ELSE (maximum density in the middle of $\mathscr{S}$)
$\quad\mathscr{S}_{RE}$ is represented on $AS_R^{n(t)}$, i.e., $\mathscr{S}_{RE} \subset AS_R^{n(t)}$
$\quad\mathscr{S}_{RC}$ is represented on $AS_R^{n(t+1)}$, i.e., $\mathscr{S}_{RC} \subset AS_R^{n(t+1)}$

As a result, the distribution of $\mathscr{S}_R$ depends on the value of the variable $density_{\mathscr{S}_R}$.

Keeping in mind the relationship between the assignable sets and the distribution of $density_{\mathscr{S}_R}$, the assignment of the semantics must follow the assignment rule shown in Table 5.1.

2. *How many terms will be assigned from each assignable set?*

The number of labels to be assigned from $AS_R^{n(t)}$ and $AS_R^{n(t+1)}$ fulfil the following lemma.

Lemma 5.1. *The number of labels assigned from each assignable set, $AS_R^{n(t)}$ and $AS_R^{n(t+1)}$, noted as lab_t and lab_{t+1}, to represent the labels of $\mathscr{S}_{RE}$ and $\mathscr{S}_{RC}$ satisfies:*

$$lab_t + lab_{t+1} = \#(S_R). \tag{5.4}$$

Therefore, the following proposition provides a way to compute lab_t and then lab_{t+1} can be inferred from Equation (5.4):

Proposition 5.1. *The number of labels utilised from $AS_R^{n(t)}$, lab_t, to represent labels of $\mathscr{S}_R$ is computed as*

$$lab_t = \frac{n(t+1)-1}{2} - \#(\mathscr{S}_R)$$

Proof. According to the linguistic hierarchy basic rules (see Section 4.2.2.1) each label $s_i^{n(t)} \in S_R^{n(t)}$ has associated two labels $\{s_{2i}^{n(t+1)}, s_{2i+1}^{n(t+1)}\} \in S_R^{n(t+1)}$. Hence,

$$lab_{t+1} = \frac{n(t+1)-1}{2} - (2 \cdot lab_t).$$

Consistent with Lemma 5.1, $lab_{t+1} = \#(\mathscr{S}_R) - lab_t$, it is thus satisfied:

$$\frac{n(t+1)-1}{2} - (2 \cdot lab_t) = \#(\mathscr{S}_R) - lab_t$$

and consequently,

$$lab_t = \frac{n(t+1)-1}{2} - \#(\mathcal{S}_R).$$

In such a case, all the labels of $\mathcal{S}_R$ can be straightforwardly represented, because it is known a priori how many labels and which ones will represent the labels of $\mathcal{S}_{RE}$ and $\mathcal{S}_{RC}$ from the initial assignable sets according to the distribution of $\mathcal{S}$.

□

Example 5.4. Using the framework of previous examples with $\mathcal{S} = \{F, D, C, B, A\}$, *density*$_{\mathcal{S}_R} = \{extreme\}$, and the assignable sets shown in Figure 5.2:

$$\mathcal{S}_R = \{C, B, A\} \quad \mathcal{S}_{RE} = \{B, A\} \quad \mathcal{S}_{RC} = \{C\}$$
$$AS_R^5 = \{s_3^5, s_4^5\}$$
$$AS_R^9 = \{s_5^9, s_6^9, s_7^9, s_8^9\}$$
$$S_{RE} \subset AS_R^9 \quad and \quad S_{RC} \subset AS_R^5$$

The cardinality and labels of $\mathcal{S}_{RE} = \{A, B\}$ and $\mathcal{S}_{RC} = \{C\}$ are computed as

$$lab_2 = \frac{9-1}{2} - 3 = 1,$$

and

$$lab_3 = 3 - 1 = 2.$$

Therefore, the linguistic term sets of the LH used to assign the semantics to $\mathcal{S}_R$ according to the assignment rule (see Table 5.1) are:

- $\{A, B\}$ will be represented with semantics from AS_R^9
- and $\{C\}$ from AS_R^5

3. *How should the semantics be assigned?*

Once the number of labels from each assignable set to be assigned is known and the assignment rule indicates if they will be assigned to $\mathcal{S}_{RE}$ or $\mathcal{S}_{RC}$, the assignment will be as detailed in Table 5.2.

Example 5.5. Following the data of Example 5.4 the semantics for the labels of $\mathcal{S}_{RE} = \{A, B\}$ and $\mathcal{S}_{RC} = \{C\}$ will be assigned according to the assigning process of Table 5.2 (shown graphically in Figure 5.3) as

- $\{A, B\}$, $A \leftarrow s_8^9$ and $B \leftarrow s_7^9$
- And $\{C\}$, $C \leftarrow s_3^5$

Table 5.2 Assigning semantics

IF $density_{\mathscr{S}_R}=$ "extreme"

THEN

$s_i \leftarrow s_j^{n(t+1)}$, $s_i \in \mathscr{S}_{RE}$ and $s_j^{n(t+1)} \in AS_R^{n(t+1)}$. The assignment is from right to left

$s_i \leftarrow s_j^{n(t)}$, $s_i \in \mathscr{S}_{RC}$ and $s_j^{n(t)} \in AS_R^{n(t)}$. The assignment is from right to left

ELSE   (maximum density in the middle of $\mathscr{S}$)

$s_i \leftarrow s_j^{n(t)}$, $s_i \in \mathscr{S}_{RE}$ and $s_j^{n(t)} \in AS_R^{n(t)}$. The assignment is from left to right

$s_i \leftarrow s_j^{n(t+1)}$, $s_i \in \mathscr{S}_{RC}$ and $s_j^{n(t+1)} \in AS_R^{n(t+1)}$. The assignment is from left to right

---

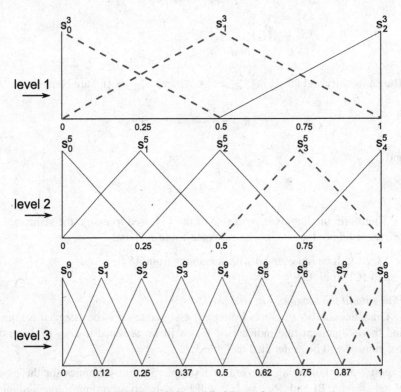

Fig. 5.3 Representation of labels A, B, C, D, and F of Figure 5.1

5.2.1.3 Representing the Central Set

Once the semantics have been assigned to the labels of the lateral subsets $\mathscr{S}_R(/\mathscr{S}_L)$, the semantics must be assigned to the central linguistic term, $\mathscr{S}_C$. In this case the semantics is assigned in two steps, assigning the downside/upside $\check{s}_C/\hat{s}_C$, parts of the

Table 5.3 Representing s_C

IF $density_{\mathscr{S}_R}=$ "extreme"	IF $density_{\mathscr{S}_L}=$ "extreme"
THEN $$\check{s}_C \leftarrow s_C^{\check{n}(t)}$$	**THEN** $$\hat{s}_C \leftarrow s_C^{\hat{n}(t)}$$
ELSE (max density in the middle of $\mathscr{S}_R$) $$\check{s}_C \leftarrow s_C^{\check{n}(t+1)}$$	**ELSE** (max density in the middle of $\mathscr{S}_L$) $$\hat{s}_C \leftarrow s_C^{\hat{n}(t+1)}$$

membership function that represents the central label. Such assignment depends on the value of the variable $density_{\mathscr{S}_R}$ of the lateral set $\mathscr{S}_R(/\mathscr{S}_L)$, according to Table 5.3.

However, if the assignment of semantics comes from just one level in the LH, the semantics of the central set will be:

$$\text{If } s_C^{n(t)} \in S^{n(t)} \text{ then } \mathscr{S}_R \Rightarrow \check{s}_C \leftarrow s_C^{\check{n}(t)} \ (/ \ \mathscr{S}_L \Rightarrow \hat{s}_C \leftarrow s_C^{\hat{n}(t)})$$

5.2.2   Unbalanced Linguistic Representation Model

Once the basics for representing the unbalanced linguistic term set, $\mathscr{S}$, have been introduced, it is necessary to formalise mathematically such ideas to develop a semantic representation algorithm for unbalanced linguistic term sets that provides a semantics for the linguistic terms belonging to an unbalanced linguistic term set. This formalisation consists of:

1. First, different representation functions that control the semantics assignment for each linguistic term according to the description of $\mathscr{S}$ and the levels of the linguistic hierarchy used for assigning the semantics must be defined.
2. According to the requirements pointed out for representing unbalanced linguistic information to achieve a fuzzy partition as a representation of $\mathscr{S}$, several steps that bridge some gaps in the initial representation obtained by the previous functions are necessary. The representation by means of a fuzzy partition guarantees that the 2-tuple linguistic model will carry out CW processes without loss of information.
3. Eventually, a formal semantics representation algorithm that assigns the semantics to the unbalanced linguistic term set is shown.

5.2.2.1 Representation Functions

According to the basics of the representation process for an unbalanced linguistic term set, the semantics assigned to each term depends on the density of the lateral set, $density_{\mathscr{S}_{R/L}} \in \{extreme, middle\}$, and on the level of the LH used to assign the semantics, t or $t + 1$.

Therefore, different representation functions must be defined in accordance with the values of *density* and the level of the LH. Four different representation functions that cover the different possibilities of such values are defined:

Definition 5.1. Let $\mathscr{S}_R$ be the right lateral set of the unbalanced linguistic term set, $\mathscr{S}$, whose semantics will be assigned from $AS_R^{n(t+1)}$. The representation function, $\mathscr{R}_{t+1}^{\mathbf{R}}(\textbf{density})$, which assigns the semantics for $s_i \in \mathscr{S}_R$ is defined as

$$\mathscr{R}_{t+1}^{R}(density) = \begin{cases} density = middle \\ \quad \mu_{s_i}(x) \leftarrow \mu_{s_j^{n(t+1)}}(x), \; s_i \in \mathscr{S}_{RC} = \{s_{c+1}, \ldots, s_{c+lab_{t+1}}\} \; and \\ \qquad\qquad s_j^{n(t+1)} \in AS_R^{n(t+1)} = \{s_{c+1}^{n(t+1)}, \ldots, s_{c+lab_{t+1}}^{n(t+1)}\} \\ density = extreme \\ \quad \mu_{s_i}(x) \leftarrow \mu_{s_j^{n(t+1)}}(x), \; s_i \in \mathscr{S}_{RE} = \{s_{g-(lab_{t+1}-1)}, \ldots, s_g\} \; and \\ \qquad\qquad s_j^{n(t+1)} \in AS_R^{n(t+1)} = \{s_{g-(lab_{t+1}-1)}^{n(t+1)}, \ldots, s_g^{n(t+1)}\} \end{cases}$$
$$(5.5)$$

Definition 5.2. Let $\mathscr{S}_R$ be the right lateral set of the unbalanced linguistic term set, $\mathscr{S}$, whose semantics will be assigned from $AS_R^{n(t)}$. The representation function, $\mathscr{R}_t^{\mathbf{R}}(\textbf{density})$, that assigns the semantics for $s_i \in \mathscr{S}_R$ is defined as

$$\mathscr{R}_t^{R}(density) = \begin{cases} density = middle \\ \quad \mu_{s_i}(x) \leftarrow \mu_{s_j^{n(t)}}(x), \; s_i \in \mathscr{S}_{RE} = \{s_{g-(lab_t-1)}, \ldots, s_g\} \; and \\ \qquad\qquad s_j^{n(t)} \in AS_R^{n(t)} = \{s_{g-(lab_t-1)}^{n(t)}, \ldots, s_g^{n(t)}\} \\ density = extreme \\ \quad \mu_{s_i}(x) \leftarrow \mu_{s_j^{n(t)}}(x), \; s_i \in \mathscr{S}_{RC} = \{s_{c+1}, \ldots, s_{c+lab_t}\} \; and \\ \qquad\qquad s_j^{n(t)} \in AS_R^{n(t)} = \{s_{c+1}^{n(t)}, \ldots, s_{c+lab_t}^{n(t)}\} \end{cases}$$
$$(5.6)$$

Definition 5.3. Let $\mathscr{S}_L$ be the left lateral set of the unbalanced linguistic term set, $\mathscr{S}$, whose semantics will be assigned from $AS_L^{n(t+1)}$. The representation function, $\mathscr{R}_{t+1}^{\mathbf{L}}(\textbf{density})$, that assigns the semantics for $s_i \in \mathscr{S}_L$ is defined as

$$\mathscr{R}_{t+1}^{L}(density) = \begin{cases} density = middle \\ \quad \mu_{s_i}(x) \leftarrow \mu_{s_j^{n(t+1)}}(x), \; s_i \in \mathscr{S}_{LC} = \{s_{c-1}, \ldots, s_{c-lab_{t+1}}\} \; and \\ \qquad\qquad s_j^{n(t+1)} \in AS_R^{n(t+1)} = \{s_{c-1}^{n(t+1)}, \ldots, s_{c-lab_{t+1}}^{n(t+1)}\} \\ density = extreme \\ \quad \mu_{s_i}(x) \leftarrow \mu_{s_j^{n(t+1)}}(x), \; s_i \in \mathscr{S}_{LE} = \{s_0, \ldots, s_{(lab_{t+1}-1)}\} \; and \\ \qquad\qquad s_j^{n(t+1)} \in AS_R^{n(t+1)} = \{s_0^{n(t+1)}, \ldots, s_{(lab_{t+1}-1)}^{n(t+1)}\} \end{cases}$$
$$(5.7)$$

Definition 5.4. Let $\mathscr{S}_L$ be the left lateral set of the unbalanced linguistic term set, $\mathscr{S}$, whose semantics will be assigned from $AS_L^{n(t)}$. The representation function, $\mathscr{R}_t^L(\textbf{density})$, that assigns the semantics for $s_i \in \mathscr{S}_L$ is defined as

$$\mathscr{R}_t^L(density) = \begin{cases} density = middle \\ \quad \mu_{s_i}(x) \leftarrow \mu_{s_j^{n(t)}}(x),\, s_i \in \mathscr{S}_{LE} = \{s_0, \ldots, s_{(lab_t - 1)}\}\ and \\ \qquad\qquad\qquad s_j^{n(t)} \in AS_R^{n(t)} = \{s_0^{n(t)}, \ldots, s_{(lab_t - 1)}^{n(t)}\} \\ density = extreme \\ \quad \mu_{s_i}(x) \leftarrow \mu_{s_j^{n(t)}}(x),\, s_i \in \mathscr{S}_{LC} = \{s_{c-1}, \ldots, s_{c-lab_t}\}\ and \\ \qquad\qquad\qquad s_j^{n(t)} \in AS_R^{n(t)} = \{s_{c-1}^{n(t)}, \ldots, s_{c-lab_t}^{n(t)}\} \end{cases}$$

$$(5.8)$$

5.2.2.2 Bridging Representation Gaps

The 2-tuple linguistic model guarantees that the CW processes are carried out in a precise way if:

1. *S is a fuzzy partition.* According to Ruspini [11], a finite family $\{s_0, \ldots, s_g\}$ of fuzzy subsets in the universe X (in our case $X = [0, 1]$) is called a fuzzy partition if $\sum_{i=0}^g \mu_{s_i}(x) = 1$, $\forall x \in X$.
2. *The membership functions of its linguistic terms are triangular;* that is, $s_i = (a_i, b_i, c_i)$.
3. $\exists x / \mu_{s_i}(x) = 1$, $s_i \in S$. There exists just one point x such that the membership function of the label $s_i \in S$ is 1.

The aim of representing the unbalanced term sets is that the CW processes with them are carried out in a precise way, but following the basic ideas shown to represent an unbalanced linguistic term set, $\mathscr{S}$, and the representation functions $\mathscr{R}_{t+1}^R(density), \mathscr{R}_t^R(density), \mathscr{R}_{t+1}^L(density), \mathscr{R}_t^L(density)$. The semantics obtained for the terms of $\mathscr{S}$ satisfy the second and third condition, but not the first one.

See Example 5.5 which uses the initial proposal for representing the unbalanced information of the right lateral set $\mathscr{S}_R = \{C, B, A\}$ shown in Figure 5.3. The labels from the LH involved in their representation are $\{s_3^5\}$ and $\{s_7^9, s_8^9,\}$ respectively (shown graphically in Figure 5.4).

In such a situation, the semantics associated with $\mathscr{S}_R$ is not a fuzzy partition, because of the representation of the downside of the label $\check{C}$. Label C represents the jump between levels t and $t + 1$, noted as s_{jump}, and whenever this type of jump occurs it then appears as the same problem regarding the fuzzy partition. Therefore, such jumps need a *bridge between the unbalanced terms*. The same situation always happens with the central label s_C, therefore a bridge processing is always necessary to obtain a fuzzy partition.

In order to obtain a fuzzy partition, the representation of the labels, s_{jump}, must follow a bridging process that assigns the semantics to the labels by splitting the

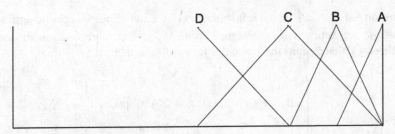

Fig. 5.4 Initial representation for $\mathscr{S}_R$

Table 5.4 Bridging the labels between levels

> **IF** *density*$_{\mathscr{S}_R}$= "extreme"
>
> **THEN**
> $$s_{j\hat{u}mp} \leftarrow s_i^{n(\hat{t})}, \quad s_{j\check{u}mp} \leftarrow s_k^{n(\check{t}+1)}, k = 2 * i$$
> **ELSE**
> $$s_{j\check{u}mp} \leftarrow s_i^{n(\check{t})}, \quad s_{j\hat{u}mp} \leftarrow s_k^{n(\hat{t}+1)}, k = 2 * i$$

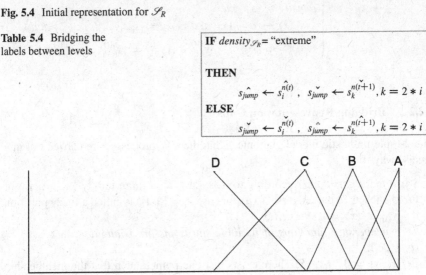

Fig. 5.5 Fuzzy partition representation for $\mathscr{S}_R$

upside and downside parts of the membership function, and it depends on the density of the lateral set (see Table 5.4).

Therefore, to represent $\mathscr{S}_R$ shown in Figure 5.4 by a fuzzy partition, it is necessary to bridge the jump that appears representing C with the following semantics.

$$\hat{C} = s_{j\hat{u}mp} \leftarrow \hat{s}_3^5, \quad \check{C} = s_{j\check{u}mp} \leftarrow \check{s}_6^9$$

Figure 5.5 shows the new representation for $\mathscr{S}_R$.

5.2.2.3 Algorithm: Semantics and Additional Information

Using the previous representation functions and the bridging process, the semantic representation algorithm is developed in Table 5.5 for unbalanced linguistic term sets that represents the unbalanced terms by means of triangular membership functions using the LH.

Table 5.5: Representation algorithm of unbalanced linguistic terms

---

INPUTS:

$\{(\#(\mathscr{S}_L), density_{\mathscr{S}_L}), \#(\mathscr{S}_C), (\#(\mathscr{S}_R), density_{S_R})\},$

$\mathscr{S} = \{s_0, \ldots, s_n\},$

$LH = \bigcup_t l(t, n(t))$

BEGIN

IF $\exists l(t, n(t))/\frac{n(t)-1}{2} = \#(\mathscr{S}_R)$

THEN

To represent $\mathscr{S}_R$ by means of $S_R^{n(t)}$: $\mathscr{S}_R \leftarrow S_R^{n(t)}$

To represent $\check{s}_C \in \mathscr{S}$ as $s_C^{\overset{\vee}{n(t)}}$: $\check{s}_C \leftarrow s_C^{\overset{\vee}{n(t)}}$

$t_{RE} = t_{RC} = t$

ELSE

To look for t and $t + 1$, such that:

$\frac{n(t)-1}{2} < \#(\mathscr{S}_R) < \frac{n(t+1)-1}{2}$

$lab_t = \frac{n(t+1)}{2} - \#(\mathscr{S}_R)$

$lab_{t+1} = \#(\mathscr{S}_R) - lab_t$

$\mathscr{R}_{t+1}^R(density_{\mathscr{S}_R})$

$\mathscr{R}_t^R(density_{\mathscr{S}_R})$

IF $density_{\mathscr{S}_R} =$ "extreme"

THEN

$s_{C+lab_t}^{\overset{\vee}{}} \leftarrow s_{n(t+1)-1-lab_{t+1}}^{n(t+1)}$; $Brid \leftarrow$ "$True$" $(**)$

$\check{s}_C \leftarrow s_C^{n(t)}$; $Brid \leftarrow$ "$True$" $(**)$

$t_{RE} = t \; t_{RC} = t + 1$

ELSE

$s_{C+1+lab_{t+1}}^{\hat{}} \leftarrow s_{C+1+lab_{t+1}}^{n(t+\hat{1})}$; $Brid \leftarrow$ "$True$" $(**)$

$\check{s}_C \leftarrow s_C^{n(t+1)}$; $Brid \leftarrow$ "$True$" $(**)$

$t_{RE} = t + 1 \; t_{RC} = t$

END-IF

END-IF

IF $\exists l(t, n(t))/\frac{n(t)-1}{2} = \#(\mathscr{S}_L)$

THEN

To represent $\mathscr{S}_L$ by means of $S_L^{n(t)}$: $\mathscr{S}_L \leftarrow S_L^{n(t)}$

To represent $\hat{s}_C \in \mathscr{S}$ as $s_C^{\hat{n(t)}}$: $\hat{s}_C \leftarrow s_C^{\hat{n(t)}}$

$t_{LE} = t_{LC} = t$

ELSE

Look for t and $t + 1$, such that:

$\frac{n(t)-1}{2} < \#(\mathscr{S}_L) < \frac{n(t+1)-1}{2}$

Table 5.5 – *Continued from previous page*

$$lab_t = \frac{n(t+1)}{2} - \#(\mathscr{S}_L)$$

$$lab_{t+1} = \#(\mathscr{S}_L) - lab_t$$

$$\mathscr{R}_{t+1}^L(density_{\mathscr{S}_L})$$

$$\mathscr{R}_t^L(density_{\mathscr{S}_L})$$

IF $density_{\mathscr{S}_L} = $ "extreme"

THEN

$$s_{C-\hat{lab}_t} \leftarrow s_{\hat{lab}_{t+1}+1}^{n(t+1)} \; ; \; Brid \leftarrow \text{``}True\text{''} \; (\ast\ast)$$

$$\hat{s_C} \leftarrow s_C^{\hat{n(t)}} \; ; \; Brid \leftarrow \text{``}True\text{''} \; (\ast\ast)$$

$$t_{LE} = t + 1 \; t_{LC} = t$$

ELSE

$$s_{C-\check{lab}_{t+1}-1} \leftarrow s_{C-lab_{t+1}-1}^{n(t+\check{1})} \; ; \; Brid \leftarrow \text{``}True\text{''} \; (\ast\ast)$$

$$\hat{s_C} \leftarrow s_C^{n(\hat{t+1})} \; ; \; Brid \leftarrow \text{``}True\text{''} \; (\ast\ast)$$

$$t_{LE} = t \; t_{LC} = t + 1$$

END-IF

END-IF

END

OUTPUTS:

$$S = \{s_0 = (a_0, b_0, c_0), \dots, s_n = (a_n, b_n, c_n)\}$$

$$LH(\mathscr{S}) = \{s_{I(i)}^{G(i)}, \; i = 0, \dots, g\}$$

$$T_{LH}$$

$$Brid$$

The representation algorithm provides the semantics for the unbalanced linguistic term set but additionally, in order to control and manage the modelling of linguistic information on any unbalanced linguistic term set $\mathscr{S}$, the algorithm also provides the following additional information.

1. *A bridge mark, Brid:* A Boolean function $Brid : \mathscr{S} \rightarrow \{False, True\}$ that indicates if $s_i \in \mathscr{S}$ is considered a s_{jump}, that is, labels whose semantic representation is achieved from two different levels in LH (including the central label s_C).

2. *A hierarchical semantic representation, $LH(\mathscr{S})$:* It provides the representation of $\mathscr{S} = \{s_i, \; i = 0, \dots, g\}$ in LH:

$$LH(\mathscr{S}) = \{s_{I(i)}^{G(i)}, \; i = 0, \dots, g\},$$

such that $\forall s_i \in \mathscr{S}, \exists S^{n(t)} \in LH$ that contains a label $s_k^{n(t)} \in S^{n(t)}$, that generates

$$I(i) = k \text{ and } G(i) = n(t),$$

with $I(\cdot)$ and $G(\cdot)$ functions that assign to each unbalanced label $s_i \in \mathscr{S}$ the index of the label that represents it in LH and the granularity of label set of LH, in which it is represented, respectively. This representation will be generated by the algorithm.

Remark 5.2. The steps of the algorithm highlighted with (**) have been included to accomplish the bridging processes. The *Brid* term assigned to *True* corresponds to the labels assigned in the same line.

Remark 5.3. If $s_i \in \mathscr{S}$ is considered a s_{jump} (i.e., $Brid(s_i) = True$) then the functions $I(\cdot)$ and $G(\cdot)$ provide two different values for s_i: one for the upside part of the membership function, $s_{I(i)}^{\hat{G}(i)}$, and another for the downside part, $s_{I(i)}^{\check{G}(i)}$.

3. *Subset ordering*: The five subsets of the unbalanced linguistic term set $\mathscr{S}$: $\mathscr{S}_{LE}, \mathscr{S}_{LC}, \mathscr{S}_C, \mathscr{S}_{RC}, \mathscr{S}_{RE}$ are ordered in increasing order.
4. *Set of levels of LH, T_{LH}*: It contains those levels used in the representation of $\mathscr{S}$: $T_{LH} = \{t_{LE}, t_{LC}, t_{RC}, t_{RE}\}$, where t_{LE} is the level of LH used to represent $\mathscr{S}_{LE}$, t_{LC} is the level of LH used to represent $\mathscr{S}_{LC}$, and so on. If $\exists S^{n(t)} / \frac{n(t)-1}{2} = \#(\mathscr{S}_R)$, then $t_{RC} = t_{RE} = t$ and $\mathscr{S}_{RC} = \mathscr{S}_{RE} = \mathscr{S}_R$. It happens similarly for $\mathscr{S}_L$.

Example 5.6. Applying the representation algorithm to a unbalanced linguistic term set shown in Figure 5.6, that is, $\mathscr{S} = \{N, L, M, AH, H, QH, VH, AT, T\}$ and the LH shown in Figure 4.7, the description of $\mathscr{S}$ is:

$$\{(2, \text{extreme}), 1, (6, \text{extreme})\},$$

with $\mathscr{S}_L = \{N, L\}$, $\mathscr{S}_C = \{M\}$, and $\mathscr{S}_R = \{AH, H, QH, VH, AT, T\}$. The representation of $\mathscr{S}$ according to the above representation algorithm is then:

1. *Representation of $\mathscr{S}_R$*: As in LH the condition

$$\exists S^{n(t)} / \frac{n(t) - 1}{2} = \#(\mathscr{S}_R)$$

is not satisfied; then it searches for two levels t and $t + 1$ such that

$$\frac{n(t) - 1}{2} < \#(\mathscr{S}_R) < \frac{n(t + 1) - 1}{2}.$$

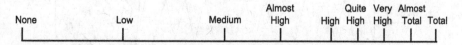

Fig. 5.6 Scale with more values on the right of the mid term

The levels that satisfy the above condition are $t = 3$ and $t + 1 = 4$ because their respective cardinalities in LH are $n(t) = 9$ and $n(t + 1) = 17$. Therefore, according to Proposition 5.1:

$$lab_t = 2 \text{ and } lab_{t+1} = 4.$$

As $density_{\mathcal{S}_R} = extreme$ the representation functions $\mathcal{R}_{t+1}^R$ and $\mathcal{R}_t^R$ represent 4 labels $\mathcal{S}_{RE} = \{T, AT, VH, QH\}$ in the level $t + 1 = 4$ and 2 labels $\mathcal{S}_{RC} = \{H, AH\}$ in the level $t = 3$, respectively. Applying both functions, the following representation of $\mathcal{S}_{RE}$ and $\mathcal{S}_{RC}$ in LH is obtained (see Figure 5.7).

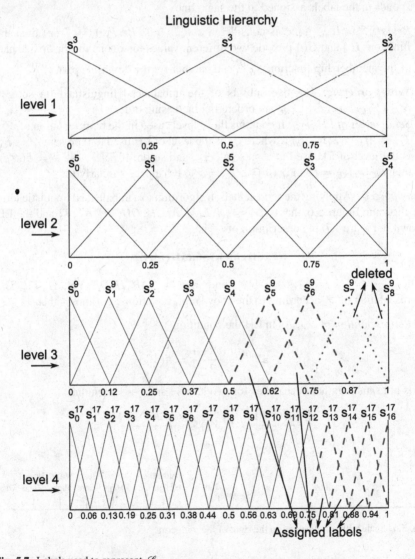

Fig. 5.7 Labels used to represent $\mathcal{S}_R$

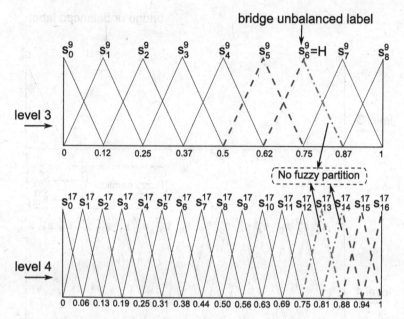

Fig. 5.8 Semantics: no fuzzy partition

$$\mathscr{S}_{RE} = \{T \leftarrow s_{16}^{17}, AT \leftarrow s_{15}^{17}, VH \leftarrow s_{14}^{17}, QH \leftarrow s_{13}^{17}\}$$
$$\mathscr{S}_{RC}\{H \leftarrow s_6^9, AH \leftarrow s_5^9, \}$$

The current representation is not a fuzzy partition, because it did not bridge the s_{jump} yet. The label H represents the s_{jump} between level $t = 3$ and level $t + 1 = 4$ (see Figure 5.8).

It is necessary to bridge the label s_{jump} by representing its semantics splitting the upside and the downside semantic representation; according to Table 5.4 the representation must be (shown graphically in Figure 5.9):

$$\hat{H} \leftarrow s_6^{\hat{9}} \text{ and } \check{H} \leftarrow s_{12}^{\check{17}}$$

2. *Representation of* $\check{\mathscr{S}}_C$: as $density_{\mathscr{S}_R} = extreme$; then following the algorithm, the downside of the central label $\check{M}$ is represented in level $t = 3$ of LH by means of $s_4^{\check{9}}$ as is shown in Figure 5.10.
3. *Representation of* $\mathscr{S}_L$: In this case, the condition:

$$\exists t \in LH \ / \ \frac{n(t) - 1}{2} = \#(\mathscr{S}_L),$$

is satisfied with $t = 2$ because $n(t) = 5$. Hence, the representation of $\mathscr{S}_L$ is obtained from the level $t = 2$ of LH as follows (see Figure 5.11): $\{L \leftarrow s_1^5, N \leftarrow s_0^5\}$.

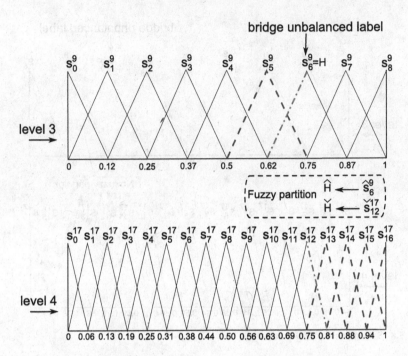

Fig. 5.9 Semantics: fuzzy partition

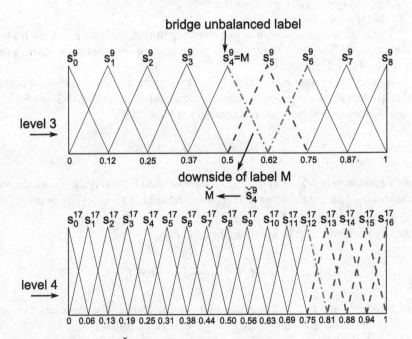

Fig. 5.10 Representation of $\check{M}$

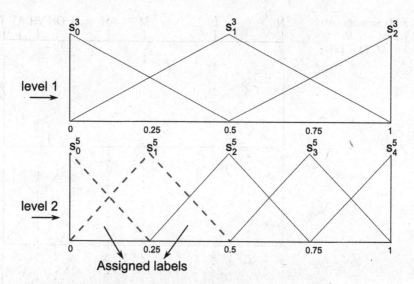

Fig. 5.11 Labels used to represent $\mathscr{S}_L$

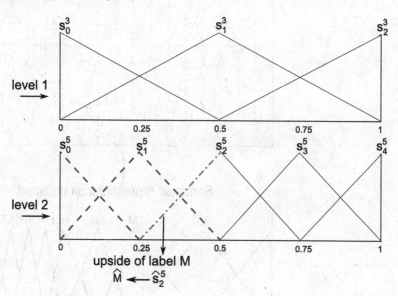

Fig. 5.12 Representation of $\hat{M}$

4. *Representation of $\hat{\mathscr{S}}_C$:* The upside of the central label $\hat{M}$ is represented in the level $t = 2$ of LH by means of $\hat{s}_2^5$ as shown in Figure 5.12.

Consequently, at the end of the representation algorithm the semantics obtained for $\mathscr{S} = \{N, L, M, AH, H, QH, VH, AT, T\}$ is (shown graphically in Figure 5.13):

Fig. 5.13 Semantics of $\mathscr{S}$ = {$N, L, M, AH, H,$ QH, VH, AT, T} in LH

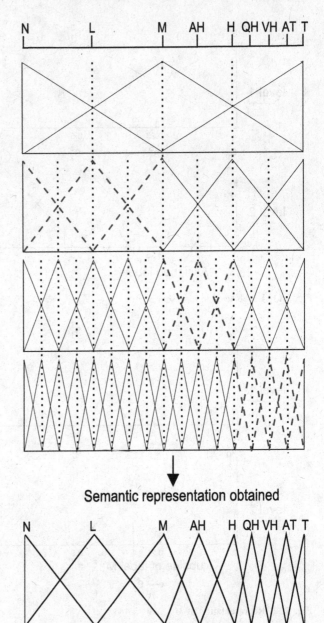

Semantic representation obtained

Table 5.6 $LH(\mathscr{S})$ and $Brid(\mathscr{S})$

$\mathscr{S}$	$LH(\mathscr{S})$	$Brid(\mathscr{S})$
$s_0 = N$	$s_{I(0)}^{G(0)} = s_0^5$	False
$s_1 = L$	$s_{I(1)}^{G(1)} = s_1^5$	False
$s_2 = M$	$s_{I(2)}^{G(2)} = \hat{s}_2^5 \text{ or } \check{s}_4^9$	True
$s_3 = AH$	$s_{I(3)}^{G(3)} = s_5^9$	False
$s_4 = H$	$s_{I(4)}^{G(4)} = \hat{s}_6^9 \text{ or } \check{s}_{12}^{17}$	True
$s_5 = QH$	$s_{I(5)}^{G(5)} = s_{13}^{17}$	False
$s_6 = VH$	$s_{I(6)}^{G(6)} = s_{14}^{17}$	False
$s_7 = AT$	$s_{I(7)}^{G(7)} = s_{15}^{17}$	False
$s_8 = T$	$s_{I(8)}^{G(8)} = s_{16}^{17}$	False

- $\mathscr{S}_L$: $\{N \leftarrow s_0^5, L \leftarrow s_1^5\}$,
- $\mathscr{S}_C$: $\{M \leftarrow \hat{s}_2^5 \bigcup \check{s}_4^9\}$,
- $\mathscr{S}_R$: $\{AH \leftarrow s_5^9, H \leftarrow \hat{s}_6^9 \bigcup \check{s}_{12}^{17}, QH \leftarrow s_{13}^{17}, VH \leftarrow s_{14}^{17}, AT \leftarrow s_{15}^{17}, T \leftarrow s_{16}^{17}\}$.

To control such a representation of $\mathscr{S}$ in the CW processes, the algorithm provides the following information.

1. $LH(\mathscr{S})$ and $Brid(\mathscr{S})$, which are given in Table 5.6.

   Remark 5.4. As can be observed in Table 5.6, some labels of $\mathscr{S}$ present two representation possibilities in LH. In such a case, one of them will be chosen according to the upside or downside part of the semantics indicated by the symbolic translation in the computational model.

2. The following five subsets of unbalanced linguistic labels are shown in increasing order.

   - $\mathscr{S}_{LE} = \mathscr{S}_{LC} = \mathscr{S}_L = \{N, L\}$.
   - $\mathscr{S}_C = \{M\}$.
   - $\mathscr{S}_{RC} = \{AH, H\}$.
   - $\mathscr{S}_{RE} = \{QH, VH, AT, T\}$.

3. The set of levels of LH used in the representation of $\mathscr{S}$, $\{t_{LE}, t_{LC}, t_{RC}, t_{RE}\} = \{2, 2, 3, 4\}$.

5.3 Unbalanced Linguistic Computational Model

Thus far, the first element of the methodology to manage unbalanced linguistic information has been developed, that is, a method to provide semantics to the terms of the unbalanced linguistic term sets, but this methodology must also provide a computational model for computing with unbalanced linguistic information without loss of information.

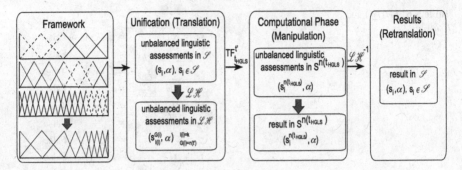

Fig. 5.14 Unbalanced linguistic computational model

It is important to keep in mind that the semantics obtained by the representation algorithm (Table 5.5) is based on a linguistic hierarchy and satisfies the requirements of the 2-tuple linguistic model to carry out accurate CW processes. Therefore, to complete the methodology for unbalanced linguistic information, the unbalanced linguistic computational model takes advantage of the computational model for linguistic hierarchies based on the 2-tuple linguistic one. Thus, it follows the scheme shown in Figure 5.14 that needs the following elements.

1. *Transformation functions*: Two transformation functions are defined, one to transform unbalanced linguistic terms into linguistic terms in the linguistic hierarchy to facilitate accurate linguistic computations, and another one to retranslate the results into linguistic terms in the unbalanced linguistic term set.
2. *Operators for unbalanced linguistic information*: Based on the transformation functions different operators for unbalanced linguistic information such as aggregation, negation, and comparison operators will be defined.

5.3.1 Unbalanced Linguistic Transformation Functions

The aim of the unbalanced linguistic transformation functions is to facilitate the computations with unbalanced linguistic information in a precise way. Given that the semantics of the unbalanced linguistic term set is based on a LH, two transformation functions will be defined to transform the semantics of the terms $s_i \in \mathcal{S}$ into its corresponding terms in the LH, $s_k^{n(t)} \in LH = \bigcup_t S^{n(t)}$, and vice versa. To do so, these functions take advantage of the 2-tuple linguistic model.

Definition 5.5. Let $\mathcal{S}$ be an unbalanced linguistic term set and the semantics of its terms $s_i \in \mathcal{S}$ obtained by the representation algorithm from a linguistic hierarchy, LH; the transformation function, $\mathcal{LH}$, uses the 2-tuple linguistic model, (s_i, α), to transform unbalanced linguistic terms $(s_i, \alpha) \in \overline{\mathcal{S}}$ into their associate ones in their respective 2-tuple linguistic values in LH, $(s_k^{n(t)}, \alpha)$, without loss of information. The transformation function, $\mathcal{LH}$ is defined as

$$\mathcal{LH} : \overline{\mathcal{S}} \to \overline{LH}$$

$$\mathcal{LH}(s_i, \alpha_i) = \begin{cases} (s_k^{n(t)}, \alpha) : \\ \quad if \; Brid(s_i) = False \\ \quad\quad s_k = s_{I(i)}^{G(i)} \; and \; \alpha = \alpha_i \\ \quad if \; Brid(s_i) = True \; and \; \alpha_i \in [-0.5, 0) \\ \quad\quad s_k = s_{I(i)}^{\hat{G}(i)} \; and \; \alpha = \alpha_i \\ \quad if \; Brid(s_i) = True \; and \; \alpha_i \in [0, 0.5) \\ \quad\quad s_k = s_{I(i)}^{\check{G}(i)} \; and \; \alpha = \alpha_i \end{cases} \quad (5.9)$$

Definition 5.6. Let $(s_k^{n(t)}, \alpha)$ be a 2-tuple linguistic value in the linguistic hierarchy, $\overline{LH}$, used to define the semantics of $s_i \in \mathcal{S}$. The transformation function, $\mathcal{LH}^{-1}$, transforms 2-tuple linguistic values, $(s_k^{n(t)}, \alpha) \in \overline{LH}$, into unbalanced terms, $(s_i, \alpha_i) \in \overline{\mathcal{S}}$ without loss of information. The transformation function, $\mathcal{LH}^{-1}$ is defined in two cases according to the condition:

$$\exists \; \hat{s}_i \; OR \; \check{s}_i \in LH(\mathcal{S}) \mid G(i) = n(t) \text{ and } I(i) = k. \quad (5.10)$$

Remark 5.5. In the output of the representation algorithm, in $LH(\mathcal{S})$ if $Brid(s_i) = False$, then both upside and downside parts of the membership function $\hat{s}_i / \check{s}_i$ belong to the same linguistic term in LH; that is, $s_{I(i)}^{\hat{G}(i)} = s_{I(i)}^{\check{G}(i)} = s_k^{n(t)}$.

1. Equation (5.10) is satisfied.

$$\mathcal{LH}^{-1} : \overline{LH} \to \overline{\mathcal{S}}$$

$$\mathcal{LH}^{-1}(s_k^{n(t)}, \alpha) = \begin{cases} (s_i, \alpha_i) : \\ \quad if \; s_k^{\hat{n}(t)} \in LH(\mathcal{S}) \\ \quad\quad s_i = \hat{s}_j \in \mathcal{S} \mid G(i) = n(t) \text{ and } I(i) = k \\ \quad\quad \alpha_i = \alpha \\ \quad if \; s_k^{\check{n}(t)} \in LH(\mathcal{S}) \\ \quad\quad s_i = \check{s}_j \in \mathcal{S} \mid G(i) = n(t) \text{ and } I(i) = k \\ \quad\quad \alpha_i = \alpha \end{cases}$$

$$(5.11)$$

2. Equation (5.10) is not satisfied.

That means that the linguistic term, $(s_k^{n(t)}, \alpha)$, obtained in the computations in the LH does not match with any semantics of the linguistic terms $s_i \in \mathscr{S}$. Therefore, it is necessary to compute the equivalent linguistic term in LH by using a transformation function of the LH such that the new term, $(s_{k'}^{n(t')}, \alpha')$, is equivalent to $(s_k^{n(t)}, \alpha)$, but the new one satisfies Equation (5.10).

Therefore, $t' \in T_{LH} = \{t_{LE}, t_{LC}, t_{RC}, t_{RE}\}$ and $(s_{k'}^{n(t')}, \alpha') = TF_{t'}^t (s_k^{n(t)}, \alpha)$. At least one of these t' must provide a term, $(s_{k'}^{n(t')}, \alpha')$, that satisfies Equations (5.10) and (5.11) can be applied.

5.3.2　Computational Model

Similarly to the 2-tuple fuzzy linguistic computational model (Chapter 2), an unbalanced linguistic computational model is developed that defines a comparison operator, a negation operator, and a tool for aggregating unbalanced linguistic information. All these operators make use of the transformation functions, $\mathscr{LH}$ and $\mathscr{LH}^{-1}$.

Definition 5.7. Let $s_i, s_j \in \overline{\mathscr{S}}$ be two unbalanced linguistic values represented by 2-tuple linguistic values. The comparison of linguistic information represented by unbalanced 2-tuple linguistic values is carried out according to an ordinary lexicographic order defined in Section 2.3.

Definition 5.8. Let $s_i \in \overline{\mathscr{S}}$ be an unbalanced linguistic value represented by a 2-tuple linguistic value. The unbalanced negation operator is defined as

$$\mathscr{NEG}(s_i, \alpha) = \mathscr{LH}^{-1}(Neg(\mathscr{LH}(s_i, \alpha))), \tag{5.12}$$

$s_i \in \overline{\mathscr{S}}$ and with Neg the 2-tuple negation operator (see Definition 2.2).

Definition 5.9. Let $A = \{(s_1, \alpha_1), \ldots, (s_p, \alpha_p)\} \in \overline{\mathscr{S}}$ be a set of unbalanced linguistic assessments to be aggregated; then a generic aggregation operator of unbalanced linguistic information,

$$\Lambda^F : \overline{\mathscr{S}}^p \to \overline{\mathscr{S}}$$

is defined according to the following expression.

$$\Lambda^F((s_1, \alpha_1), \ldots, (s_p, \alpha_p)) = F((s_1, \alpha_1), \ldots, (s_p, \alpha_p)) \tag{5.13}$$

$$F(TF_{t_{HGLS}}^{t'}(\mathscr{LH}(s_1, \alpha_1)), \ldots, TF_{t_{HGLS}}^{t'}(\mathscr{LH}(s_p, \alpha_p))) = (s_k^{n(t_{HGLS})}, \alpha)$$

with $t_{HGLS} = \max\{t_{LE}, t_{LC}, t_{RC}, t_{RE}\}$ the level of LH in which all linguistic values are conducted before their aggregation, $t' \in \{t_{LE}, t_{LC}, t_{RC}, t_{RE}\}$, and F any aggregation operator of 2-tuple linguistic values. $(s_k^{n(t_{HGLS})}, \alpha)$ is the 2-tuple linguistic value obtained by aggregating the unified unbalanced linguistic values.

$$\mathscr{L}\mathscr{H}^{-1}(s_k^{n(t_{HGLS})}, \alpha)) = (s_i, \alpha) \in \overline{\mathscr{S}}$$

In the following section an illustrative example of the application of the methodology for managing unbalanced linguistic information is shown, both the representation and the computational model.

5.4 Illustrative Example: Best Paper Award

Let us suppose that in an international conference the conference committee comprises three researchers $\{r_1, r_2, \text{ and } r_3\}$, and has to select the best paper to grant the best paper award. There are three selected papers, {Anne's paper, John's paper, and Michael's paper} and the researchers have to provide their assessments over the papers taking into account four criteria {clarity, innovation, motivation, and originality}. In this problem, it is necessary that the assessments scale has greater granularity on the right side on the left.

A. Framework

First of all, the framework is defined. In this problem, the assessments are expressed using the unbalanced linguistic term set shown in Figure 5.15, $\mathscr{S} = \{None(N), Bad(B), Medium(M), Almost\ Good(AG), Good(G), Quite\ Good(QG), Very\ Good(VG), Almost\ Perfect(AO), Perfect(P)\}$.

The assessments obtained by the researchers are shown in Tables 5.7, 5.8, and 5.9.

. In order to obtain a global assessment for each selected paper, the methodology to deal with unbalanced linguistic information developed in this chapter must be applied.

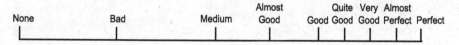

Fig. 5.15 Unbalanced linguistic term set to assess the selected papers

Table 5.7 Assessments from researcher r_1

r_1	Clarity	Innovation	Motivation	Originality
Anne's paper	AG	VG	M	AP
John's paper	VG	QG	QG	VG
Michael's paper	B	QG	M	G

Table 5.8 Assessments from researcher r_2

r_2	Clarity	Innovation	Motivation	Originality
Anne's paper	B	QG	M	P
John's paper	G	QG	M	M
Michael's paper	B	G	G	M

Table 5.9 Assessments from researcher r_3

r_3	Clarity	Innovation	Motivation	Originality
Anne's paper	M	G	AG	QG
John's paper	VG	VG	QG	M
Michael's paper	M	QG	M	AG

B. Representation in the LH

The representation algorithm represents the unbalanced linguistic terms of $\mathscr{S}$ as shown in Figure 5.16.

Consequently, the semantic representation is:

- $\mathscr{S}_L$: $\{N \leftarrow s_0^5, B \leftarrow s_1^5\}$,
- $\mathscr{S}_C$: $\{M \leftarrow s_2^5 \cup \check{s}_4^9\}$, and
- $\mathscr{S}_R$: $\{AG \leftarrow s_5^9, G \leftarrow \hat{s}_6^9 \cup s_{12}^{17}, QG \leftarrow s_{13}^{17}, VG \leftarrow s_{14}^{17}, AP \leftarrow s_{15}^{17}, P \leftarrow s_{16}^{17}\}$.

And the additional information to control the representation of $\mathscr{S}$ in the CW processes provided by the algorithm is:

1. $LH(\mathscr{S})$ and $Brid(\mathscr{S})$, which are given in Table 5.10.
2. The following five subsets of unbalanced linguistic terms are ordered in increasing order.

   - $\mathscr{S}_{LE} = \mathscr{S}_{LC} = \mathscr{S}_L = \{N, B\}$,
   - $\mathscr{S}_C = \{M\}$,
   - $\mathscr{S}_{RC} = \{AG, G\}$,
   - $\mathscr{S}_{RE} = \{QG, VG, AP, P\}$.

3. The set of levels of LH used in the representation of $\mathscr{S}$, is:
   $\{t_{LE}, t_{LC}, t_{RC}, t_{RE}\} = \{2, 2, 3, 4\}$.

Fig. 5.16 Semantics of $\mathscr{S}$ = $\{N, B, M, AG, G, QG, VG, AP, P\}$ in LH

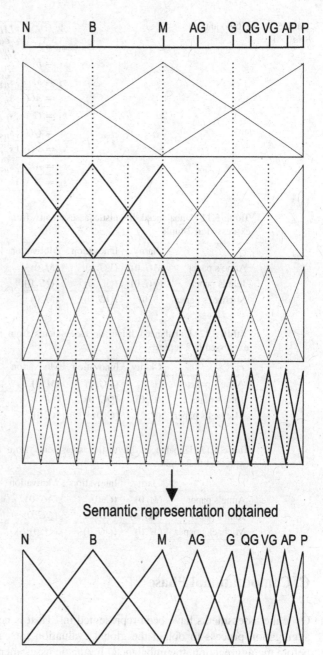

Semantic representation obtained

Table 5.10 $LH(\mathscr{S})$ and $Brid(\mathscr{S})$

$\mathscr{S}$	$LH(\mathscr{S})$	$Brid(\mathscr{S})$
$s_0 = N$	$s^{G(0)}_{I(0)} = s^5_0$	False
$s_1 = B$	$s^{G(1)}_{I(1)} = s^5_1$	False
$s_2 = M$	$s^{G(2)}_{I(2)} = s^5_2$ or s^9_4	True
$s_3 = AG$	$s^{G(3)}_{I(3)} = s^9_5$	False
$s_4 = G$	$s^{G(4)}_{I(4)} = s^9_6$ or s^{17}_{12}	True
$s_5 = QG$	$s^{G(5)}_{I(5)} = s^{17}_{13}$	False
$s_6 = VG$	$s^{G(6)}_{I(6)} = s^{17}_{14}$	False
$s_7 = AP$	$s^{G(7)}_{I(7)} = s^{17}_{15}$	False
$s_8 = P$	$s^{G(8)}_{I(8)} = s^{17}_{16}$	False

Table 5.11 Unbalanced linguistic assessments from researcher r_1 expressed in 2-tuple

r_1	Clarity	Innovation	Motivation	Originality
Anne's paper	$(AG, 0)$	$(VG, 0)$	$(M, 0)$	$(AP, 0)$
John's paper	$(VG, 0)$	$(QG, 0)$	$(QG, 0)$	$(VG, 0)$
Michael's paper	$(B, 0)$	$(QG, 0)$	$(M, 0)$	$(G, 0)$

Table 5.12 Unbalanced linguistic assessments from researcher r_2 expressed in 2-tuple

r_2	Clarity	Innovation	Motivation	Originality
Anne's paper	$(B, 0)$	$(QG, 0)$	$(M, 0)$	$(P, 0)$
John's paper	$(G, 0)$	$(QG, 0)$	$(M, 0)$	$(M, 0)$
Michael's paper	$(B, 0)$	$(G, 0)$	$(G, 0)$	$(M, 0)$

Table 5.13 Unbalanced linguistic assessments from researcher r_3 expressed in 2-tuple

r_3	Clarity	Innovation	Motivation	Originality
Anne's paper	$(M, 0)$	$(G, 0)$	$(AG, 0)$	$(QG, 0)$
John's paper	$(VG, 0)$	$(VG, 0)$	$(QG, 0)$	$(M, 0)$
Michael's paper	$(M, 0)$	$(QG, 0)$	$(M, 0)$	$(AG, 0)$

C. Computational Phase

Once the assessments have been represented in LH, it is necessary to carry out an aggregation process to obtain the global evaluation for each selected paper. But before the aggregation, the unbalanced linguistic assessments are transformed into 2-tuple linguistic values (see Tables 5.11, 5.12, and 5.13).

The aggregation process is divided into two steps:

1. Firstly, researchers' assessments are aggregated by means of an aggregation operator of unbalanced linguistic information Λ^F, in this case $F = L2TOWA$, that

Table 5.14 Global	Anne's paper	$(AG, 0.31)$
assessments in $\mathscr{S}$	John's paper	$(G, -0.35)$
	Michael's paper	$(M, 0.35)$

is, L2TOWA operator (see Definition 2.5) whose weighting vector W is obtained by using the linguistic quantifier *most* (see Equations (2.6) and (2.7) to obtain the OWA weights). The weighting vector obtained is $W = \{0.07, 0.66, 0.27\}$.

2. Afterwards, the criteria are aggregated by $F = \bar{x}^e$, that is, the arithmetic mean for 2-tuple given in Definition 2.3.

D. Retranslation Phase

Table 5.14 shows the global assessment represented in the unbalanced linguistic term set $\mathscr{S}$, for each selected paper.

E. Exploitation Phase

Finally, in the exploitation phase, the global assessments are ordered to get the *best paper award*,

$$John's\ paper > Anne's\ paper > Michael's\ paper$$

which in this case is {**John's paper$=$(G,-0.35)**}.

References

1. M.A. Abchir and I. Truck. Towards an extension of the 2-tuple linguistic model to deal with unbalanced linguistic term sets. *Kybernetika*, 49(1):164–180, 2013.
2. P.P. Bonissone and K.S. Decker. *Selecting Uncertainty Calculi and Granularity: An Experiment in Trading-Off Precision and Complexity*. In L.H. Kanal and J.F. Lemmer, Editors., Uncertainty in Artificial Intelligence. North-Holland, 1986.
3. C.H. Cheng and Y. Lin. Evaluating the best main battle tank using fuzzy decision theory with linguistic criteria evaluation. *European Journal of Operational Research*, 142(1):174–186, 2002.
4. N. Fenton and W. Wang. Risk and confidence analysis for fuzzy multicriteria decision making. *Knowledge-Based Systems*, 19(6):430–437, 2006.
5. F. Herrera, E. Herrera-Viedma, and L. Martínez. A fuzzy linguistic methodology to deal with unbalanced linguistic term sets. *IEEE Transactions on Fuzzy Systems*, 16(2):354–370, 2008.

6. F. Herrera and L. Martínez. An approach for combining linguistic and numerical information based on 2-tuple fuzzy representation model in decision-making. *International Journal of Uncertainty, Fuzziness and Knowledge-Based Systems*, 8(5):539–562, 2000.

7. E. Herrera-Viedma and A.G. López-Herrera. A model of an information retrieval system with unbalanced fuzzy linguistic information. *International Journal of Intelligent Systems*, 22(11):1197–1214, 2007.

8. L. Martínez. Sensory evaluation based on linguistic decision analysis. *International Journal of Approximate Reasoning*, 44(2):148–164, 2007.

9. L. Martínez, M. Espinilla, J. Liu, L.G. Pérez, and P.J. Sánchez. An evaluation model with unbalanced linguistic information: Applied to olive oil sensory evaluation. *Journal of Multiple-Valued Logic and Soft Computing*, 15(2–3):229–251, 2009.

10. M. Roham, A.R. Gabrielyan, and N.P. Archer. Fuzzy linguistic modeling of ease of doing business indicators. *International Journal of Uncertainty, Fuzziness and Knowledge-Based Systems*, 17(4):531–557, 2009.

11. E.H. Ruspini. A new approach to clustering. *Inform. Control*, 15:22–32, 1969.

12. V. Torra. Aggregation of linguistic labels when semantics is based on antonyms. *International Journal of Intelligent Systems*, 16:513–524, 2001.

Chapter 6
Dealing with Hesitant Fuzzy Linguistic Information in Decision Making

6.1 Introduction

Thus far, the decision problems reviewed have been defined under uncertain conditions that are common in real-world decision-making problems, but quite challenging because of the difficulty of modelling and coping with them. This book is centered on 2-tuple linguistic modelling for dealing with such uncertainty; however, as pointed out in Chapter 4, different fuzzy based tools and models have been used to handle imperfect, vague, and imprecise information [20]. Notwithstanding, the management of vague and imprecise information in which two or more sources of vagueness appear simultaneously is limited in the fuzzy based modelling of ordinary fuzzy sets. Because of this, different decision generalisations and extensions of fuzzy sets have been introduced in the literature, such as

- *Type 2 fuzzy sets* [18], and *type n fuzzy sets* [9] that introduce uncertainty about the membership function in their definition.
- *Nonstationary fuzzy sets* [12] that incorporate into the membership functions a connection that expresses a slight variation in the membership function.
- *Intuitionistic fuzzy sets (IFSs)* [2] that extend the fuzzy sets by an additional degree, called degree of uncertainty.
- *Fuzzy multisets* [30] based on multisets that allow repeated elements in the set.
- *Hesitant fuzzy sets* recently introduced by Torra [25] as an extension of fuzzy sets. They try to manage those situations where a set of values is possible in the definition process of the membership of an element.

In [7] can be found a historical review on the generalisations and extensions of fuzzy sets, analysing the relationships among them.

Previous extensions suit problems defined in quantitative situations, but it has already been pointed out that uncertainty is often due to the vagueness of meanings used by experts in problems whose nature is rather qualitative. In such situations, the fuzzy linguistic approach [32] dealing with type 1 and type 2 fuzzy sets have

© Springer International Publishing Switzerland 2015
L. Martínez et al., *The 2-tuple Linguistic Model*, DOI 10.1007/978-3-319-24714-4_6

provided very good results in many fields and applications [3, 13, 16, 28]. However, in a similar way to fuzzy sets, the use of the fuzzy linguistic approach presents some limitations, mainly regarding information modelling due to the lack of flexibility and rigid syntax.

Reviewing the fuzzy linguistic approach and the different linguistic extensions and generalisations, it is observed that despite the improvements introduced the modelling of linguistic information is still *limited*, mainly because it is based on the elicitation of either single or very simple terms that should encompass and express the information elicited by the experts regarding a linguistic variable. In many problems experts cannot easily provide a single term as an expression of their knowledge or preference, because they are thinking of a bunch of terms at the same time or looking for a more complex linguistic construction. Initial approaches can be found in [15, 24, 26]. Another possibility is the use of linguistic expressions as the comparative linguistic expressions that are not usually defined in the linguistic term set, but quite common in real-world decision making.

This chapter aims at overcoming such limitations, taking into account the idea under the concept of hesitant fuzzy sets introduced by Torra [25] to deal with several values in a membership function in quantitative settings but in qualitative ones. It presents the concept of *hesitant fuzzy linguistic term set* (HFLTS) based on the fuzzy linguistic approach that serves as the basis of increasing the flexibility of eliciting linguistic information by means of comparative linguistic expressions. Additionally, different computational functions for HFLTS are introduced, and it is then shown how the use of HFLTS can improve the elicitation of linguistic information by using the fuzzy linguistic approach and context-free grammars. This is a crucial point, because if necessary it allows experts the use of different comparative linguistic expressions to represent experts' knowledge/preferences in decision making. Once all the necessary machinery to model comparative linguistic expressions and compute with them have been detailed, a 2-tuple based multicriteria decision-making model in which experts can elicit either single or comparative linguistic expressions is then shown. Finally, an illustrative example of a multicriteria decision-making problem is described.

6.2   Hesitant Fuzzy Sets: Concepts and Basic Operations

HFS have recently been introduced as an extension of fuzzy sets that aims to model the uncertainty provoked by the expert's hesitation that might arise in the assignment of the membership degrees of an element to a fuzzy set.

Formally, a HFS is defined in terms of a function that returns a set of membership values for each element in the domain.

Definition 6.1 ([25]). Let X be a reference set; a HFS on X is a function $\mathfrak{h}$ that returns a non-empty subset of values in [0,1]:

$$\mathfrak{h} : X \to \wp([0, 1]) \tag{6.1}$$

A HFS can also be defined from a set of fuzzy sets.

Definition 6.2 ([25]). Let $M = \{\mu_1, \ldots, \mu_n\}$ be a set of n membership functions. The HFS associated with M, $\mathfrak{h}_M$, is defined as follows.

$$\mathfrak{h}_M : X \to \wp([0, 1])$$
$$\mathfrak{h}_M(x) = \bigcup_{\mu \in M} \{\mu(x)\} \tag{6.2}$$

where $x \in X$.

The previous definition is quite suitable for decision making when experts have to provide their assessments over a set of alternatives or criteria. In such a case, M represents the assessments of the experts for each alternative or criterion, and $\mathfrak{h}_M$ the assessments elicited by the set of experts.

Afterwards, Xia and Xu [29] modified the original definition of a HFS by including its mathematical representation as

$$E = \{\langle x, h_E(x)\rangle : x \in X\},$$

where $h_E(x)$ is a set of some values in [0,1], representing the possible membership degrees of the element $x \in X$ to the set E. For convenience, Xia and Xu noted $h = h_E(x)$ the so-called hesitant fuzzy element (HFE) of E, and $H = \cup h_E(x)$, the set of all HFEs of E.

Therefore, a HFS is a set of subsets in the interval [0,1], one set for each element of the reference set X, and a HFE is one of such sets, the one for a particular $x \in X$.

Given a function ϕ on n HFEs, the following definition shows how to build a function ϕ' on HFS from ϕ.

Definition 6.3 ([23]). Let $\{H_1, \ldots, H_n\}$ be a set of n HFSs on X, and ϕ an n-ary function on HFEs,

$$\phi'(H_1, \ldots, H_n)(x) = \phi(H_1(x), \ldots, H_n(x)). \tag{6.3}$$

Recently [4] proposed a specific case of HFS, the typical hesitant fuzzy set, that is, when $H(x)$ is a finite nonempty subset of the interval [0,1] for all $x \in X$.

Several basic operations and properties of HFEs were introduced in [25], although originally they were not called HFEs.

Definition 6.4 ([25]). Given a HFE, h, its lower and upper bounds are as follows.

$$h^- = inf\{\gamma|\gamma \in h\} \tag{6.4}$$

$$h^+ = sup\{\gamma|\gamma \in h\} \tag{6.5}$$

Definition 6.5 ([25]). Let h be a HFE; its complement is defined as

$$h^c = \bigcup_{\gamma \in h}\{1 - \gamma\} \tag{6.6}$$

Definition 6.6 ([25]). Let h_1 and h_2 be two HFEs; their union is defined as

$$h_1 \cup h_2 = \cup_{\gamma_1 \in h_1, \gamma_2 \in h_2} max\{\gamma_1, \gamma_2\} \tag{6.7}$$

Definition 6.7 ([25]). Let h_1 and h_2 be two HFEs; their intersection is defined as

$$h_1 \cap h_2 = \cup_{\gamma_1 \in h_1, \gamma_2 \in h_2} min\{\gamma_1, \gamma_2\} \tag{6.8}$$

Torra also discussed the relation between Atanassov's IFS and HFS and proved that the envelope of a HFS built from the envelope of a HFE is an Atanassov's IFS.

Definition 6.8 ([25]). Let h be a HFE; the envelope of h, $A_{env}(h)$, is defined as

$$A_{env}(h) = \{x, \mu_A(x), \nu_A(x)\} \tag{6.9}$$

with $A_{env}(h)$ being the Atanassov's IFS [2] of h, and μ and ν defined as

$$\mu_A(x) = h^- \qquad \nu_A(x) = 1 - h^+$$

The relationship between HFEs and fuzzy multisets was also studied in [25].

6.3 Hesitant Fuzzy Linguistic Term Sets

Similarly to the hesitant situations managed by HFSs in [25] where experts can consider several values to define a membership function, in qualitative contexts it might happen that experts hesitate among several linguistic terms to assess a linguistic variable because they do not have enough knowledge or information to provide their assessment using only one linguistic term.

Let's suppose the following example to understand easily the necessity of modelling multiple linguistic terms in hesitant decision situations.

Example 6.1. Let us suppose an evaluation committee composed of three experts in art who have to provide their preferences and select the best painting in an exhibition. There are 20 paintings in the exhibition and three of them have been selected for the evaluation. Therefore, experts have to assess these three paintings by using the linguistic term set $S = \{nothing, very\ bad, bad, medium, good, very\ good, perfect\}$ taking into account the criteria $\{colour, movement, harmony\}$. Each expert has an art specialty, such as colour, dynamism, and so on. Thus, each expert finds it easier to evaluate the associated criteria according to his or her expertise than other criteria in which he or she could hesitate among several linguistic terms. For instance, an expert specialist in colour usually would not have any hesitation to provide his assessment regarding the colour criterion, and he uses only one linguistic term. However, when he has to elicit his preference over the movement criterion, he might hesitate among $\{medium, good, very\ good\}$.

In such hesitant decision situations, experts hesitate among different linguistic terms and they would like to use more complex linguistic expressions which cannot be built by the classical linguistic approaches. This limitation is due to the use of linguistic terms defined a priori and because most of the linguistic approaches model the information by using only one linguistic term. In order to overcome this limitation, different proposals have been presented in the literature [15, 24, 26] to provide more flexible linguistic expressions that can include more than one linguistic term. In spite of these proposals improving the flexibility to provide linguistic expressions, they are either not close to the human cognitive model or are not formally defined.

Keeping in mind the idea of HFS [25], the concept of HFLTS based on the fuzzy linguistic approach was introduced in [21].

6.3.1 HFLTSs: Concept and Basic Operations

Definition 6.9 ([21]). Let S be a linguistic term set, $S = \{s_0, \ldots, s_g\}$, an HFLTS, and H_S is an ordered finite subset of consecutive linguistic terms of S:

$$H_S = \{s_i, s_{i+1}, \ldots, s_j\} \quad such\ that\ s_k \in S, \ k \in \{i, \ldots, j\} \tag{6.10}$$

The use of consecutive linguistic terms in HFLTS is because of a cognitive point of view in which in a discrete domain with a short number of terms (usually not more than 9) makes no sense to hesitate among arbitrary and total different linguistic terms, $\{low, high, very\ high\}$, and not hesitate in their middle terms.

Example 6.2. Let S be a linguistic term set, $S = \{nothing, very\ low, low, medium, high, very\ high, perfect\}$, and ϑ a linguistic variable; an HFLTS could be:

$$H_S(\vartheta) = \{very\ low, low, medium\}$$

By using this example, it is easy to show that it does not make sense to hesitate between {very low, medium}, because according to the linguistic term set S, the expert is also considering {low} that is in the middle of *very low* and *medium*.

Some basic operators to compute with HFLTS and several properties were presented in [21].

Let S be a linguistic term set; $S = \{s_0, \ldots, s_g\}$; and H_S, H_S^1, and H_S^2 three HFLTS:

Definition 6.10 ([21]). The upper bound, H_{S+}, and lower bound, H_{S-}, of the HFLTS, H_S, are defined as

$$H_{S+} = max(s_i) = s_j, \ s_i \in H_S \ and \ s_i \le s_j \ \forall i \tag{6.11}$$

$$H_{S-} = min(s_i) = s_j, \ s_i \in H_S \ and \ s_i \ge s_j \ \forall i \tag{6.12}$$

Definition 6.11 ([21]). The complement of HFLTS, H_S, is defined as

$$H_S^c = S - H_S = \{s_i/s_i \in S \ and \ s_i \notin H_S\} \tag{6.13}$$

Definition 6.12 ([21]). The union between two HFLTS, H_S^1 and H_S^2 is defined as

$$H_S^1 \cup H_S^2 = \{s_i/s_i \in H_S^1 \ or \ s_i \in H_S^2\} \tag{6.14}$$

Definition 6.13 ([21]). The intersection of two HFLTS, H_S^1 and H_S^2 is:

$$H_S^1 \cap H_S^2 = \{s_i/s_i \in H_S^1 \ and \ s_i \in H_S^2\} \tag{6.15}$$

The result of this operation is another HFLTS.

In order to facilitate the computation with HFLTS, the concept of an envelope of a HFLTS was introduced.

Definition 6.14 ([21]). The envelope of the HFLTS, $env(H_S)$, is a linguistic interval whose limits are obtained by means of the upper bound (*max*) and lower bound (*min*), respectively.

$$env(H_S) = [H_{S-}, H_{S+}], \ H_{S-} <= H_{S+} \tag{6.16}$$

6.3.2   *Elicitation of Linguistic Information Based on HFLTS: Linguistic Expressions*

Throughout this chapter, it has been pointed out that the main purpose of the HFLTS is to improve the elicitation of linguistic information when experts hesitate among different linguistic terms to assess a linguistic variable. Nevertheless, experts usually do not use multiple linguistic terms to express their preferences, but more complex expressions similar to the ones used by human beings.

Following Example 6.1, let's suppose that the committee member $\{e_1\}$ specialist in colours, has to express her preference over the criteria {Colour, Movement, Harmony} for the painting $\{x_1\}$. Due to her knowledge, it might occur that to assess the *movement* criterion the specialist hesitates among the linguistic terms {good, very good, perfect}. In such a case, it is common to provide linguistic expressions such as, "greater than medium" or "at least good".

Bearing in mind this basic idea and considering the main goal of improving the flexibility of the elicitation of the linguistic information, the use of context-free grammars to generate linguistic expressions close to the human reasoning model was proposed.

The context-free grammar was introduced by Chomsky [8] and it is defined as follows.

Definition 6.15 ([8]). A context-free grammar G is a 4-tuple (V_N, V_T, I, P), where V_N is the set of nonterminal symbols, V_T is the set of terminal symbols, I is the starting symbol, and P the production rules defined in an extended Backus-Naur Form [6]. Thus, choosing I as any nonterminal symbol and using P linguistic expressions could be generated such as

$$\{lower\ than\ medium, greater\ than\ good, \ldots\}.$$

The language generated by G must be wide enough to describe any situation of the problem.

Therefore, the use of context-free grammars supports the generation of simple but rich linguistic expressions close to human beings' cognitive processes, that can be easily modelled by HFLTS. Hence, a general context-free grammar G_H [21, 22], was defined to build common *comparative* linguistic expressions in decision-making problems when experts hesitate among several single terms.

Definition 6.16 ([22]). Let G_H be a context-free grammar and $S = \{s_0, \ldots, s_g\}$ a linguistic term set. The elements of $G_H = (V_N, V_T, I, P)$ are defined as follows.

$V_N = \{\langle primary\ term\rangle, \langle composite\ term\rangle, \langle unary\ relation\rangle, \langle binary\ relation\rangle,$
$\langle conjunction\rangle\}$
$V_T = \{lower\ than, greater\ than, at\ least, at\ most, between, and, s_0, s_1, \ldots, s_g\}$
$I \in V_N$

The production rules are defined in an extended Backus-Naur Form so that the brackets enclose optional elements and the symbol | indicates alternative elements [6]. For the context-free grammar, G_H, the production rules are:

$P = \{I ::= \langle primary\ term\rangle | \langle composite\ term\rangle$
$\langle composite\ term\rangle ::= \langle unary\ relation\rangle\langle primary\ term\rangle | \langle binary\ relation\rangle$
$\langle primary\ term\rangle\langle conjunction\rangle\langle primary\ term\rangle$
$\langle primary\ term\rangle ::= s_0 | s_1 | \ldots | s_g$
$\langle unary\ relation\rangle ::= lower\ than | greater\ than | at\ least | at\ most$
$\langle binary\ relation\rangle ::= between$
$\langle conjunction\rangle ::= and\}$

Remark 6.1. The *unary relation* has some limitations. If the nonterminal symbol is *lower than* or *at most*, the *primary term* cannot be s_0 and if the nonterminal symbol is *greater than* or *at least* the *primary term* cannot be s_g.

Remark 6.2. In the *binary relation* the *primary term* of the left side must be less than the *primary term* of the right side.

Example 6.3. Let $S = \{nothing, very\ low, low, medium, high, very\ high, perfect\}$ be a linguistic term set; some comparative linguistic expressions obtained by means of the context-free grammar, G_H, might be:

$ll_1 = very\ low$
$ll_2 = lower\ than\ medium$
$ll_3 = at\ least\ high$
$ll_4 = between\ medium\ and\ very\ high$

Due to the flexibility that provides the definition of a context-free grammar, the definition of its elements and production rules will depend on the specific problem to solve.

The use of HFLTS allows representing the expert's hesitation among multiple linguistic terms, and thus facilitates the computing processes with such expressions. Therefore, a transformation function E_{G_H}, that converts the comparative linguistic expressions into HFLTS, is necessary.

Definition 6.17 ([22]). Let E_{G_H} be a function that transforms comparative linguistic expressions, $ll \in S_{ll}$, obtained by G_H, into HFLTS, H_S. S is the linguistic term set used by G_H and S_{ll} is the expression domain generated by G_H.

$$E_{G_H} : S_{ll} \longrightarrow H_S$$

The comparative linguistic expressions generated through the production rules are transformed into HFLTS in different ways according to their meaning. Next, the transformations of the comparative linguistic expressions generated by the context-free grammar G_H, introduced in Definition 6.16 are:

- $E_{G_H}(s_i) = \{s_i | s_i \in S\}$
- $E_{G_H}(at\ most\ s_i) = \{s_j | s_j \in S\ and\ s_j \leq s_i\}$
- $E_{G_H}(lower\ than\ s_i) = \{s_j | s_j \in S\ and\ s_j < s_i\}$
- $E_{G_H}(at\ least\ s_i) = \{s_j | s_j \in S\ and\ s_j \geq s_i\}$
- $E_{G_H}(greater\ than\ s_i) = \{s_j | s_j \in S\ and\ s_j > s_i\}$
- $E_{G_H}(between\ s_i\ and\ s_j) = \{s_k | s_k \in S\ and\ s_i \leq s_k \leq s_j\}$

Example 6.4. By using the comparative linguistic expressions obtained in Example 6.3, $ll_1, ll_2, ll_3,$ *and* ll_4 their transformation into HFLTS by the transformation function E_{G_H}, is:

$E_{G_H}(very\ low) = \{very\ low\}$
$E_{G_H}(lower\ than\ medium) = \{nothing, very\ low, low\}$

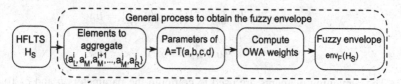

Fig. 6.1 General process to compute the fuzzy envelope

$E_{G_H}(at\ least\ high) = \{high, very\ high, perfect\}$
$E_{G_H}(between\ medium\ and\ very\ high) = \{medium, high, very\ high\}$

Other approaches have recently been introduced to manage linguistic expressions more complex than a linguistic term [1, 10, 17, 19].

6.3.3   A New Fuzzy Envelope for Comparative Linguistic Expressions

Consider the Computing with Words (CW) scheme introduced in Chapter 1 (see Figure 1.6), where the linguistic inputs should be translated into a format based on fuzzy tools in which the computations are carried out. Liu and Rodríguez have recently introduced a proposal in which the semantics of the comparative linguistic expressions are represented by fuzzy membership functions instead of linguistic intervals, because the concept of HFLTS is based on a fuzzy linguistic approach, and the linguistic terms are defined by a syntax and fuzzy semantics. Therefore, a new fuzzy envelope for HFLTS represents the semantics of the comparative linguistic expressions by means of a fuzzy membership function obtained by aggregating the linguistic terms that compound the HFLTS was proposed in [14]. This fuzzy envelope is obtained by a four-step process (see Figure 6.1).

Let $H_S = \{s_i, s_{i+1}, \ldots, s_j\}$ be a HFLTS, so that $s_k \in S = \{s_0, \ldots, s_g\}$, $k \in \{i, \ldots, j\}$.

1. *Obtain the elements for the aggregation*: All the linguistic terms that compound the HFLTS are considered in the aggregation process. Assuming that all linguistic terms $s_k \in S$ are defined by trapezoidal or triangular membership functions $A^k = T(a_L^k, a_M^k, a_M^k, a_R^k)$, $k = \{0, \ldots, g\}$, the set of elements to aggregate is:

$$T = \{a_L^i, a_M^i, a_M^{i+1}, \ldots, a_M^j, a_R^j\}$$

2. *Compute the parameters of the trapezoidal fuzzy membership function*: Keeping in mind that a trapezoidal fuzzy membership function $A = T(a, b, c, d)$ is used as the representation of a comparative linguistic expression based on HFLTS H_S, the left and right limits of A are obtained through the maximum and minimum operators.

$$a = min\{a_L^i, a_M^i, a_M^{i+1}, \ldots, a_M^j, a_R^j\} = a_L^i$$

$$d = max\{a_L^i, a_M^i, a_M^{i+1}, \ldots, a_M^j, a_R^j\} = a_R^j$$

The remaining elements are used to compute the parameters b and c. To do so, the OWA operator [31] is used which allows us to reflect different importance in the linguistic terms of a HFLTS generated from a comparative linguistic expression.

$$b = OWA_{W^s}\{a_M^i, a_M^{i+1}, \ldots, a_M^j\}$$

$$d = OWA_{W^t}\{a_M^i, a_M^{i+1}, \ldots, a_M^j\}$$

The OWA weighting vectors are in the form of W^s and W^t with $s, t = 1, 2$, $s \neq t$, or $s = t$.

3. *Compute the OWA weights*: Due to the hesitation among the linguistic terms that compound a HFLTS, such terms might have different importance which can be reflected by the OWA weights. Two different types of OWA weights W^1 and W^2 [11] are used to aggregate the elements $\{a_M^i, a_M^{i+1}, \ldots, a_M^j\}$ and compute the parameters b and c.

4. *Obtain the fuzzy envelope*: The fuzzy envelope $env_F(H_S)$ is defined as the trapezoidal fuzzy membership function.

$$env_F(H_S) = T(a, b, c, d) \tag{6.17}$$

6.4   Linguistic Decision Making with Comparative Linguistic Expressions

Once the concept of HFLTS and how to build comparative linguistic expressions through a context-free grammar is clear, this section shows a 2-tuple based multicriteria decision-making model in which experts can provide their assessments by means of either single linguistic terms or if necessary comparative linguistic expressions. This model uses the 2-tuple linguistic model to obtain linguistic results easy to understand by experts involved in the decision-making problem. Eventually, an example of a multicriteria decision-making problem is solved by the presented model.

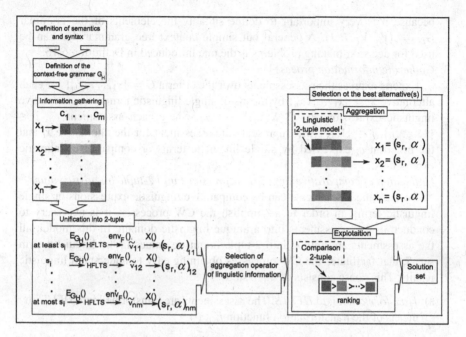

Fig. 6.2 Scheme of the 2-tuple based multicriteria decision-making model

6.4.1 A 2-Tuple Based Multicriteria Decision-Making Model Dealing with Comparative Linguistic Expressions

In the real world there are many decision-making problems in which the alternatives are defined by multiple criteria. There are different multicriteria decision-making models that deal with comparative linguistic expressions and single linguistic terms [5, 14, 27], but they do not consider the retranslation process of the CW scheme to obtain linguistic results easily understood by human beings. Therefore, we show here a multicriteria decision-making model that deals with comparative linguistic expressions and uses the 2-tuple linguistic model to carry out the CW processes obtaining linguistic results comprehensible by experts involved in the problem. It consists of six phases (graphically shown in Figure 6.2).

1. *Definition of semantics and syntax*
   In this phase, the linguistic term set $S = \{s_0, \ldots, s_g\}$ is defined which will be used by experts to assess the criteria of the decision-making problem. To do so, it is necessary to fix the syntax of the linguistic terms and define their semantics.
2. *Definition of the context-free grammar*
   Once the syntax and semantics of the linguistic term set, S, are fixed the context-free grammar G_H to generate comparative linguistic expressions is defined. The definition of the context-free grammar will depend on the specific problem,

because it is very important to define suitably the elements of the grammar $G_H = (V_N, V_T, P, I)$. A general but simple context-free grammar that can be used for decision-making problems is the one introduced in Definition 6.16.

3. *Gathering information process*

Experts express their assessments over the criteria $C = \{c_1, \ldots, c_m\}$ for each alternative $X = \{x_1, \ldots, x_n\}$ by means of single linguistic terms or comparative linguistic expressions $\mu_V : X \times C \rightarrow S_{ll}$, where each assessment v_{ij}, $i \in \{1, \ldots, n\}, j \in \{1, \ldots, m\}$, represents the assessment for the alternative x_i and the criterion c_j expressed by single linguistic terms or comparative linguistic expressions.

4. *Unification of comparative linguistic expressions into 2-tuple linguistic values*

Because the assessments can be comparative linguistic expressions or single linguistic terms, in order to accomplish the CW processes, it is necessary to conduct all the assessments into a unique linguistic domain. In this model, all the assessments are unified into 2-tuple linguistic values in the linguistic term set, S, that facilitates the CW processes obtaining easy to understand linguistic results. This phase consists of three steps.

(a) *Transformation into HFLTS*: The assessments are transformed into HFLTS by means of the transformation function $E_{G_H}(\cdot)$.

$$E_{G_H}(v_{ij}) = H_S(v_{ij}) \tag{6.18}$$

where H_S is the HFLTS obtained according to the function $E_{G_H}(\cdot)$.

(b) *Computation of the fuzzy envelope*: For each HFLTS its fuzzy representation by $env_F(\cdot)$ is obtained.

$$env_F(H_S(v_{ij})) = T(a, b, c, d) \tag{6.19}$$

where $T(a, b, c, d)$ is a trapezoidal fuzzy membership function (see Section 6.3.2).

(c) *Obtaining a 2-tuple linguistic value*: The trapezoidal fuzzy membership function is transformed into a 2-tuple linguistic value by using the transformation function τ_{TS} that computes a fuzzy set of S in the fuzzy envelope and afterwards, the function $\chi(\cdot)$ (see Definition 4.2) is applied that computes its central value to obtain a 2-tuple linguistic value in S (see Figure 6.3).

$$\tau_{TS} : T \rightarrow F(S)$$

$$\tau(T(a, b, c, d)) = \sum_{k=0}^{g} s_k / \gamma_k \tag{6.20}$$

$$\gamma_k = \max_y \min\{\mu_T(y), \mu_{s_k}(y)\}$$

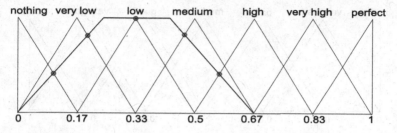

Fig. 6.3 Transformation of a fuzzy envelope into a 2-tuple linguistic value

5. *Selection of a linguistic aggregation operator*

Taking into account that this model uses the 2-tuple linguistic model to carry out the CW processes to obtain easy to understand linguistic results, a linguistic aggregation operator based on 2-tuple, φ, is chosen in this phase. There are different aggregation operators for the 2-tuple as reviewed in Chapter 2, inasmuch as the choice will depend on the specific problem to solve.

6. *Selection of the best alternative*

The solution set of alternatives is obtained in the selection process. Such a process is divided into two steps.

- *Aggregation of linguistic information*

  The assessments represented by 2-tuple linguistic values are aggregated by means of the aggregation operator for the 2-tuple chosen previously, to obtain a collective value for each alternative.

$$(s_r, \alpha)_i = \Delta(\varphi(\Delta^{-1}(s_r, \alpha)_{ij})) \quad \forall j \in \{1, \dots, m\} \tag{6.21}$$

- *Exploitation*

  The comparison operator for 2-tuple linguistic values is used to obtain a ranking of alternatives (see Section 2.3). Finally, the solution set of alternative(s) is selected for the decision-making problem as the alternative that maximises the collective value.

$$X_{sol} = \{x_i \in X | i = \max_j \{(s_r, \alpha)_j\}\} \tag{6.22}$$

6.4.2 Illustrative Example: 2-Tuple Based Multicriteria Decision-Making Model

Let us suppose that the head of a research group has to evaluate the proposals presented by four PhDs {*David, Helen, John, Sarah*} to apply for a postdoc position in the research group. The head of the research group will consider three criteria

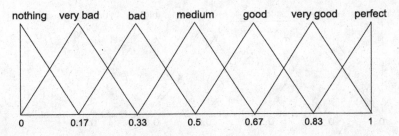

Fig. 6.4 Semantics and syntax of the linguistic term set S

Table 6.1 Assessments provided by the head of the research group

	c_1	c_2	c_3
David	Between g and vg	vg	g
Helen	m	Between m and vg	At most m
John	vg	g	Lower than m
Sarah	g	Greater than g	b

Table 6.2 Assessments
unified into HFLTS

	c_1	c_2	c_3
David	$\{g, vg\}$	$\{vg\}$	$\{g\}$
Helen	$\{m\}$	$\{m, g, vg\}$	$\{n, vb, b, m\}$
John	$\{vg\}$	$\{g\}$	$\{n, vb, b\}$
Sarah	$\{g\}$	$\{vg, p\}$	$\{b\}$

$\{c_1 : \textit{international experience}, c_2 : \textit{journal publications}, c_3 : \textit{research projects}\}$
for the evaluation. The head of the research group can elicit their assessments by
using single linguistic terms or may hesitate among different linguistic terms by
comparative linguistic expressions.

1. *Definition of semantics and syntax*
    A linguistic term set S, appropriate for this problem is shown in Figure 6.4.
2. *Definition of the context-free grammar*
    The context-free grammar G_H, introduced in Definition 6.16 is suitable to
    generate comparative linguistic expressions which can be used by the head of the
    research group in case of hesitation.
3. *Gathering information process*
    The assessments provided by the head of the research group about the criteria
    defined for the alternatives are shown in Table 6.1.
4. *Unification of comparative linguistic expressions into 2-tuple linguistic values*

    (a) *Transformation into HFLTS*
        The assessments are transformed into HFLTS by means of the function
        $E_{G_H}(\cdot)$. Table 6.2 shows the comparative linguistic expressions and single
        linguistic terms unified into HFLTS.

Table 6.3 Assessments represented by 2-tuple linguistic values

	c_1	c_2	c_3
David	$(vg, -0.5)$	$(vg, 0)$	$(g, 0)$
Helen	$(m, 0)$	$(g, 0)$	$(b, 0.12)$
John	$(vg, 0)$	$(g, 0)$	$(vb, -0.11)$
Sarah	$(g, 0)$	$(p, -0.16)$	$(b, 0)$

Table 6.4 Collective values for the alternatives

David	$(vg, -0.4)$
Helen	$(m, 0.22)$
John	$(g, -0.22)$
Sarah	$(g, 0.34)$

(b) *Computation of the fuzzy envelope*

In this phase, the fuzzy envelope for the HFLTS obtained in the previous phase is computed.

$$\tilde{v}_{11} = T(0.5, 0.67, 0.83, 1)$$
$$\tilde{v}_{22} = T(0.33, 0.64, 0.7, 1)$$
$$\tilde{v}_{23} = T(0, 0, 0.35, 0.67)$$
$$\tilde{v}_{33} = T(0, 0, 0.15, 0.5)$$
$$\tilde{v}_{42} = T(0.67, 0.97, 1, 1)$$

It is not necessary to compute the fuzzy envelope for the HFLTS compound by only one linguistic term inasmuch as they can be directly transformed into 2-tuple linguistic values by adding the value 0 as symbolic translation.

(c) *Obtaining a 2-tuple linguistic value*

The 2-tuple linguistic values are obtained by means of the functions τ_{TS} and $\chi(\cdot)$. Table 6.3 shows the assessments represented by 2-tuple linguistic values.

5. *Selection of a linguistic aggregation operator*

This model carries out the CW processes using the 2-tuple linguistic model upon which the aggregation operator must be based. Without loss of generality, the operator used is the 2-tuple weighted average (see Definition 2.4), and the weighting vector is $W = (0.4, 0.4, 0.2)$.

6. *Selection of the best alternative*

- Aggregation of linguistic information

  The assessments represented by 2-tuple linguistic values are aggregated to obtain a collective value for each alternative (see Table 6.4).

- Exploitation

  Finally, the solution set of alternatives is:

$$X_{sol} = \{x_i \in X | i = \max_{j \in \{1,2,3,4\}} \{(vg, -0.4)_1, (m, 0.22)_2, (g, -0.22)_3, (g, 0.34)_4\}\} = x_1$$

Therefore, the PhD selected for the postdoc position is:

David=(vg,-0.4).

As can be seen, this model provides a final result that is a linguistic value close to the easy to understand human cognitive model and the use of the symbolic translation shows that the result is accurate.

References

1. N. Agell, M. Sánchez, F. Prats, and L. Roselló. Ranking multi-attribute alternatives on the basis of linguistic labels in group decisions. *Information Sciences*, 209(1):49–60, 2012.
2. K.T. Atanassov. Intuitionistic fuzzy sets. *Fuzzy Sets and Systems*, 20:87–96, 1986.
3. H. Becker. Computing with words and machine learning in medical diagnosis. *Information Sciences*, 134:53–69, 2001.
4. B. Bedregal, R. Reiser, H. Bustince, C. López-Molina, and V. Torra. Aggregating functions for typical hesitant fuzzy elements and the action of automorphisms. *Information Sciences*, 256(1):82–97, 2014.
5. I. Beg and T. Rashid. TOPSIS for hesitant fuzzy linguistic term sets. *International Journal of Intelligent Systems*, 28:1162–1171, 2013.
6. G. Bordogna and G. Pasi. A fuzzy linguistic approach generalizing boolean information retrieval: A model and its evaluation. *Journal of the American Society for Information Science*, 44:70–82, 1993.
7. H. Bustince, E. Barrenechea, M. Pagola, J. Fernández, Z. Xu, B. Bedregal, J. Montero, H. Hagras, F. Herrera, and B. De Baets. A historical account of types of fuzzy sets and their relationships. *IEEE Transactions on Fuzzy Systems*, DOI:10.1109/TFUZZ.2015.2451692, 2015.
8. N. Chomsky. Three models for the description of language. *IRE Transactions on Information Theory*, 2(3):113–124, 1956.
9. D. Dubois and H. Prade. *Fuzzy Sets and Systems: Theory and Applications*. Kluwer Academic., New York, 1980.
10. E. Falcó, J. L. García-Lapresta, and L. Roselló. Allowing agents to be imprecise: A proposal using multiple linguistic terms. *Information Sciences*, 258:249–265, 2014.
11. D. Filev and R. Yager. On the issue of obtaining OWA operator weights. *Fuzzy Sets and Systems*, 94:157–169, 1998.
12. J.M. Garibaldi, M. Jaroszewski, and S. Musikasuwan. Nonstationary fuzzy sets. *IEEE Transactions on Fuzzy Systems*, 16(4):1072–1086, 2008.
13. H. Ishibuchi, T. Nakashima, and M. Nii. *Classification and Modeling with Linguistic Information Granules: Advanced Approaches to Linguistic Data Mining*. Springer, Berlin, 2004.
14. H. Liu and R.M. Rodríguez. A fuzzy envelope for hesitant fuzzy linguistic term set and its application to multicriteria decision making. *Information Sciences*, 258:266–276, 2014.
15. J. Ma, D. Ruan, Y. Xu, and G. Zhang. A fuzzy-set approach to treat determinacy and consistency of linguistic terms in multi-criteria decision making. *International Journal of Approximate Reasoning*, 44(2):165–181, 2007.
16. L. Martínez. Sensory evaluation based on linguistic decision analysis. *International Journal of Approximate Reasoning*, 44(2):148–164, 2007.

17. S. Massanet, J.V. Riera, J. Torrens, and E. Herrera-Viedma. A new linguistic computational model based on discrete fuzzy numbers for computing with words. *Information Sciences*, 258:277–290, 2014.
18. M. Mizumoto and K. Tanaka. Some properties of fuzzy sets of type 2. *Information Control*, 31:312–340, 1976.
19. C.H. Nguyen, V.N. Huynh, and W. Pedrycz. A construction of sound semantic linguistic scales using 4-tuple representation of term semantics. *International Journal of Approximate Reasoning*, 55(3):763–786, 2014.
20. S. Parsons. Current approaches to handling imperfect information in data and knowledge bases. *IEEE Transactions on Knowledge Data Engineering*, 8(3):353–372, 1996.
21. R.M. Rodríguez, L. Martínez, and F. Herrera. Hesitant fuzzy linguistic term sets for decision making. *IEEE Transactions on Fuzzy Systems*, 20(1):109–119, 2012.
22. R.M. Rodríguez, L. Martínez, and F. Herrera. A group decision making model dealing with comparative linguistic expressions based on hesitant fuzzy linguistic term sets. *Information Sciences*, 241(1):28–42, 2013.
23. R.M. Rodríguez, L. Martínez, V. Torra, Z.S. Xu, and F. Herrera. Hesitant fuzzy sets: state of the art and future directions. *International Journal of Intelligent Systems*, 29(6):495–524, 2014.
24. Y. Tang and J. Zheng. Linguistic modelling based on semantic similarity relation among linguistic labels. *Fuzzy Sets and Systems*, 157(12):1662–1673, 2006.
25. V. Torra. Hesitant fuzzy sets. *International Journal of Intelligent Systems*, 25(6):529–539, 2010.
26. J.H. Wang and J. Hao. A new version of 2-tuple fuzzy linguistic representation model for computing with words. *IEEE Transactions on Fuzzy Systems*, 14(3):435–445, 2006.
27. C. Wei, Z. Ren, and R.M. Rodríguez. A hesitant fuzzy linguistic TODIM method based on a score function. *International Journal of Computational Intelligence Systems*, 8(4):701–712, 2015.
28. D. Wu and J.M. Mendel. Computing with words for hierarchical decision making applied to evaluating a weapon system. *IEEE Transactions on Fuzzy Systems*, 18:441–460, June 2010.
29. M.M. Xia and Z.S. Xu. Hesitant fuzzy information aggregation in decision making. *International Journal Approximate Reasoning*, 52:395–407, 2011.
30. R.R. Yager. On the theory of bags. *International Journal Generation System*, 13:23–37, 1986.
31. R.R. Yager. On ordered weighted averaging aggregation operators in multicriteria decision making. *IEEE Transactions on Systems, Man, and Cybernetics*, 18:183–190, 1988.
32. L.A. Zadeh. The concept of a linguistic variable and its applications to approximate reasoning. *Information Sciences, Part I, II, III*, 8,8,9:199–249,301–357,43–80, 1975.

Chapter 7
2-Tuple Linguistic Decision Based Applications

7.1 Introduction

The 2-tuple linguistic model has had a great impact in the last decade and it has been used by many researchers to define new theoretical models and approaches, and it has also been used by practitioners to solve problems in a wide variety of real-world applications, mainly based on decision making and decision analysis, because a common activity for human beings in their daily lives is to make decisions under uncertainty, in which they select the best from a set of possible alternatives.

The areas in which the 2-tuple linguistic model has been applied cover a wide range; among others the following are highlighted.

- Multicriteria decision making
- Decision analysis
- E-services
- Fuzzy rule based systems
- Image processing

But not only the 2-tuple linguistic model has been used to solve real-world problems, also its extensions such as the use of nonhomogeneous information and the management of linguistic term sets with different granularity or unbalanced information.

This chapter reviews the applications in which the 2-tuple linguistic model or any of the 2-tuple linguistic based approaches have been used to solve real-world problems.

© Springer International Publishing Switzerland 2015
L. Martínez et al., *The 2-tuple Linguistic Model*, DOI 10.1007/978-3-319-24714-4_7

7.2 Applications

This section presents a review of the most important applications in which the 2-tuple linguistic model and its extensions have been used. Therefore, for each application a brief description about it is introduced and a table showing the papers related to such an application and which 2-tuple linguistic based approach has been used to solve the problem.

7.2.1 Multicriteria Decision Making

Human beings make decisions in their daily lives, for example, choosing the best car according to their requirements, selecting the best candidate for a position in a company, establishing the most suitable alternative for an emergency situation, and so forth.

Multicriteria decision-making models have been widely used to deal with decision-making problems where several criteria are considered to select the best alternative. Different approaches to cope with multicriteria decision-making problems have been introduced in the literature such as PROMETHEE [25], TOPSIS [27], AHP [47], VIKOR [7], and so on. Traditionally, such approaches have been used in quantitative contexts, however, many authors have used the 2-tuple linguistic model to extend and define new multicriteria decision-making models based on such approaches to manage not only linguistic information but also multigranular, heterogeneous, and unbalanced information (see Table 7.1). These models have been applied to different decision problems such as selecting the best experts to take part in the R&D project selection in a government funding agency [60], choosing the most suitable material for a specific product [39], personal selection [13, 19, 62, 63, 74], and so on.

7.2.2 Decision Analysis

Decision analysis is a systematic and quantitative approach to address and evaluate important choices. Decision analysis utilises a variety of tools to evaluate all relevant information to support the decision-making process. It is applied to many different areas; here only those are shown in which the 2-tuple linguistic model has been used.

- *Performance appraisal*
  The main purpose of a company is to be competitive and most of them know that competitiveness depends on continuous development of human resources. In order to accomplish correct management of human resources it is necessary to quantify and qualify employees' aims. To do so, companies utilise methods to

Table 7.1 Decision applications based on the use of the 2-tuple linguistic model

Application	Papers	2-tuple based approach	Year
Multicriteria decision making	Sun et al. [60]	2-tuple	2008
	Halouani et al. [28]	Non-homogeneous	2009
	De Andrés and García-Lapresta [13]	LH	2010
	Dursun and Karsak [19]	2-tuple	2010
	Moreno et al. [49]	2-tuple	2010
	Balezentis and Balezentis [8]	Non-homogeneous	2011
	Zhang [73]	2-tuple	2011
	Carrasco et al. [10]	2-tuple	2012
	Ju and Wang [33]	2-tuple	2013
	Ju and Wang [34]	2-tuple	2013
	Liu et al. [39]	2-tuple	2013
	Park et al. [52]	2-tuple	2013
	Ruan et al. [58]	2-tuple	2013
	Xu and Wu [69]	2-tuple	2013
	Xu et al. [70]	2-tuple	2013
	Wan [62]	2-tuple	2013
	Wan [63]	2-tuple	2013
	Wei [67]	2-tuple	2013
	Dhouib [15]	Non-homogeneous	2014
	Li and Dong [36]	Unbalanced	2014
	Zhao et al. [74]	2-tuple	2014
	Espinilla et al. [21]	Non-homogeneous	2015
	Montes et al. [48]	2-tuple	2015

Note: *2-tuple* stands for 2-tuple linguistic model, *LH* stands for the 2-tuple linguistic based model that deals with multigranular linguistic information by using linguistic hierarchies, *nonhomogeneous* stands for the 2-tuple linguistic based model that deals with nonhomogeneous information, and *unbalanced* stands for the 2-tuple linguistic based model that deals with unbalanced information

evaluate relationships between their fixed aims and human resources. A procedure used for companies to evaluate their employees is *performance appraisal*. Some companies use formal methods to carry out such an evaluation, but the results obtained are difficult to understand, because the methods only model numerical information, although indicators to be evaluated are qualitative in nature. In order to obtain easy to understand linguistic results, different proposals for performance appraisal have been introduced by using the 2-tuple linguistic based approaches (see Table 7.2).

• *Risk evaluation*
  Risk is the probability of an undesirable situation in a system, process, design, or service in which a failure can happen. Failure modes and effects analysis (FMEA) is a widely used tool to identify and prioritise potential failure modes for risk analysis. The main objective of FMEA is to evaluate, analyse, and determine

Table 7.2 Decision analysis applications based on the use of the 2-tuple linguistic model

Applications	Papers	2-tuple based approach	Year
Performance appraisal	De Andrés et al. [14]	LH	2010
	Espinilla et al. [20]	LH and non-homogeneous	2013
Risk evaluation	Lin [38]	2-tuple	2009
	Chang and Wang [11]	2-tuple	2010
	Wei [68]	2-tuple	2010
	Pei and Shi [53]	Unbalanced	2011
	Zhou et al. [75]	2-tuple	2011
	Ko [35]	2-tuple	2013
Product development	Wang [65]	2-tuple	2009
evaluation	Wang [66]	LH and non-homogeneous	2009
	Dhouib and Elloumi [16]	2-tuple	2011
	Ngan [50]	2-tuple	2011
	Wang [64]	ELH	2013
Knowledge evaluation	Fan et al. [23]	2-tuple	2009
	Tai and Chen [61]	2-tuple	2009
Sensorial evaluation	Martínez et al. [44]	LH	2008
	Martínez et al. [43]	Unbalanced	2009
	Estrella et al. [22]	Unbalanced	2014
Nuclear safeguards	Liu et al. [40]	2-tuple	2002
evaluation	Rodríguez et al. [57]	2-tuple	2010
Engineering systems	Martínez et al. [46]	LH	2005
	Martínez et al. [45]	Non-homogeneous	2006
Supply chain management	Yeh et al. [71]	2-tuple	2007
	Li and Xie [37]	2-tuple	2009
Sustainable development	Costa and Menichini [12]	2-tuple	2013
	Doukas et al. [17]	2-tuple	2014

Note: *ELH* stands for the 2-tuple linguistic based model that deals with multigranular linguistic information by using extended linguistic hierarchies.

the risk priority number for each potential failure mode to decrease or remove the potential risk. Several researchers pointed out that conventional methods had some disadvantages such as loss of information due to the approximation processes or the use of quantitative information instead of qualitative. Different methods that use the 2-tuple linguistic based approaches have been proposed to avoid the drawbacks mentioned and improve the results (see Table 7.2).

• *Product development evaluation*
New *product development* is the cornerstone for companies to keep and improve competitiveness. The development of new products is a complex process which should be evaluated by multiple experts taking into account not only the customers' demands, but also delivery time, price, and so on. In the literature different evaluation models for product development can be found that use the

2-tuple linguistic based approaches to avoid the loss of information, obtain results
that are easy to understand, and model multigranular information (see Table 7.2).

- *Knowledge evaluation*

  Knowledge management capability is a key source for organisations to gain
  sustainable competitive advantages. Knowledge management capability has a
  great effect on organisational competitiveness and it is a tool to retain information
  and knowledge that will help employees to work more efficiently. Knowledge
  management evaluation considers different attributes which are usually assessed
  by numerical values. However, it is difficult for experts to express their opinions
  based on human perceptions by using numerical values. Thus, several *knowledge
  evaluation* approaches that deal with linguistic information have been introduced
  in the literature. Such approaches use the 2-tuple linguistic model to avoid the
  loss of information and lack of precision in the results (see Table 7.2).

- *Sensory evaluation*

  The information gathered in an evaluation process is usually provided by a
  group of experts, called an expert panel, where each expert expresses his or
  her assessments about a set of items according to his or her knowledge and
  perceptions. In *sensory evaluation* the expert panel provides their assessments
  by using their human senses such as sight, smell, taste, touch, and hearing.
  In evaluation processes the assessments are usually expressed by numerical
  values to assess criteria which are quantitative in nature. Nevertheless, in sensory
  evaluation the assessments are based on perceptions which are of a qualitative
  nature. In such cases, the use of the fuzzy linguistic approach to model linguistic
  information has provided good results. However, it is common that experts
  involved in the evaluation process have different degrees of knowledge about
  the items. Therefore, the use of multigranular linguistic information to express
  the assessments might improve the results. To do so, different proposals that deal
  with 2-tuple linguistic based approaches have been proposed (see Table 7.2).

- *Nuclear safeguards evaluation*

  Among their different tasks the International Atomic Energy Agency (IAEA)
  carries out a *nuclear safeguards evaluation* with the goal of detecting nondiver-
  sion of nuclear materials and verifying that a state is living up to its international
  undertaking without using nuclear programs for nuclear weapons purposes [31].
  As part of its efforts to strengthen international safeguards, the IAEA includes
  the enhancement of its ability to provide believable assurance of the absence
  of undeclared nuclear activities. To do so, the IAEA uses huge amounts of
  information on states' nuclear and related nuclear activities. Some researchers
  pointed out that the evaluation model proposed by the IAEA [31] was not suitable
  to manage the available information, because such information is usually vague,
  imprecise, too complex, ill-defined, and so on. Therefore, some proposals based
  on the 2-tuple linguistic model to manage this type of information in a proper
  way have been proposed to obtain accurate results that are easy to understand
  (see Table 7.2).

- *Engineering systems*
  Usually, in the design of *engineering systems* the main objective is to reach
  high safety and technical performance levels while keeping the cost low. This
  implies the evaluation of several criteria to select the most suitable design.
  The study, analysis, and evaluation of the criteria involved in the selection
  of different design options imply that in this type of problem several experts
  with different backgrounds and knowledge about the criteria (which might be
  of a different nature, qualitative, or quantitative) take part. Most of evaluation
  approaches defined for this type of problem force experts to express their
  assessments using only one domain and one utility space. Nevertheless, it seems
  more suitable to define a framework that depends on the knowledge area of
  experts and the nature of the criteria in order that experts can use numerical
  values to assess quantitative criteria and linguistic values for qualitative ones.
  In addition, it is necessary to deal with different linguistic scales according to the
  knowledge level of experts. To deal with such issues, different proposals that deal
  with 2-tuple linguistic based approaches have been presented (see Table 7.2).
- *Supply chain management*
  Nowadays, companies have to face many changes because of technological innovation and additionally they have to satisfy customer requirements. In order to
  survive in a competitive world, companies try to reach some objectives including
  effectiveness, rapidity, responsiveness, and customer satisfaction. These goals are
  fixed in the elements of *supply chain management* such as acquisition of raw
  material, production planning, capacity of enhancement, timely production, on-
  time delivery, satisfactory services, and so on. Many companies have identified
  the achievement of the goals of supply chain management as a strategy to be
  competitive and it is very important for them. Consequently, many researchers
  have paid attention to this topic and have proposed performance evaluation
  models for supply chain management. Some of them have used the 2-tuple
  linguistic model to accomplish the Computing with Words processes without
  loss of information (see Table 7.2).
- *Sustainable development*
  Green economy is defined as an economy that improves human well-being
  and social equity while reducing environmental risk. The European Union has
  launched the Europe 2020 strategy to overcome the crisis and strengthen the
  economy for the coming future giving priority to a low-carbon economy and
  green growth. Companies have to integrate social and environmental concerns
  in their business and in their interaction with stakeholders on a voluntary basis.
  Hence, it is necessary for the state to support small to medium companies in
  these tasks through the development and adoption of suitable policies. Therefore,
  new tools and methods are necessary to relate indicators to policies to define the
  state's strategies for fostering green entrepreneurship and green energy growth.
  The 2-tuple linguistic model has been used to propose evaluation methods for
  sustainable development (see Table 7.2).

Table 7.2 shows the above-mentioned applications including their publications
and the 2-tuple linguistic approach used.

7.2.3   E-services

Advanced communications development with the adoption in the daily life of Internet services have contributed to a remarkable revolution that characterises modern times. *E-services* are tools or systems that manage information by communication technologies. Some applications that belong to the e-service area and use the 2-tuple linguistic model or any of its extensions are introduced below.

• *Recommender systems*
  In the e-commerce area customers face huge amounts of information about items that are hard to check in an affordable time to buy the most suitable item(s). The most successful tool in this field has been the *recommender systems* that try to lead customers to the most suitable items according to their requirements, needs, tastes, preferences, and so on. The general scheme of a recommender system consists of building an item database and a customer database that store the items and customers' profiles, respectively, and perform a filtering process by matching a customer profile and the items' profiles. This allows finding those items that better serve the customers' needs expressed by their profiles. There are different types of recommender systems, but all of them gather the information about items, users, and their needs to select the most suitable items for a specific user. Usually, the information related to users' needs is vague and imprecise. Nevertheless, most recommender systems use numerical values in the information-gathering process. Therefore, different researchers have proposed recommender systems that deal with a linguistic framework to model the user's preferences. In such proposals the 2-tuple linguistic model and the 2-tuple linguistic based multigranular linguistic model are used (see Table 7.3).
• *Information retrieval*
  An information retrieval system gathers the most relevant documents that best satisfy the user information requirements which are called queries. An information retrieval system consists of three components: a documents database which stores documents and the representation of their information contents, a

Table 7.3 E-services applications based on the use of the 2-tuple linguistic model

Applications	Papers	2-tuple based approach	Year
Recommender systems	Martínez et al. [42]	2-tuple	2008
	Rodríguez et al. [56]	2-tuple	2010
	Porcel and Herrera-Viedma [54]	LH	2010
	Porcel et al. [55]	LH	2012
	Serrano-Guerrero et al. [59]	LH	2013
Information retrieval	Herrera-Viedma et al. [30]	2-tuple	2007
	Herrera-Viedma and López-Herrera [29]	Unbalanced	2007
Networks	Gramajo and Martínez [26]	ELH	2012

query which allows users to make queries by means of a query language, and an evaluation process which evaluates the relevance of each document for the user's query computing a retrieval status value.

One way to improve the effectiveness of an information retrieval system is to consider weights in the user's query. Some authors have provided weighted models based on fuzzy sets theory [72] which assume that the weights are numerical values. However, it seems more natural to use linguistic terms to provide the importance of a query instead of numbers. Therefore, new linguistic information retrieval systems based on a 2-tuple linguistic model have been proposed. Such models use the 2-tuple linguistic model to accomplish the Computing with Words processes without loss of information (see Table 7.3).

• *Networks*
Nowadays *network* technology is very important in efficiently developing tasks in organisations, companies, universities, and the like. The Internet based networks provide a service which does not guarantee that data are delivered or that a user receives a quality of service level or priority. Therefore, all users get the best possible service without planning from the network. Nevertheless, the commercial use of Internet and the increasing demand of resources make companies require a best guarantee of quality of service to face problems such as delivery delays, loss of data, low bandwidth, and so on. Therefore, it is necessary to control traffic prioritisation according to user needs. This is a complex task for the network administrators who have to make decisions regarding the design of networks to improve the productivity of companies and get a high level of efficiency. A linguistic decision support system for quality of service priorities for network traffic that uses the 2-tuple linguistic based multigranular linguistic model has been proposed to help administrators make better decisions dealing with users' knowledge which is vague and imprecise (see Table 7.3).

7.2.4   Fuzzy-Rule Based Systems

Fuzzy Rule Based Systems (FRBSs) represent experts' knowledge by means of linguistic rules *IF A THEN B*, where A and B are (collections of) propositions containing linguistic variables. Usually these rules are provided by experts who can link the evidence with conclusions. The FRBSs are well-known tools in data mining [32] and intelligent control [18].

The 2-tuple linguistic model has been used to improve the FRBSs' behaviour using this representation to tune the linguistic variables representation, calling it a lateral tuning [2, 3]. It has been applied to improve fuzzy models in different problems such as control systems [1], association rules [5], classification problems [4, 6], imbalanced classification problems [24, 41], and subgroup discovery [9] (Table 7.4).

Table 7.4 FRBSs applications based on the use of the 2-tuple linguistic model

Applications	Papers	2-tuple based approach	Year
Control systems	Alcalá et al. [1]	2-tuple	2009
Association rules	Alcalá-Fdez et al. [5]	2-tuple	2009
Classification problems	Alcalá et al. [4]	2-tuple	2011
	Alcalá-Fdez et al. [6]	2-tuple	2011
Imbalanced classification	Fernández et al. [24]	2-tuple	2012
problems	López et al. [41]	2-tuple	2013
Subgroup discovery	Carmona et al. [9]	2-tuple	2012

Table 7.5 Image processing applications based on the use of the 2-tuple linguistic model

Applications	Papers	2-tuple based approach	Year
Image processing	Orduna et al. [51]	2-tuple	2014

7.2.5 Image Processing

Image processing is processing of images using mathematical operations by utilising any form of signal processing for which the input is an image, such as a photograph, and the output may be an image or a set of characteristics or parameters related to the image. The 2-tuple linguistic model has been applied to a specific problem of image processing, segmentation of images, that consists of dividing an image into disjoint and homogeneous regions (see Table 7.5). In such a problem, a set of experts expresses their preference degrees of each pixel for each object in the image by using linguistic terms. The 2-tuple linguistic model was used to carry out the Computing with Words processes without loss of precision.

References

1. R. Alcalá, J. Alcalá-Fdez, M.J. Gacto, and F. Herrera. Improving fuzzy logic controllers obtained by experts: a case study in HVAC systems. *Applied Intelligence*, 31(1):15–30, 2009.
2. R. Alcalá, J. Alcalá-Fdez, and F. Herrera. A proposal for the genetic lateral tuning of linguistic fuzzy systems and its interaction with rule selection. *IEEE Transactions on Fuzzy Systems*, 15(4):616–635, 2007.
3. R. Alcalá, J. Alcalá-Fdez, F. Herrera, and J. Otero. Genetic learning of accurate and compact fuzzy rule based systems based on the 2-tuples linguistic representation. *International Journal of Approximate Reasoning*, 44(1):45–64, 2007.
4. R. Alcalá, Y. Nojima, F. Herrera, and H. Ishibuchi. Multiobjective genetic fuzzy rule selection of single granularity-based fuzzy classification rules and its interaction with the lateral tuning of membership functions. *Soft Computing*, 15(12):2303–2318, 2011.
5. J. Alcalá-Fdez, R. Alcalá, M.J. Gacto, and F. Herrera. Learning the membership function contexts for mining fuzzy association rules by using genetic algorithms. *Fuzzy Sets and Systems*, 160(7):905–921, 2009.

6. J. Alcalá-Fdez, R. Alcalá, and F. Herrera. A fuzzy association rule-based classification model for high-dimensional problems with genetic rule selection and lateral tuning. *IEEE Transactions on Fuzzy Systems*, 19(5):857–872, 2011.

7. M. Bahraminasab and A. Jahan.
Material selection for femoral component of total knee replacement using comprehensive VIKOR. *Materials & Design*, 32(8–9):4471–4477, 2011.

8. A. Balezentis and T. Balezentis. An innovative multi-criteria supplier selection based on two tuple MULTIMOORA and hybrid data.
Economic Computation and Economic Cybernetics Studies and Research, 45:1–20, 2011.

9. C.J. Carmona, P. González, M.J. Gacto, and M.J. del Jesus. Genetic lateral tuning for subgroup discovery with fuzzy rules using the algorithm NMEEF-SD. *International Journal of Computational Intelligence Systems*, 5(2):355–367, 2012.

10. R.A. Carrasco, P. Villar, M.J. Hornos, and E. Herrera-Viedma. A linguistic multicriteria decision-making model applied to hotel service quality evaluation from web data sources. *International Journal of Intelligent Systems*, 27(7):704–731, 2012.

11. T.H. Chang and T.C. Wang. A novel efficient approach for DFMEA combining 2-tuple and the OWA operator. *Expert Systems with Applications*, 37(3):2362–2370, 2010.

12. R. Costa and T. Menichini. A multidimensional approach for CSR assessment: The importance of the stakeholder perception. *Expert Systems with Applications*, 40(1):150–161, 2013.

13. R. de Andrés and J.L. García-Lapresta. An endogenous human resources selection model based on linguistic assessments. *Neural network world*, 20(1):91–111, 2010.

14. R. de Andrés, J.L. García-Lapresta, and L Martínez. A multi-granular linguistic model for management decision-making in performance appraisal. *Soft Computing*, 14(1):21–34, 2010.

15. D. Dhouib. An extension of MACBETH method for a fuzzy environment to analyze alternatives in reverse logistics for automobile tire wastes. *Omega*, 42(1):25–32, 2014.

16. D. Dhouib and S. Elloumi. A new multi-criteria approach dealing with dependent and heterogeneous criteria for end-of-life product strategy. *Applied Mathematics and Computation*, 218(5):1668–1681, 2011.

17. H. Doukas, A. Tsiousi, V. Marinakis, and J. Psarras. Linguistic multi-criteria decision making for energy and environmental corporate policy. *Information Sciences*, 258:328–338, 2014.

18. D. Driankov, H. Hellendoorn, and M. Reinfrank. *An introduction to fuzzy control*. Springer-Verlag, 1996.

19. M. Dursun and E.E. Karsak. A fuzzy MCDM approach for personnel selection. *Expert Systems with Applications*, 37(6):4324–4330, 2010.

20. M. Espinilla, R. de Andrés, F.J. Martínez, and L. Martínez. A 360-degree performance appraisal model dealing with heterogeneous information and dependent criteria. *Information Sciences*, 222:459–471, 2013.

21. M. Espinilla, N. Halouani, and H. Chabchoub. Pure linguistic PROMETHEE I and II methods for heterogeneous MCGDM problems. *International Journal of Computational Intelligence Systems*, 8(2):250–264, 2015.

22. F.J. Estrella, M. Espinilla, and L. Martínez. Fuzzy linguistic olive oil sensory evaluation model based on unbalanced linguistic scales. *Journal of Multiple-Valued Logic and Soft Computing*, 22:501–520, 2014.

23. Z.P. Fan, B. Feng, Y.H. Sun, and W. Ou. Evaluating knowledge management capability of organizations: A fuzzy linguistic method. *Expert Systems With Applications*, 36(2, Part 2):3346–3354, 2009.

24. A. Fernández, M.J. del Jesus, and F. Herrera. On the 2-tuples based genetic tuning performance for fuzzy rule based classification systems in imbalanced data-sets. *Information Sciences*, 180(8):1268–1291, 2010.

25. M. Goumas and V. Lygerou. An extension of PROMETHEE method for decision making in fuzzy environment: Ranking of action energy exploitation projects. *European Journal of Operational Research*, 123:347–357, 2000.

26. S. Gramajo and L. Martínez. A linguistic decision support model for QoS priorities in networking. *Knowledge-based Systems*, 32(1):65–75, 2012.

27. N. Gupta. Material selection for thin-film solar cells using multiple attribute decision making approach. *Materials & Design*, 32(3):1667–1671, 2011.
28. N. Halouani, H. Chabchoub, and J.M. Martel. PROMETHEE-MD-2T method for project selection. *European Journal of Operational Research*, 195(3):841–849, 2009.
29. E. Herrera-Viedma and A.G. López-Herrera. A model of an information retrieval system with unbalanced fuzzy linguistic information. *International Journal of Intelligent Systems*, 22(11):1197–1214, 2007.
30. E. Herrera-Viedma, A.G. López-Herrera, M. Luque, and C. Porcel. A fuzzy linguistic IRS model based on a 2-tuple fuzzy linguistic approach. *International Journal of Uncertainty, Fuzziness and Knowledge-based Systems*, 15(2):225–250, 2007.
31. IAEA. *IAEA Bulletin, Annual Report*, volume 43, chapter Nuclear Security and Safeguards. 2001.
32. H. Ishibuchi, T. Nakashima, and M. Nii. *Classification and Modeling with Linguistic Information Granules: Advanced Approaches to Linguistic Data Mining*. Springer, Berlin, 2004.
33. Y. Ju and A. Wang. Extension of VIKOR method for multi-criteria group decision making problem with linguistic information. *Applied Mathematical Modelling*, 37(5):3112–3125, 2013.
34. Y. Ju and A. Wang. Projection method for multiple criteria group decision making with incomplete weight information in linguistic setting. *Applied Mathematical Modelling*, 37(20–21):9031–9040, 2013.
35. W.C. Ko. Exploiting 2-tuple linguistic representational model for constructing HOQ-based failure modes and effects analysis. *Computers & Industrial Engineering*, 64(3):858–865, 2013.
36. C.C. Li and Y. Dong. Unbalanced linguistic approach for venture investment evaluation with risk attitudes. *Progress in Artificial Intelligence*, 3(1):1–13, 2014.
37. Y.F. Li and Q.H. Xie. A method of identifying supply chain risk factors. In D. Tran and S.M. Zhou, editors, *World Congress on Software Engineering*, volume 4, pages 369–373, 2009.
38. Y. Lin. Method for risk evaluation of high-technology with 2-tuple linguistic information. In *Third International Symposium on Intelligent Information Technology Application,2009*, pages 261–264, 2009.
39. H.C. Liu, L. Liu, and J. Wu. Material selection using an interval 2-tuple linguistic VIKOR method considering subjective and objective weights. *Materials & Design*, 52:158–167, 2013.
40. J. Liu, D. Ruan, and R. Carchon. Synthesis and evaluation analysis of the indicator. *International Journal of Applied Mathematics and Computer Science*, 12(3):449–462, 2002.
41. V. López, A. Fernández, M.J. del Jesus, and F. Herrera. A hierarchical genetic fuzzy system based on genetic programming for addressing classification with highly imbalanced and borderline data-sets. *Knowledge-Based Systems*, 38(0):85–104, 2013.
42. L. Martínez, M. Barranco, L.G. Pérez, and M. Espinilla. Improving the effectiveness of knowledge based recommender systems using incomplete linguistic preference relations. *International Journal of Uncertainty, Fuzziness and Knowledge-Based Systems*, 16:33–56, 2008.
43. L. Martínez, M. Espinilla, J. Liu, L.G. Pérez, and P.J. Sánchez. An evaluation model with unbalanced linguistic information: Applied to olive oil sensory evaluation. *Journal of Multiple-Valued Logic and Soft Computing*, 15(2–3):229–251, 2009.
44. L. Martínez, M. Espinilla, and L.G. Pérez. A linguistic multigranular sensory evaluation model for olive oil. *International Journal of Computational Intelligence Systems*, 1(2):148–158, 2008.
45. L. Martínez, J. Liu, and J. B. Yang. A fuzzy model for design evaluation based on multiple criteria analysis in engineering systems. *International Journal of Uncertainty, Fuzziness and Knowledge-Based Systems*, 14(3):317–336, 2006.
46. L. Martínez, J. Liu, J.B. Yang, and F. Herrera. A multigranular hierarchical linguistic model for design evaluation based on safety and cost analysis. *International Journal of Intelligent Systems*, 20(12):1161–1194, 2005.

47. A. Mayyas, Q. Shen, A. Mayyas, M. Abdelhamid, D. Shan, A. Qattawi, and M. Omar. Using quality function deployment and analytical hierarchy process for material selection of body-in-white. *Materials & Design*, 32(5):2771–2782, 2011.
48. R. Montes, A.M. Sánchez, P. Villar, and F. Herrera. A web tool to support decision making in the housing market using hesitant fuzzy linguistic term sets. *Applied Soft Computing*, DOI:10.1016/j.asoc.2015.01.030, 2015.
49. J.M. Moreno, J.M. Morales del Castillo, C. Porcel, and E. Herrera-Viedma. A quality evaluation methodology for health-related websites based on a 2-tuple fuzzy linguistic approach. *Soft Computing*, 14(8):887–897, 2010.
50. S.C. Ngan. Decision making with extended fuzzy linguistic computing, with applications to new product development and survey analysis. *Expert Systems with Applications*, 38(11):14052–14059, 2011.
51. R. Orduna, A. Jurio, D. Paternain, H. Bustince, P. Melo-Pinto, and E. Barrenechea. Segmentation of color images using a linguistic 2-tuples model. *Information Sciences*, 258:339–352, 2014.
52. J.H. Park, J.M. Park, and Y.C Kwun. 2-tuple linguistic harmonic operators and their applications in group decision making. *Knowledge-Based Systems*, 44(0):10–19, 2013.
53. Z. Pei and P. Shi. Fuzzy risk analysis based on linguistic aggregation operators. *International Journal of Innovative Computing, Information and Control*, 7(12):7105–7117, 2011.
54. C. Porcel and E. Herrera-Viedma. Dealing with incomplete information in a fuzzy linguistic recommender system to disseminate information in university digital libraries. *Knowledge-based systems*, 23(1):32–39, 2010.
55. C. Porcel, A. Tejeda-Lorente, M.A. Martìnez, and E. Herrera-Viedma. A hybrid recommender system for the selective dissemination of research resources in a technology transfer office. *Information Sciences*, 184(1):1–19, 2012.
56. R.M. Rodríguez, M. Espinilla, P.J. Sánchez, and L. Martínez. Using linguistic incomplete preference relations to cold start recommendations. *Internet Research*, 20(3):296–315, 2010.
57. R.M. Rodríguez, L. Martínez, D. Ruan, and J. Liu. Using collaborative filtering for dealing with missing values in nuclear safeguards evaluation. *International journal of uncertainty fuzziness and knowledge-based systems*, 18(4):431–449, 2010.
58. Y. Ruan, Z. Pei, and Z. Gao. Linguistic interval 2-tuple power aggregation operators and their applications. *International Journal of Computational Intelligence Systems*, 6(2):381–395, 2013.
59. J. Serrano-Guerrero, F.P. Romero, and J.A. Olivas. Hiperion: A fuzzy approach for recommending educational activities based on the acquisition of competences. *Information Sciences*, 248:114–129, 2013.
60. Y.H. Sun, J. Ma, Z.P. Fan, and J. Wang. A group decision support approach to evaluate experts for R&D project selection. *IEEE Transactions on Engineering Management*, 55(1):158–170, 2008.
61. W.S. Tai and C.T. Chen. A new evaluation model for intellectual capital based on computing with linguistic variable. *Expert Systems with Applications*, 36(2):3483–3488, 2009.
62. S.P. Wan. Some hybrid geometric aggregation operators with 2-tuple linguistic information and their applications to multi-attribute group decision making. *International Journal of Computational Intelligence Systems*, 6(4):750–763, 2013.
63. S.P. Wan. Some hybrid geometric aggregation operators with 2-tuple linguistic information and their applications to multi-attribute group decision making. *International Journal of Computational Intelligence Systems*, 6(4):750–763, 2013.
64. S.Y. Wang. Applying the superior identification group linguistic variable to construct kano model oriented quality function deployment. *Technological and Economic Development of Economy*, 19(sup1):S304–S325, 2013.
65. W.P. Wang. Evaluating new product development performance by fuzzy linguistic computing. *Expert Systems with Applications*, 36(6):9759–9766, 2009.
66. W.P. Wang. Toward developing agility evaluation of mass customization systems using 2-tuple linguistic computing. *Expert Systems with Applications*, 36(2):3439–3447, 2009.

67. G. Wei. Some linguistic power aggregating operators and their application to multiple attribute group decision making. *Journal of Intelligent and Fuzzy Systems*, 25(3):695–707, 2013.

68. J. Wei. A risk evaluation method for the high-technology project investment based on ET-WA operator with 2-tuple linguistic information. *Journal of Convergence Information Technology*, 5(10):176–180, 2010.

69. J. Xu and Z. Wu. A maximizing consensus approach for alternative selection based on uncertain linguistic preference relations. *Computers & Industrial Engineering*, 64(4): 999–1008, 2013.

70. Y. Xu, H. Wang, and D. Palacios-Marqués. An interactive approach based on alternative achievement scale and alternative comprehensive scale for multiple attribute decision making under linguistic environment. *International Journal of Computational Intelligence Systems*, 6(1):87–95, 2013.

71. D.Y. Yeh, C.H. Cheng, and M.L. Chi. A modified two-tuple FLC model for evaluating the performance of SCM: By the six sigma DMAIC process. *Applied Soft Computing*, 7(3):1027–1034, 2007.

72. L.A. Zadeh. Fuzzy sets. *Information and Control*, 8:338–353, 1965.

73. S. Zhang. A model for evaluating computer network security systems with 2-tuple linguistic information. *Computers & Mathematics with Applications*, 62(4):1916–1922, 2011.

74. X. Zhao, Q. Li, and G. Wei. Some prioritized aggregating operators with linguistic information and their application to multiple attribute group decision making. *Journal of Intelligent & Fuzzy Systems*, 26(4):1619–1630, 2014.

75. S. Zhou, W. Chang, and Z. Xiong. Risk assessment model with 2-tuple temporal linguistic variable. *Applied Mechanics and Materials*, 58–60:2540–2545, 2011.

Chapter 8
Flintstones: A Fuzzy Linguistic Decision Tools Enhancement Suite

8.1 Introduction

Throughout the book it has been shown that there are many linguistic computational models and they can be applied to many decision-based applications. Also it has been stated that despite the existence of many models dealing with linguistic information not all of them fulfil the requirements of the Computing with Words (CW) paradigm (see Figure 1.6) unlike the 2-tuple linguistic model that fulfils such requirements (see Chapter 2).

In spite of the popularity and use of linguistic decision making in many decision-based problems such as sustainable energy [4], recommender systems [15], sensory evaluation [6, 13], personnel selection [11], quality of service [7], performance appraisal [2], vendor selection problems [1], soft consensus [10, 14, 17], or software project selection [18], there is a lack of software tools that facilitate the solving processes based on linguistic decision making.

The lack of decision software tools within the CW paradigm for solving linguistic decision problems has provoked the development of a reusable and easy to extend software suite, called *Fuzzy LINguisTic deciSion TOols eNhancEment Suite* (*Flintstones*)[1] [5]. It is based on the 2-tuple linguistic model and its extensions in order to support the solution of those problems defined in linguistic and complex frameworks, such as

- *Heterogeneous frameworks*
- *Multigranular linguistic frameworks*
- *Unbalanced linguistic frameworks*
- *Hesitant fuzzy linguistic information*

Additionally the methodology applied in *Flintstones* fulfils the CW paradigm and provides accurate, interpretable, and easily understandable linguistic results.

---

[1]http://sinbad2.ujaen.es/flintstones/.

L. Martínez et al., *The 2-tuple Linguistic Model*, DOI 10.1007/978-3-319-24714-4_8

145

Furthermore, this chapter not only introduces a linguistic decision software tool but also presents the *Flintstones* website in which the current and past releases can be downloaded together with a repository of datasets for decision-making problems defined in linguistic and complex frameworks.

The coming sections explain the architecture of the tool, the technologies used for its development, its functionality, and how to use it. Afterwards, the *Flintstones* website is introduced in brief.

8.2   *Flintstones*: Architecture and Technologies

The software *Flintstones* not only aims at facilitating the decision-solving process of linguistic decision-making problems by using the 2-tuple linguistic model and its extensions, but also at facilitating the reusability of its components and hence extending their current components with others, for solving different types of problems dealing with linguistic information, by using extension points in its implementation process. Therefore, first it is interesting to show the architecture and technologies used in its development.

Flintstones has been developed as an *Eclipse Rich Client Platform* (Eclipse RCP)[2] application, that is, a platform to build and deploy rich client applications developed by IBM and maintained by the Eclipse community. The key value of Eclipse RCP is that it allows us quickly to develop professional applications with a native look and feel on multiple platforms which can be easily extended, modified, and reused. Eclipse RCP is based on a *component-based architecture*, which tries to solve some common problems in software development such as reusing, maintaining, extending, and modifying.

An Eclipse RCP application consists of several *Eclipse components*, also called *plug-ins*, *bundles*, or *OSGi components*. *Flintstones* includes more than 100 components, which can be grouped into nine basic component types (see Figure 8.1):

- *Core*: Provides structures and procedures with the aim of supporting the resolution of linguistic decision problems. These components include elements such as experts, criteria and alternatives, support for undo and redo actions, and functionalities for storing and exporting data.
- *Graphical user interface* (GUI): Allows users to interact with the software suite of tools.
- *Resolution Phases*: Phases of decision-solving method.
- *Resolution Schemes*: Ordered set of resolution phases that carry out the decision-solving method.
- *Domains*: The set of domains in which experts can provide their assessments.

---

[2]http://www.eclipse.org/home/categories/rcp.php.

Fig. 8.1 Component types in
Flintstones

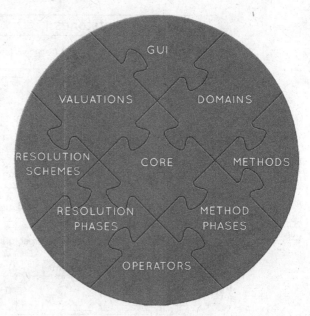

- *Valuations*: Support for specific types of assessments such as linguistic, numerical, or interval-valued.
- *Method Phases*: Specific phases of the 2-tuple decision methods.
- *Methods*: Such a module develops the 2-tuple linguistic computational model and its extensions for solving decision-making problems with linguistic and complex contexts (see Chapters 4 and 5).
- *Operators*: Aggregation operators that can be used to aggregate the information involved in the decision problem.

A further detailed architectonic diagram of *Flintstones*, which shows several components implemented in it, can be seen in Figure 8.2.

The component-based architecture provides several advantages based on its architecture and technologies:

- *Flintstones* has been developed with an RCP based on Java. Therefore, it is a multiplatform suite of tools that can be used on any machine with Java virtual machine (JVM), disregarding the operating system.
- The software suite is divided in separated modules. Thus it is possible to upgrade the software suite just by making changes in a particular module.
- The structure of *Flintstones* is ready to include new functionalities or elements such as new aggregation operators, new solving processes, or new preference modelling, without changing its components in a fast and simple way by means of *extension points*, which are interfaces or abstract classes that model an aspect of a build system.

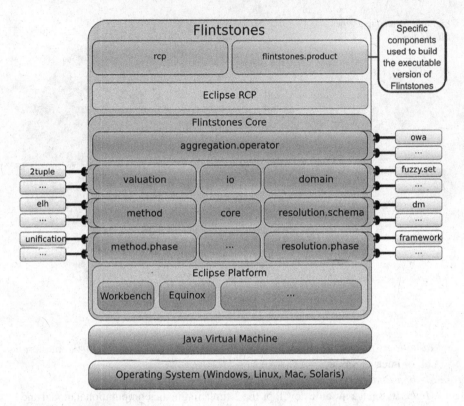

Fig. 8.2 Flintstones architecture

8.2.1   Extension Points in Flintstones

In order to avoid tight coupling between components, *Eclipse* provides the concept of *extension points* and *extension*. When it is desirable for the functionality of a given component to be extended or customised, this component will declare an extension point. An extension point defines a contract to which extensions must conform. Components that want to extend or customise the functionality provided by the component must implement that contract in their extension. The general scheme of an extension point can be seen in Figure 8.3.

Flintstones makes an intensive use of these concepts, providing at its core a total of seven extension points: *Resolution phases*, *Resolution schemes*, *Domains*, *Valuations*, *Method phases*, *Methods*, and *Aggregation operator*.

Each of the above extensions is defined in separate components as shown in Figure 8.2. Each component which defines extension points manages the life cycle of all extensions that implement this extension point. The internal implementation of extension points in these components is similar to the scheme shown in Figure 8.3, but adapted to the specific needs of the extended functionality.

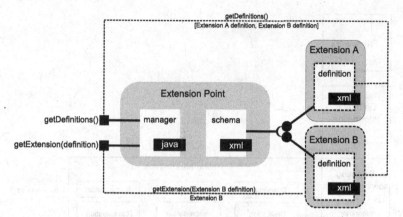

Fig. 8.3 Extension point scheme

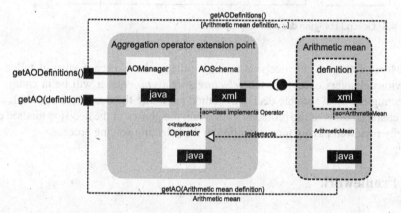

Fig. 8.4 Aggregation operator extension point

Figure 8.4 shows the scheme implemented by one of these extension points, specifically the extension point defined for extending aggregation operators.

8.3 General Common Decision-Solving Method Based on the 2-Tuple Linguistic Model and Its Extensions

Flintstones aims at solving linguistic decision-making problems under uncertainty and complex frameworks by using the 2-tuple linguistic model and its extensions. Initially, it was developed including the different linguistic decision methods presented in Chapters 2, 4 and 5 which shared a general common decision-solving method (see Figure 8.5) that follows the CW scheme, but with specific characteristics according to the framework in which the decision problem is defined that will choose the solving process used in each decision problem.

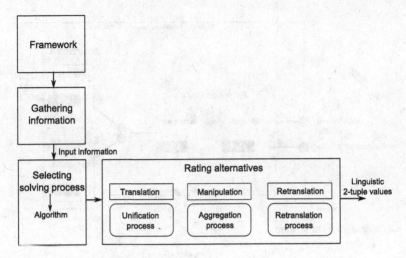

Fig. 8.5 General common decision-solving method

Most phases of the decision-making scheme have been further detailed in previous chapters except for the *selecting solving process*. It will be in charge of selecting the most suitable decision method attending the decision framework and the characteristics of the problem. Following, the phases of the decision method are briefly reviewed paying more attention to the selecting solving process.

A. Framework

It defines the elements involved in the decision-making problem:

- A finite set of alternatives $X = \{x_1, \ldots, x_h\}$
- A set of criteria $C = \{c_1, \ldots, c_n\}$ that might be grouped
- A set of experts $E = \{e_1, \ldots, e_m\}$ that could also be grouped
- The set of expression domains D in which experts can elicit their assessments, including numerical (*num*), interval-valued (*int*), linguistic (*lin*), and unbalanced linguistic domains (*linUnb*)

B. Gathering Information

In this phase, each expert e_k, elicits the assessments by means of assessment vectors

$$U^k = (v_{ij}^k : i = 1, \ldots, n, j = 1, \ldots, m : v_{ij}^k \in D)$$

Let v_{ij}^k be the assessment provided by expert e_k, for the criterion c_i of the alternative x_j that will belong to an expression domain in the framework D.

C. Selecting a Solving Process

A decision-solving process based on the 2-tuple linguistic model should be selected to solve the decision problem. The selection of a suitable solving process depends on the elements and expression domains in the framework. Hence, according to these domains and elements the use of the 2-tuple linguistic model or one of its extensions is chosen to solve the linguistic decision problem. Therefore, to select the right solving process it is necessary to have the following information about the framework.

- *edNum* $\in$ *{True, False}* indicates if a numerical expression domain *num* was defined in *D*.
- *edInt* $\in$ *{True, False}* establishes if an interval expression domain *int* was defined in *D*.
- *edLinUnb* $\in$ *{True, False}* determines if an unbalanced linguistic domain defined with a *linguistic hierarchy linUnb* was fixed in *D*.
- *tamEdLinLis* $\in$ $\mathbb{N}^+$ defines the number of linguistic scales established in the set of expression domains *D*, with $\mathbb{N}^+$ any positive integer number.
- *edLin* $= \{card, 2T\}$ describes a linguistic domain *lin* fixed in the framework that is characterised by two values. First, *card* $\in \mathbb{N}^+$ that indicates the cardinality of the linguistic domain and, the second value, $2T \in$ *{True, False}* that establishes if the linguistic domain can be represented by 2-tuple linguistic values; that is, the linguistic term set has an odd value of granularity and whose membership functions are triangular-shaped and symmetrically and uniformly distributed in the unit interval.
- *edLinList* $= \{edLin_i; i = 1, \ldots, tamEdLinLis\}$ is a vector of *edLin* that provides information about the linguistic scales established in *D*.

The algorithm presented in Table 8.1 illustrates a procedure to select the suitable solving process for linguistic decision-making problems. The algorithm selects the *id* $\in \{1, 2, 3, 4, 5, 6\}$ that identifies the solving process according to the following references.

1. *2-Tuple linguistic computational model*
2. *Fusion approach for managing multigranular linguistic information*
3. *Linguistic hierarchies*
4. *Extended linguistic hierarchies*
5. *Fusion approach for managing heterogeneous information*
6. *Fuzzy linguistic methodology to deal with unbalanced linguistic term sets*

Table 8.1: Algorithm to select the suitable solving process

```
INPUTS:
    edNum, edInt, edLinUnb, tamEdLinLis, edLinList
BEGIN
IF   (edLin[1].2T=true) and (tamEdLinLis=1)
THEN
    RETURN 1
ELSE
    IF (edNum=true) or (edInt=true)
    THEN
        RETURN 5
ELSE
    IF (edLinUnb=true)
    THEN
        RETURN 6
ELSE
    edLinListShortCard ⇐ short(edLinList,edLinList.card)
    i⇐1
    WHILE (i<tamEdLinLis) DO
        IF (edLinListShortCard.edLin[i].2T=false)
        THEN
            RETURN 2
        ELSE
            IF (edLinListShortCard[i+1].card≠((edLinListShortCard[i].card)-1)·2+1)
            THEN
                RETURN 4
        ELSE
            i⇐i+1
        END-IF
    END-WHILE
    RETURN 3
END-IF
END
OUTPUT:
    id
```

D. Rating Alternatives

The aim of this phase is to obtain the solution for the decision problem. Therefore, the solving process will obtain a linguistic assessment for each alternative which will be used to choose the solution set of alternatives for the problem. Each solving process follows the common scheme with the following three processes (see Figure 8.5).

1. *Unification process.* Decision-making problems defined in linguistic complex frameworks (multigranular linguistic, heterogeneous, or unbalanced linguistic) solved by the 2-tuple linguistic model based models initially conduct all input information into a unified linguistic domain.
2. *Aggregation process.* The unified information is aggregated to obtain a global assessment for each alternative.
3. *Retranslation process.* It is used to express the global assessments for each alternative in a linguistic expression domain that can be easily interpreted by experts, keeping the CW scheme (see Figure 1.6).

8.4 On the Use of Flintstones

To facilitate the understanding of elements and the use of *Flintstones*, a multigranular linguistic decision-making problem (see Chapter 4) and how it is solved by it is described here. It shows the elements of *Flintstones* that define a multigranular linguistic *framework*, the way of gathering the information, the selection, and run of the suitable decision method and finally the rating of alternatives.

8.4.1 Framework

Let us suppose a decision problem with four possible alternatives $X = \{x_1, \ldots, x_4\}$ in which the decision lies with four experts $E = \{e_1, \ldots, e_4\}$ who evaluate the alternatives according to four criteria $C = \{c_1, \ldots, c_4\}$. Due to the uncertainty that involves the decision problem the experts will assess the criteria in a linguistic domain.

In this problem, the experts have different degrees of knowledge about the set of criteria. Therefore, they will express their preferences in two different linguistic term sets based on their own knowledge: one set with five labels and another with seven labels. Both linguistic term sets are distributed symmetrically and uniformly around the central label. The elements involved in the framework are defined in *Flintstones* and shown in Figure 8.6.

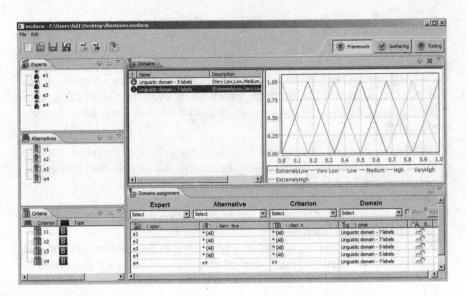

Fig. 8.6 Framework

8.4.2　Gathering Information

In this phase, the assessments elicited by experts for each criterion for each alternative are provided, according to the expression domains fixed in the framework as shown in Figure 8.7.

8.4.3　Selecting a Solving Process

Here, *Flintstones* carries out the algorithm shown in Table 8.1 to select the suitable solving process for the decision-making problem, taking into account the expression domains established in the framework. The input information for the algorithm is:

edNum = False, edInt = False, edLinUnb = False, tamEdLinLis = 2 and *edLinList = ((5, True), (7, True))*.

The problem is defined in a multigranular linguistic framework. Therefore, the algorithm returns the value *4* that corresponds to the solving process based on *extended linguistic hierarchies*.

Remark 8.1. It is noteworthy that the extension based on the *fusion approach for managing multigranular linguistic information* could also be applied to solve the problem (see Figure 8.8).

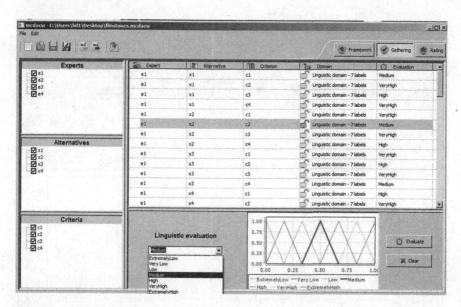

Fig. 8.7 Gathered information

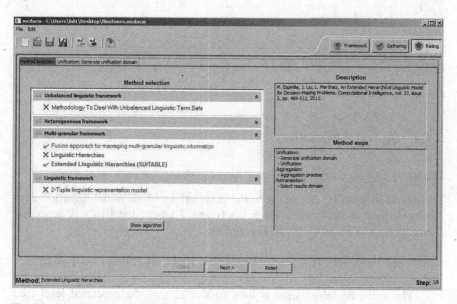

Fig. 8.8 Selection of the suitable solving process

However, as was reviewed in Section 4.2, the methodologies based on the *fusion approach* can provide inaccurate linguistic results. Therefore, the selected suitable solving process is based on *extended linguistic hierarchies* because this extension provides precise linguistic results without loss of information.

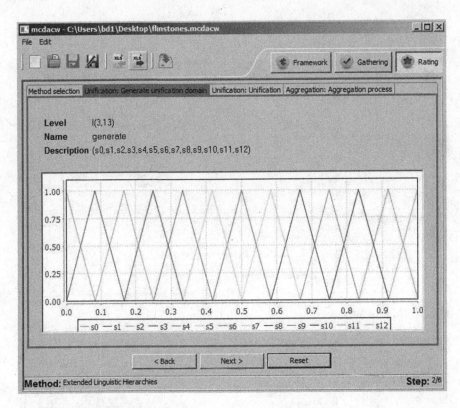

Fig. 8.9 New generated level

8.4.4 Rating Alternatives

The rating process computes the linguistic assessments for each alternative:

1. *Unification process.* According to the granularities of the initial linguistic term sets defined in the framework, 5 labels and 7 labels, the BLTS is generated according to Section 4.2.3 (see Figure 8.9):

$$n(t^*) = lcm(n(1) - 1, n(2) - 1) + 1 = lcm(4, 6) + 1 = 12 + 1 = 13$$

   The gathered information is then conducted into the generated level (see Figure 8.10).

2. *Aggregation process.* It aggregates the information by using aggregation operators for 2-tuple linguistic values (see Figure 8.11). In this problem, the *2-tuple linguistic weighted average operator* is selected to aggregate the preferences provided by experts for each criterion with the following weighting vector $w_e = (0.2, 0.3, 0.3, 0.2)$. On the other hand, the *2-tuple linguistic arithmetic mean operator* is used to compute a collective value for each alternative,

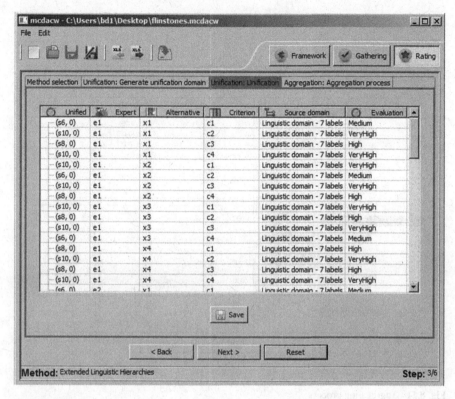

Fig. 8.10 Unified information

aggregating its collective assessments. The computed global assessments for each alternative are expressed in the unified level t^* that corresponds to $\overline{S}^{13}$.

3. *Retranslation process*: The global assessments in $\overline{S}^{13}$ are expressed in the initial expression domains used by the experts applying a retranslation process for ELH (see Figure 8.12).

8.5 *Flintstones*: Adding New Functionalities

The integration of new functionalities or elements in *Flintstones* involves adding multiple new features. Let's exemplify this process with the integration of HFLTS in *Flintstones* that implies the development of tools that provide:

- *Support for hesitant fuzzy linguistic assessments*: *Flintstones* provides an extension point to extend the types of assessments supported, the *valuation extension point*. The functionalities implemented to support hesitant fuzzy linguistic assessments were added to *Flintstones* using a new component that extends

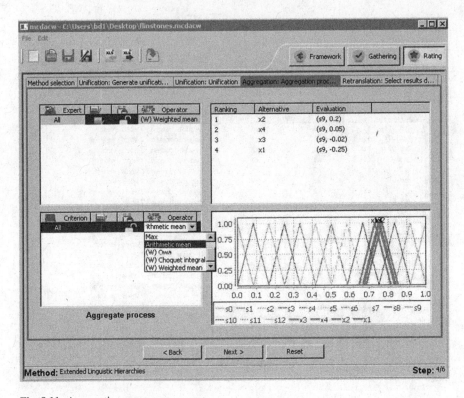

Fig. 8.11   Aggregation process

this extension point, *flintstones.valuation.hesitant*. This component allows future development of new solving processes based on HFLTS and new aggregation operators that can operate with this type of information. The component adds the following functionality to *Flintstones*.

- Ability to use valuation of this nature in the suite.
- Support for saving hesitant valuations; thus it is possible to save and to load these kinds of valuations.
- Adding a hesitant assessment panel, so that it is possible to gather assessments of this nature in a simple way (see Figure 8.13).
- Adding a graph visualisation of hesitant assessments in order to visualise these assessments clearly (see Figure 8.13).

- *Hesitant fuzzy linguistic decision-solving process*: At least a solving decision-making problem for HFLTS is included in *Flintstones* using the *method extension point*. The hesitant solving process developed was added to *Flintstones* using a new component that extends this extension point, the *flintstones.method.hesitant* component which fulfils the contract imposed by *method extension point*. In the case of this solving process, it specifies:

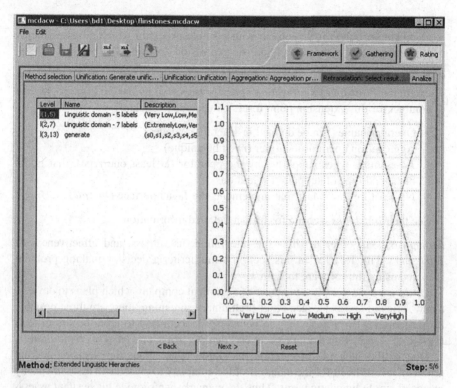

Fig. 8.12 Retranslation process

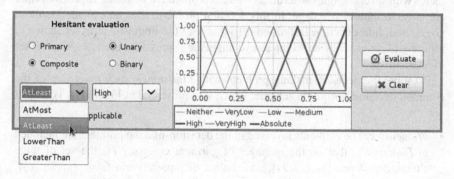

Fig. 8.13 Hesitant assessment panel

- A single *method phase* to solving a decision-making problem, the aggregation of the assessments, which takes as input the assessments provided by experts for each criterion of each alternative, and the aggregation operators to use and return the collective valuation for each alternative.

– The condition that the solving process only can be carried out if the decision-making problem is a problem with a single expert in which all assessments are expressed in the same linguistic expression domain.

• *Aggregation operators*: The creation of an aggregation operator is carried out extending *Flintstones aggregation operator extension point* (see Figure 8.4). The contract for this extension point forces extensions to declare:

– Operator name (can be defined in several languages)
– Aggregation operator identifier (must be unique)
– Assessment types supported by the operator (at least one type), that is, its name and type of supported valuations
– Name of the Java class that implements the Java interface *Operator*

See the *Flintstones* website for further detailed information.

Example 8.1. In order to show the integration, usefulness, and effectiveness of *Flintstones* with HFLTS, in this section a multicriteria decision-making problem is solved using the software tool suite.

Let us suppose there is a manager of a garment company which plans to develop a new series of sports jackets. After preliminary screening, there are three possible textile fabrics $X = \{x_1, \ldots, x_3\}$ to be assessed, according to three benefit criteria $C = \{c_1, \ldots, c_3\}$, which are respectively: *quality, price,* and *business reputation.*

Due to the lack of information and knowledge about the decision-making problem, it is difficult for the manager of the company to provide all assessments by means of single linguistic terms. Thus the manager can provide his hesitant assessments with several linguistic terms as well as comparative linguistic expressions that are close to natural language. In this decision problem, the context-free grammar G_H is used, introduced in Definition 6.16 that uses the linguistic term set shown in Figure 8.14, to generate the comparative linguistic expressions used to assess the set of alternatives.

To solve the decision-making problem with *Flintstones*, each main step of the common decision resolution scheme, which was presented in Figure 1.4, is carried out.

• *Framework.* The elements involved in the decision-making problem are included in *Flintstones*, that is, the manager of garment company e_1, the set of three alternatives $X = \{x_1, \ldots, x_3\}$, and the set of three criteria $C = \{c_1, \ldots, c_3\}$. Figure 8.15 illustrates the framework of this illustrative example.
• *Gathering Information*
  Once the framework has been defined to assess the different alternatives, the manager elicits his preferences by single linguistic terms and hesitant fuzzy linguistic assessments (comparative linguistic expressions) in S (see Figure 8.16).

  For example, the assessment provided by the manager e_1 for the alternative x_2 about the criterion c_3 is expressed by means of the expression: *Al least High.*

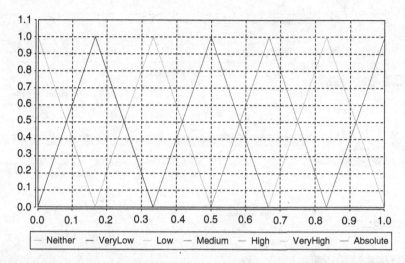

Fig. 8.14 Linguistic term set with seven labels

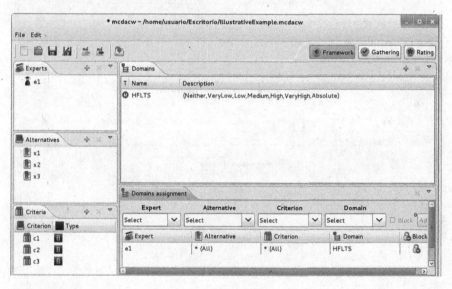

Fig. 8.15 Framework

- Selecting a solving process to rate the alternatives

  This example is defined to deal with hesitant linguistic assessments. In this step, a solving process for a decision-making problem with hesitant linguistic information must be carried out (see Figure 8.17) to conduct the rating process.

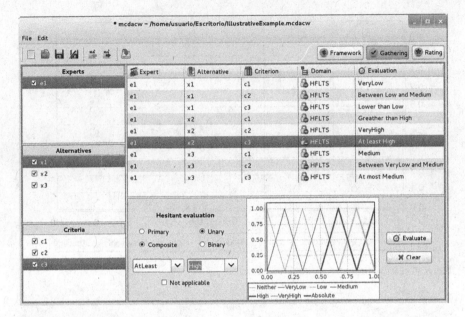

Fig. 8.16 Hesitant assessments

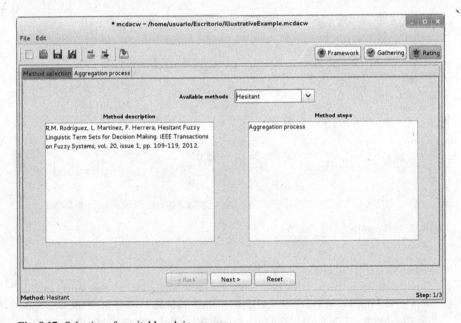

Fig. 8.17 Selection of a suitable solving process

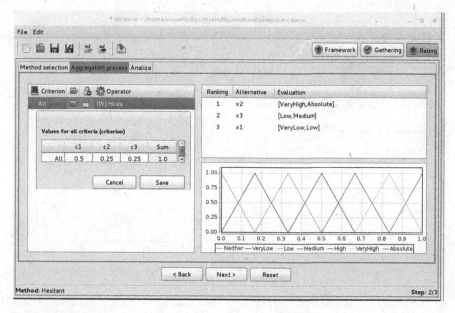

Fig. 8.18 Rating process—HLWA

The solving process for hesitant fuzzy linguistic information includes an aggregation phase to obtain a result for each alternative which is used to rank the set of alternatives. Transparently to the user, in this phase the suite converts the comparative linguistic expressions into HFLTS by means of the transformation function $E_{G_H}(\cdot)$ (see Definition 6.17).

Currently, *Flintstones* has implemented different aggregation operators for HFLTS: *min_upper, max_lower, HLWA* and *HLOWA*. Note that the HLWA and HLOWA aggregation operators, Figures 8.18 and 8.19, have been used with the following weighting vector $w = (0.5, 0.25, 0.25)^T$.

Finally, in view of the results, a ranking among the alternatives is established with the purpose of identifying the best one. Although the obtained results are different in some cases, depending on the aggregation operator used, we can see that the set of alternatives keeps the same ranking without depending on the aggregation operator used,

$$x_2 > x_3 > x_1$$

Therefore, the best alternative is the second textile fabric x_2.

With this illustrative example, it has been shown that *Flintstones* obtains the results of a decision-making problem, using different aggregation operators. Therefore, *Flintstones* is an excellent option to make comparisons among aggregation operators in a decision-making problem in an easy way.

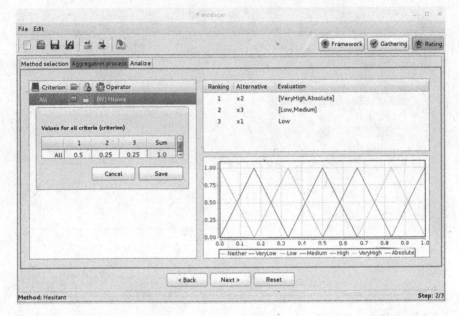

Fig. 8.19 Rating process—HLOWA

8.6 *Flintstones* Website: Case Studies and Datasets

The development of a software suite of tools is very important, but it is not enough if users cannot use it to verify its performance with real datasets in order to make comparisons with their own proposals or problems. Therefore, *Flintstones* is not only a decision software suite, but it has also been deployed the *Flintstones* website[3] that includes a repository of case studies and their corresponding datasets as well as different interesting sections (see Figure 8.20). Here the *Flintstones* website and its elements are described.

The website has been designed with the aim of publishing all *Flintstones* released versions and a repository of case studies with real datasets that can be solved with the software suite of tools. Furthermore, different interesting sections with theoretical foundations as well as video tutorials about the software suite of tools can be found on the website. Each section of the website is described briefly below:

- *Description.* In order to provide the theoretical foundations of *Flintstones*, the main theoretical concepts are briefly introduced in this section of the website. Examples of these concepts are the *CW paradigm* or the 2-tuple linguistic model.
- *Software tool.* All *Flintstones* released versions will be available on the website. The current version, v1.0, has all the functionality to create, manage, and solve

---

[3]http://sinbad2.ujaen.es/flintstones/.

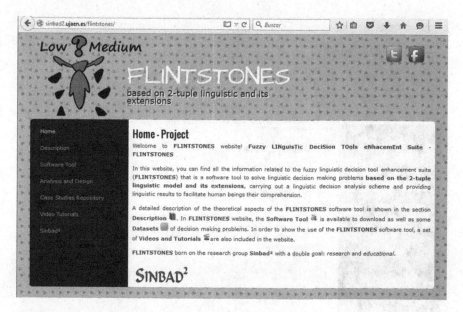

Fig. 8.20 *Flintstones* website

decision-making problems with linguistic and complex frameworks. In order to run *Flintstones*, it is only necessary to download and unpack the *zip* file and execute the *flintstones.jar* file. This file can be used on any machine with JVM, independently of the operating system. The software tool is licensed under the terms of the GNU General Public License.[4]

- *Analysis and Design*. Technical aspects related to the analysis and design of the suite are provided in order to offer a complete view of the internal structure of the suite. Therefore this website section shows the architecture of the suite as well as the package and class diagrams.

- *Case studies repository*. Case studies of decision-making problems are available on the website, which are categorised by the type of framework (multigranular linguistic framework, heterogeneous framework, and unbalanced linguistic framework). Each case study is associated with its datasets for *Flintstones* that includes the definition of the framework and the set of assessments provided by experts. Furthermore, each case study is associated with the research paper in which the use of the 2-tuple linguistic model or any of its extensions has been successfully applied to it. The repository is alive and new datasets will be included; Table 8.2 shows a summary of the case studies currently incorporated in the repository (see Figure 8.21).

---

[4]http://www.gnu.org.

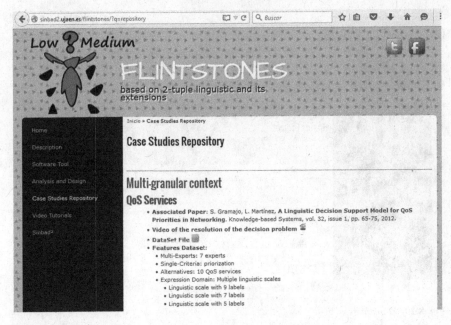

Fig. 8.21 *Flintstones* datasets

Table 8.2 Repository of case studies and datasets

Framework	Extension	Application	Year
Linguistic	Fusion for multigranular information	Decision making [3]	2011
Multigranular	Linguistic hierarchies	Decision making [9]	2001
		Sensory evaluation [13]	2008
	Extended linguistic hierarchies	Decision making [3]	2011
		Quality of services in networking [7]	2012
Heterogeneous	Fusion for heterogeneous information	360-degree performance appraisal [2]	2013
		Sustainable energy evaluation [4]	2012
		ERP evaluation processes [16]	2009
Unbalanced Linguistic	Methodology to deal with unbalanced scales	Sensory evaluation [12]	2009
		Decision making [8]	2008

- *Video tutorials.* A set of video tutorials that illustrate the functionality of *Flintstones* are shown in this section. Each basic functionality has been briefly described and has been illustrated in a video tutorial, which can be directly reproduced from the website (see Figure 8.22).

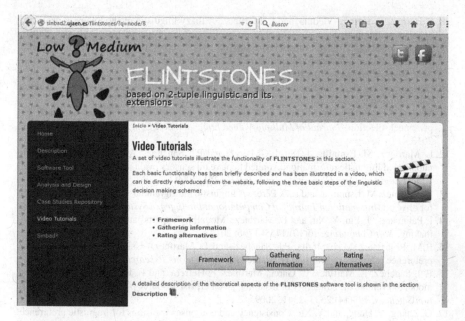

Fig. 8.22 *Flintstones* video tutorials

Acknowledgements The authors want to highlight and thank Francisco J. Estrella and Macarena Espinilla for their hard work and cooperation in developing *Flintstones*.

References

1. S. Aydin and C. Kahraman. A new fuzzy analytic hierarchy process and its application to vendor selection problem. *Journal of Multiple-Valued Logic and Soft Computing*, 20(3–4): 353–371, 2013.
2. M. Espinilla, R. de Andrés, F.J. Martínez, and L. Martínez. A 360-degree performance appraisal model dealing with heterogeneous information and dependent criteria. *Information Sciences*, 222:459–471, 2013.
3. M. Espinilla, J. Liu, and L. Martínez. An extended hierarchical linguistic model for decision-making problems. *Computational Intelligence*, 27(3):489–512, 2011.
4. M. Espinilla, I. Palomares, L. Martínez, and D. Ruan. A comparative study of heterogeneous decision analysis approaches applied to sustainable energy evaluation. *International Journal on Uncertainty, Fuzziness and Knowledge-based Systems*, 20(supp01):159–174, 2012.
5. F.J. Estrella, M. Espinilla, F. Herrera, and L. Martínez. FLINTSTONES: a fuzzy linguistic decision tools enhancement suite based on the 2-tuple linguistic model and extensions. *Information Sciences*, 280:152–170, 2014.
6. F.J. Estrella, M. Espinilla, and L. Martínez. Fuzzy linguistic olive oil sensory evaluation model based on unbalanced linguistic scales. *Journal of Multiple-Valued Logic and Soft Computing*, 22:501–520, 2014.
7. S. Gramajo and L. Martínez. A linguistic decision support model for QoS priorities in networking. *Knowledge-based Systems*, 32(1):65–75, 2012.

8. F. Herrera, E. Herrera-Viedma, and L. Martínez. A fuzzy linguistic methodology to deal with unbalanced linguistic term sets. *IEEE Transactions on Fuzzy Systems*, 16(2):354–370, 2008.

9. F. Herrera and L. Martínez. A model based on linguistic 2-tuples for dealing with multigranular hierarchical linguistic context in multi-expert decision making. *IEEE Transactions on Systems, Man, And Cybernetics - Part B: Cybernetics*, 31(2):227–234, 2001.

10. E. Herrera-Viedma, F.J. Cabrerizo, J. Kacprzyk, and W. Pedrycz. A review of soft consensus models in a fuzzy environment. *Information Fusion*, 17(0):4–13, 2014.

11. M. Kabak. A fuzzy DEMATEL-ANP based multi criteria decision making approach for personnel selection. *Journal of Multiple-Valued Logic and Soft Computing*, 20(5–6):571–593, 2013.

12. L. Martínez, M. Espinilla, J. Liu, L.G. Pérez, and P.J. Sánchez. An evaluation model with unbalanced linguistic information: Applied to olive oil sensory evaluation. *Journal of Multiple-Valued Logic and Soft Computing*, 15(2–3):229–251, 2009.

13. L. Martínez, M. Espinilla, and L.G. Pérez. A linguistic multigranular sensory evaluation model for olive oil. *International Journal of Computational Intelligence Systems*, 1(2):148–158, 2008.

14. I. Palomares, J. Liu, Y. Xu, and L. Martínez. Modelling experts' attitudes in group decision making. *Soft Computing*, 16(10):1755–1766, 2012.

15. R.M. Rodríguez, M. Espinilla, P.J. Sánchez, and L. Martínez. Using linguistic incomplete preference relations to cold start recommendations. *Internet Research*, 20(3):296–315, 2010.

16. P. J. Sánchez, L. Martínez, C. García-Martínez, F. Herrera, and E. Herrera-Viedma. A fuzzy model to evaluate the suitability of installing an enterprise resource planning system. *Information Sciences*, 179(14):2333–2341, 2009.

17. G. Zhang, Y. Dong, and Y. Xu. Consistency and consensus measures for linguistic preference relations based on distribution assessments. *Information Fusion*, 17(0):46–55, 2014.

18. Y. Zhang and Z.P. Fan. Uncertain linguistic multiple attribute group decision making approach and its application to software project selection. *Journal of Software*, 6(4):662–669, 2011.

Printed in the United States
By Bookmasters

Printed in the United States
By Bookmasters